ANCIENTS AND MODERNS

ANCIENTS AND MODERNS
AN ANTHOLOGY OF POETRY

Edited by
Stewart A. Baker
Rice University

Harper & Row, Publishers
New York, Evanston, San Francisco, London

ACKNOWLEDGMENTS

Grateful acknowledgment is made to the publishers and individuals who granted permission to reprint the following poems.

EMILY DICKINSON
"Success is counted sweetest," "I died for Beauty," "I heard a Fly buzz—when I died," "Because I could not stop for Death," "I taste a liquor never brewed," "A narrow Fellow in the Grass," "I dreaded that first Robin, so," and "Death is the supple Suitor" reprinted by permission of the publishers and the Trustees of Amherst College from Thomas H. Johnson, Editor, *The Poems of Emily Dickinson*, Cambridge, Mass., The Belknap Press of Harvard University Press, copyright 1951, 1955 by the President and Fellows of Harvard College.
"Forever is composed of Nows" reprinted by permission of the publishers and the Trustees of Amherst College from Thomas H. Johnson, Editor, *The Poems of Emily Dickinson*, Cambridge, Mass., The Belknap Press of Harvard University Press, Copyright 1951, 1955 by the President and Fellows of Har-

vard College; and by permission of Little, Brown and Co. from *The Complete Poems of Emily Dickinson* edited by Thomas H. Johnson.

WILLIAM BUTLER YEATS
"The Wild Swans at Coole" reprinted with permission of The Macmillan Company from *Collected Poems* by William Butler Yeats, copyright 1919 by The Macmillan Company, renewed 1947 by Bertha Georgie Yeats; and from *Collected Poems of W. B. Yeats* by permission of Michael Butler Yeats, A. P. Watt & Son, and The Macmillan Company of Canada Limited.
"Leda and the Swan," "Among School Children," and "Sailing to Byzantium" reprinted with permission of The Macmillan Company from *Collected Poems* by William Butler Yeats, copyright 1928 by The Macmillan Company, renewed 1956 by Georgie Yeats; and from *Collected Poems of W. B. Yeats* by permission of Michael Butler Yeats, A. P. Watt & Son, and The Macmillan Company of Canada Limited.
"A Stick of Insense," "Sweet Dancer," "The Lover's Song," "The Chambermaid's First Song," "The Chambermaid's Second Song," "Long-Legged Fly," and "Lapis Lazuli" reprinted with permission of The Macmillan Company from *Collected Poems* by William Butler Yeats, copyright 1940 by Georgie Yeats, renewed 1968 by Bertha Georgie Yeats, Michael Butler Yeats, and Anne Yeats; and from *Collected Poems of W. B. Yeats* by permission of Michael Butler Yeats, A. P. Watt & Son, and The Macmillan Company of Canada Limited.
"The Second Coming" reprinted with permission of The Macmillan Company from *Collected Poems* by William Butler Yeats, copyright 1924 by The Macmillan Company, renewed 1952 by Bertha Georgie Yeats; and from *Collected Poems of W. B. Yeats* by permission of Michael Butler Yeats, A. P. Watt & Son, and The Macmillan Company of Canada Limited.
"Crazy Jane and the Bishop" and "Crazy Jane Talks with the Bishop" reprinted with permission of The Macmillan Company from *Collected Poems* by William Butler Yeats, copyright 1933 by The Macmillan Company, renewed 1961 by Bertha Georgie Yeats; and from *Collected Poems of W. B. Yeats* by permission of Michael Butler Yeats, A. P. Watt & Son, and The Macmillan Company of Canada Limited.

ROBERT FROST
"Nothing Gold Can Stay," "Out, Out—," "The Wood-Pile," "Fire and Ice," "An Old Man's Winter Night," "The Strong Are Saying Nothing," "Design," and "Forgive, O Lord" reprinted by permission of Holt, Rinehart and Winston, Inc., from *The Poetry of Robert Frost*, edited by Edward Connery Lathem, copyright 1916, 1923, 1930, 1939 by Holt, Rinehart and Winston, Inc.; copyright, 1936, 1944, 1951, © 1958, 1962 by Robert Frost; copyright © 1964, 1967 by Lesley Frost Ballantine.

T. S. ELIOT
"The Naming of Cats" reprinted by permission of Harcourt Brace Jovanovich, Inc., from *Old Possum's Book of Practical Cats* by T. S. Eliot, copyright 1939 by T. S. Eliot, copyright 1967 by Esme Valerie Eliot; and by permission of Faber and Faber Ltd. from *Old Possum's Book of Practical Cats*.

"The Hippopotamus," "The Hollow Men," "La Figlia Che Piange," "The Love Song of J. Alfred Prufrock," "Sweeney Erect," and "Gerontion" reprinted by permission of the publishers from *Collected Poems 1909–1962* by T. S. Eliot, copyright 1939 by Harcourt Brace Jovanovich, Inc., copyright © 1963, 1964 by T. S. Eliot; and by permission of Faber and Faber Ltd. from *Collected Poems 1909–1962*.

WALLACE STEVENS
"The Emperor of Ice-Cream" and "Peter Quince at the Clavier" reprinted by permission of Alfred A. Knopf, Inc., from *The Collected Poems of Wallace Stevens*, copyright 1923, renewed 1951 by Wallace Stevens.
"The Idea of Order at Key West" reprinted by permission of Alfred A. Knopf, Inc., from *The Collected Poems of Wallace Stevens*, copyright 1936, renewed 1964 by Elsie Stevens and Holly Stevens Stephenson.

JOHN CROWE RANSOM
"Bells for John Whiteside's Daughter" reprinted by permission of the publisher from *Selected Poems*, 3rd Revised Edition, by John Crowe Ransom, copyright 1924 by Alfred A. Knopf, Inc., renewed 1952 by John Crowe Ransom.

e. e. cummings
"plato told him" reprinted by permission of Harcourt Brace Jovanovich, Inc., from *Poems 1923–1954* by e. e. cummings, copyright 1944 by e. e. cummings.
"here is little Effie's head" and "i like my body when it is with your body" reprinted by permission of Harcourt Brace Jovanovich, Inc., from *Poems 1923–1954* by e. e. cummings, copyright 1925 by e. e. cummings.
"anyone lived in a pretty how town" and "my father moved through dooms of love" reprinted by permission of Harcourt Brace Jovanovich, Inc., from *Poems 1923–1954* by e. e. cummings, copyright 1940 by e. e. cummings, copyright 1968 by Marion Morehouse Cummings.
"love is more thicker than forget" reprinted by permission of Harcourt Brace Jovanovich, Inc., from *Poems 1923–1954* by e. e. cummings, copyright 1939 by e. e. cummings, copyright 1967 by Marion Morehouse Cummings.
"my sweet old etcetera" reprinted by permission of Harcourt Brace Jovanovich, Inc., from *Poems 1923–1954* by e. e. cummings, copyright 1926 by Horace Liveright, copyright 1954 by e. e. cummings.

MARIANNE MOORE
"Poetry" reprinted with permission of The Macmillan Company from *Collected Poems* by Marianne Moore, copyright 1935 by Marianne Moore, renewed 1963 by Marianne Moore and T. S. Eliot.

W. H. AUDEN
"Musée des Beaux Arts" reprinted by permission of Random House, Inc., from *Collected Shorter Poems 1927–1957* by W. H. Auden, copyright 1940, renewed 1968 by W. H. Auden; and by permission of Faber and Faber Ltd. from *Collected Shorter Poems 1927–1957*.
"The Voice of Caesar" reprinted by permission of Random House, Inc., from *The Collected Poetry of W. H. Auden*, copyright 1944 by W. H. Auden; and by permission of Faber and Faber Ltd. from *For the Time Being*.
"The Fall of Rome" reprinted by permission of Random House, Inc., from *Collected Shorter Poems 1927–1957* by W. H. Auden, copyright 1947 by W. H. Auden.

& Row, Publishers, Inc., from *Ariel* by Sylvia Plath, copyright © 1963 by Ted Hughes, and by permission of Miss Olywn Hughes.
"Words" and "Ariel" reprinted by permission of Harper & Row, Publishers, Inc., from *Ariel* by Sylvia Plath, copyright © 1965 by Ted Hughes, and by permission of Miss Olywn Hughes.

WELDON KEES
"White Collar Ballad," "The Patient Is Rallying," "Crime Club," "Aspects of Robinson," "Robinson," "Robinson at Home," "Relating to Robinson," and "Saratoga Ending" reprinted by permission of the publisher from *The Collected Poems of Weldon Kees,* copyright 1962 by The University of Nebraska Press. All rights reserved.

WILLIAM STAFFORD
"Tornado" reprinted by permission of Harper & Row, Publishers, Inc., from *Traveling Through the Dark* by William Stafford, copyright © 1962 by Harper & Row, Publishers, Inc.
"Aunt Mabel," copyright © 1963 by William E. Stafford; "At the Chairman's Housewarming," copyright © 1952 by William Stafford; "The Summons in Indiana," copyright © 1960 by William E. Stafford; and "Written on the Stub of the First Paycheck," copyright © 1960 by William Stafford; reprinted by permission of Harper & Row, Publishers, Inc., from *The Rescued Year* by William Stafford.

RICHARD WILBUR
"The Death of a Toad" and "Still, Citizen Sparrow" reprinted by permission of Harcourt Brace Jovanovich, Inc., from *Ceremony and Other Poems* by Richard Wilbur, copyright 1948, 1949, 1950 by Richard Wilbur.
"Love Calls Us to the Things of This World" reprinted by permission of Harcourt Brace Jovanovich, Inc., from *Things of This World* by Richard Wilbur, copyright © 1956 by Richard Wilbur.
"She" reprinted by permission of Harcourt Brace Jovanovich, Inc., from *Advice to a Prophet and Other Poems* by Richard Wilbur, copyright © 1958 by Richard Wilbur.

ALLEN GINSBERG
Part I of "Howl" reprinted by permission of City Lights Books, copyright © 1956, 1959 by Allen Ginsberg.

DENISE LEVERTOV
"Come into Animal Presence," "Resting Figure," and "The Jacob's Ladder" reprinted by permission of New Directions Publishing Corporation from *The Jacob's Ladder* by Denise Levertov, copyright © 1960, 1961 by Denise Levertov Goodman.
"Losing Track," "The Secret," "Our Bodies," "A Psalm Praising the Hair of Man's Body," "Hypocrite Women," and "Song for Ishtar" reprinted by permission of New Directions Publishing Corporation from *O Taste and See* by Denise Levertov, copyright © 1962, 1963, 1964 by Denise Levertov Goodman. "Losing Track" and "Our Bodies" were first published in *Poetry*.
"Bedtime," "A Day Begins," and "The Mutes" reprinted by permission of New Directions Publishing Corporation from *The Sorrow Dance* by Denise Levertov, copyright © 1966 by Denise Levertov Goodman.

CONTENTS

PREFACE

The students for whom this anthology is intended are engaged today in action as well as inquiry and reflection. The modern temper demands involvement and a sense of present relevance. It also, I think, requires an awareness of the past and its giants (as the Ancients would say) on whose shoulders we stand. But we do not, and perhaps we should not, have time for the poetry of nostalgia or the pedantry of the antiquarian. The mode of our poetry, as of our lives, is engagement and action.

The poetry of engagement and action, however, is not exclusively modern. A reader who compares the older poets with the large selection of modern writers in this volume will discover that the Ancients are often directly engaged with their experience, whereas the Moderns are sometimes absorbed in reflection. For the Moderns, however, reflection may create a basis for action. For the Ancients, action and engagement are often vehicles for reflection.

The eighteenth century resolved its debate over the relative value of its modern writers and the ancient Greeks and Romans by deciding that both had their special relevance. ANCIENTS AND MODERNS is an anthology that presents equal selections from the older and newer writers of British and American poetry, beginning with Donne and concluding with extensive selections from contemporary poets. The poems are chosen for their sense of their particular present, even when they also reflect the most acute awareness of the meaning of the past. These poems will be found to evoke comparisons and meaningful contrasts. The relevance of their experience to us, I think, is often immediate and deep. At the same time, many of them also require that we examine the relevance and individuality of our own experience.

My introduction does not attempt to say all that should be said about poetry. It concentrates instead on the way poems convey the immediacy of their experience. Interpretation and stylistic analysis should only, I think, be ways to become engaged in the action of the poem.

I owe a special debt of thanks to the friends who have taught me, especially Robert S. Cox, Jr. In addition, Mrs. Ronald Brown gave invaluable assistance in the preparation of the manuscript. I owe an even greater and continuing debt to my students.

STEWART A. BAKER

discipulus discipulis

AN INTRODUCTION

POEMS

A poem is the voice of a person speaking to a person listening. This voice, through the uniqueness of its perception and the intensity of its language, attempts to penetrate the barriers of psyche and society that separate speaker and listener. A successful poem differs from other forms of speech chiefly through its power to relate the inner man conceiving the message to the other inner man who interprets it. A poem is a voice that threatens the silences of everyday speech.

Prose conveys information; poems communicate experience. In its most discursive forms, prose conveys the things that we can know with relative dispassion, without involvement. Poetry involves another kind of knowing: the acquaintance with and experience of things, as we know people by acquaintance. This kind of knowing, this meaning that a poem communicates through acquaintance, is not reducible, reproducible, or abstractable. A poem's meaning is itself.

But the printed text of a poem is not the poem itself. A poem *is* what it *does*—communicating its experience, mediating between speaker and listener. A poem happens.

A poem happens each time it is spoken and heard. It happens each time with a different intensity and hence becomes each time a different experience. This is a volume of ancient and modern poems that keep happening with intensity and meaning, even for very different people. Both groups of poems, old and new, emphasize poems which are intended to be exploratory, innovative, and calculated to challenge conventional attitudes. For the most part, they communicate powerful experiences through a language and form that shatter intellectual resistance and complacency. By breaking older forms or creating new ones, these poems attempt to communicate their sense of their present to the reader in his present. These are poems that, both in the past and present, have transformed men's experience and perceptions.

My short introduction could not attempt a comprehensive discussion of these poems. Instead, I have tried to emphasize the features of language that make them uniquely powerful, those features of rhythm, rhyme, and diction that communicate the wholeness and integrity of a poem's experience, and the features of metaphor, symbol, and genre that communicate the quality of that experience and the nature of the mind that perceives it. In short, I have attempted to emphasize those qualities of voice that make poems happen.

WORDS

Each poem that happens is both conventional and unique. In effect, it employs the conventions of language and conceptualization to create a unique statement. Each time this statement is read or performed, each time it happens, its own conventionality is renewed and transformed by the voice of the speaker and the understanding of the listener.

Words, basically, are compressed ideas—concepts reduced to conventions of sound and regulated by conventions of grammar. Simple words like *two* and *zebra* are relatively fixed in their conventional meanings. More complex words like *children, neighbor*, and *love* embody multiple personal and social meanings and attitudes. Others, such as *implicate, imply*, and *complex* contain submerged metaphors. Many others, such as *light* and *dark, straight* and *crooked*, have allegorical or moral implications which can easily be either revealed or repressed by their context. These more complex words, by embodying complex concepts, have a greater flexibility and range that allows them to overcome or expand conventional meanings. Poems use the conventions of words both to exploit their complex meanings and out of them to evolve new meanings.

To create a unique meaning out of its use of conventions, a poem must somehow overcome the barriers of conventional understanding. For a poet like Sylvia Plath, who uses words with a special intensity to analyze and communicate her own attitudes, words in the process of becoming poems are simultaneously destructive and creative. Words, she says, are

Axes
After whose stroke the wood rings.

For Sylvia Plath, the words of a poem, like the ax on the tree, commit an act of violence upon the minds of both speaker and listener. The ringing of the wood suggests the reverberations of associated meanings and feelings that an intense statement causes in the mind of a listener. But the effect of the ax on the tree is small, she implies, in comparison to the ringing that redoubles itself like concentric circles on a pond:

And the echoes!
Echoes travelling
Off from the centre like horses.

The echoes that a poem creates in a listener's consciousness partly reflect his individual experience that the words have evoked. If his experience is deep and broad, he will respond to many kinds of poems, and he will respond to each poem in a more intense way. His ability to understand the experience of the poem and to contribute his own experience to it determines the resonance of its echoes. The listener's relevance to the experience of the poem is just as crucial as the poem's relevance to the listener. When a poem creates a deep reverberation in his thinking and feeling, he begins to cooperate in its creative process. The echoes traveling off from the center assume, like the horses, an energy of their own.

For Sylvia Plath, whose words strike with an intensity far beyond the reach and intention of most poets, the consciousness of both speaker and listener must be, like the tree, wounded:

The sap
Wells like tears, like the
Water striving
To re-establish its mirror
Over the rock.

The listener's response to the violence of words is, like this sap wel-
ling like tears, the means by which he strives to reestablish his sense
of the real, as the water reforms its smooth mirror over the rock
that has shattered its surface. Through the words' act of violence,
he has been forced to attain, or regain, a renewed and heightened
awareness.

This awareness of reality includes both the perceiver's reality and
the reality of what he perceives. But the things he perceives, the
world of measurable facts, can never be for the poet as important
as the perceiver and the nature of his acts of perception. For Sylvia
Plath, this consciousness which perceives is defined in terms of its
perception of the physical body and the threat of death. The rock
that has shattered the mind's mirror, she reminds us,

    drops and turns,
A white skull,
Eaten by weedy greens.

Machines measure mechanically; men perceive according to the
measure of their humanity.

Poems, then, attempt to renew awareness while exploring or communicating acts of perception. This renewed awareness may
prolong the experience of a poem; if the ax has cut deeply, the experience stays with us, like the rock that shines from the bottom of the
pond. The words themselves have lost their force; we have used
them and put them aside. But the self and its perceptions that they
have helped to shape and define retain their complex integrity:

Years later I
Encounter them on the road——

Words dry and riderless,
The indefatigable hoof-taps.
While
From the bottom of the pool, fixed stars
Govern a life.

("Words," p. 302)

STYLE

Style derives from an Indo-European action verb meaning *to prick* or *to stab*. The Roman *stilus* was the sharp pointed tool used for carving letters upon wax tablets. Figuratively, then, style became a way of describing a speaker's voice—how it transforms the conventions of language to create a unique meaning and impress it upon his listener. Thus style reflects the essential process of a poem, what happens between speaker and listener.

The uniqueness of a poem derives chiefly from its style. What is said may resemble things said before, but each voice, through the integrity of its style, expresses the personality behind it. This personality, shaped by its experiences, projects its individual perceptions and meanings through the way it organizes language.

The important experiences of a poem, then, and the subtle individuality of its speaker, are communicated through style. Style is the means by which the speaker closes the gap between the privacy of his experiences and the privacy of his listener's mind. Thus style reflects both the process of perception, the quality of the speaker's experience, and the process of communication. To a large extent, therefore, we can say that style is meaning.

If style is meaning, then the meaning of a poem can be shared only through the experience of its style. It follows that poems cannot be abstracted or paraphrased without some loss of meaning. It is impossible to say the same thing in different ways.

STYLE AND RHYTHM

The most basic—and least analyzable—element of style is rhythm. As an element of style, rhythm carries part of its implicit meaning. We understand the meanings implicit in rhythm intuitively, largely through the conventional but unanalyzed meanings which rhythms have in the functions of the body, in music and dance, in nature and machines, and in all the conversations we have ever heard. Without rhythm, conversational speech loses its clarity and force. Similarly, a poet controls the rhythms of his language in order to limit and define the meanings that his poem may have.

The meanings implicit in rhythm become apparent in Howard Nemerov's conundrum, "A Life":

Innocence?
In a sense.
In no sense!

Was that it?
Was that *it?*
Was *that it?*

That was it.

(p. 289)

The meaning of each line clearly depends upon where the speaker places the stress. The meaning of the poem, its quizzical attitude toward life's meaning and value, is inseparable from the comically arbitrary repetition of sounds in different stress patterns. As the stress pattern changes, the meaning of innocence is transvalued, and the meaningfulness of the question is transformed. That, in any case, was it.

RHYTHM AND METER

Meter is an academic concept which attempts to regulate or describe the rhythm of a spoken line. The conventions of meter are notoriously unable to reflect adequately the modulations of the voice. One need only compare the irregular curve of a voice on an oscillograph to the simplicities of conventional metrics in order to recognize their inadequacy. Nevertheless, metrical descriptions of rhythm can help to define the possible meanings of a poem.

Stress patterns are intimately related to the syntactic structure of a line or sentence. For instance, a word like *no* can receive varying stresses, but in the statement "In no sense!" both syntax and meaning require that it receive maximum stress.

Stress is produced in several ways. The speaker obviously increases the actual volume of his voice. But he also heightens its pitch and lengthens the sound of the vowel in the stressed syllable. Musically, in the line above, *no* would be several tones higher than *in*, and it would take at least twice as long to pronounce. The stress on *no* is also emphasized, of course, by contrast with the weaker volume and lower pitch of the word that precedes it. Consequently, we must say that stress is relative to its context. Thus it is partly a physical phenomenon and partly a psychological phenomenon because it requires the listener to assess its relation to its context. Stress, we might say, reinforces meaning, but meaning and context help to make us aware of stress.

Older concepts of meter assume a simpler concept of stress patterns. Usually only two forms of stress are recognized: stress (′) and unstress (ˣ), which are naïvely modeled on the Greek and Latin metrics of long (−) and short (˘) syllables. If meter is to attempt to describe the complexities of voice modulation, clearly more degrees of stress must be recognized. But since stress is partly psychological, a system of meter need not be as sensitive as an oscillograph. It need only register the *relative* degrees of stress which the ear can recognize as significant.

The most practical system available recognizes four degrees of relative stress. These range from minimum stress (1) to maximum stress (4), with moderately stressed syllables in between (2 and 3). This makes it possible to clarify the distinction between *incident* and
$$\overset{4\ 1\ 3}{}$$
incident and
$$\overset{3\ 1\ 4\ 1\ 2}{incidentally},\ \text{or between}\ \overset{4\ \ \ 1\ \ \ 4}{have\ the\ meat}\ \text{and}\ \overset{4\ \ \ 3\ \ \ 4}{have\ them\ eat.}$$

This four-stress system also helps to describe what is going on in Nemerov's poem, which I usually read in this way:

$$\overset{4\ \ 1\ \ 3}{Innocence?}$$

$$\overset{3\ \ 1\ \ 4}{In\ a\ sense.}$$

$$\overset{3\ \ 4\ \ 3}{In\ no\ sense!}$$

The first two lines can sound very much alike, although their meanings are comically different. But the question form of the first line requires a heavier stress on the first syllable than on the last. In reading the second line, I find that I both stress and lengthen the last syllable. Thus the difference in meaning is underscored by a rhythmic inversion from 413 to 314.

The first two lines, by being so alike, create a complex set of expectations. Repetition, we might say, establishes a tentative norm. The listener's response to this norm is to expect that it will be either repeated or varied. Meter and rhythm, in this way, help to create meaning by organizing a listener's expectations of rhythmic repetition and variation. In Nemerov's poem, for instance, the stress on *no* in line three is emphasized because it provides a variation to the repetition of the unstressed second syllables in the first two lines. Moreover, the first and third syllables, which alternate values of 3 and 4 in the first two lines, attain an equal stress in line three.

Thus the apparent nonsense of the poem's word-play is contradicted by its systematic rhythmic structure. This is even more obvious in the second stanza, where the maximum stress moves regularly from the third to the second to the first syllable. Having established this pattern of expectation, Nemerov then resolves it with the change of stress and tone in "That was it," which the speaker is free to stress and interpret as he pleases. But whatever meaning he places on the innocence of this life, the last line at least asserts that it had meaning and a perceptible integrity of its own.

Most poems, of course, have more complex and less systematic rhythms than "A Life." Even with the very regular five-stress lines of the poetry of Pope, one quickly discovers the difficulty of describing speech rhythms through rigid metrical patterns. This difficulty increases in the conversational rhythms of much modern poetry, but even in modern poetry patterns emerge from metrical analysis.

In William Stafford's poem "Written on the Stub of the First Paycheck" (p. 330), for instance, there is much informal variety in line length and rhythm. But lines of very different lengths and rhythms are often equated by having an equal number of maximum stresses. This equality of heavy stresses encourages the speaker to give these lines equal time. For instance:

```
  3    2   4   2  1 4  4  4
There were peaks to the left so high
```

. . . .

```
 3   2   4   1 4    4    4
It has been a long day, Bing.
```

```
  3 4 2 3  3 42  4    4
Wherever I go is your ranch.
```

One also senses a recurrent rhythm in each line, e.g., 324 214 44; or 324 144 4 and 342 342 44, which partially equates the lines by strengthening their rhythmical relationships.

A similar rhythmic pattern is observable in Stafford's line:

 4   2   4   1   4   2   1   4   2   1   4
breathing fumes and reading the snarl of a map.

Since a long line like this tends to break in two parts, we might want to describe it as 42   4[] 142   142   14. The break, or caesura ([]), creates a pause which takes the place of the second element in the second rhythmic section. Rhythm thus employs silences as well as sounds.

In a poem like Stafford's, it is very apparent that meter describes a speaker's choice of possible meanings by describing his choice of rhythms. Even in a fairly simple line, we are forced to make a choice:

4   3   2   1 4 2   4 2
I stood in the filling station

is significantly different from

3   4   2   1 4 2   4 2
I stood in the filling station.

And we would certainly want to reject the reading

2   3   4   1 4 2   4 2
I stood in the filling station.

In the first reading, the heavy stress on *I* emphasizes the difference between the speaker who travels west looking for a job and the *someone* who shot a wildcat. Two concepts of the value of human action are being contrasted, and two attitudes toward the American West. If the maximum stress is placed on *stood*, as in the second reading, the speaker's inaction and his difficulties with the map are clarified. The third reading, which suggests that it was somehow important that he was *in* the filling station, is not supported by the context. I prefer the first reading because it retains some of the meaning of the second reading while insisting upon the more important contrast between the speaker and the hunter. A reading of the line is the most effective way of describing its meter, but an effective reading depends upon an interpretation of its meaning.

RHYTHM AND RHYME

Rhythm and rhyme are derived, significantly, from the same Greek and Latin words. Rhythm describes a sound pattern measurable in terms of relative stress. Rhyme describes the patterned repetition of another kind of sound measurable in terms of vowels and consonants—or in terms of the phonetic units which linguists call phonemes and morphemes. Both rhythm and rhyme, then, describe patterns of sound. Often they reinforce one another, since rhymed words are usually stressed in the same way. Both rhythm and rhyme employ patterns of sound to create expectations of repetition and significant variation.

Through repetition of the same sound, rhyme suggests that words "belong" together. This may mean simply that they are felt to be appropriate and adequate for the occasion, or it may imply a definite logical relationship between them. For instance, the life Nemerov describes is defined by the question "Innocence?" and its rhyming answer, "In a sense." The rhyme indicates a logical relationship between *innocence* and *sense:* the meaning (sense) of innocence can be grasped by the mind (sense) and the senses only in a special way. *Innocence* exists here only *in a sense*.

Whereas repetition encourages logical equations or analogies, variation suggests logical antithesis or opposition. Hence "In no sense," by rhyming the first and third syllables but not the second, underscores its contradiction of the first two lines. Thus rhyme can express either analogies or antitheses. It can show that ideas and words belong together, or by comparing them it can underscore a significant contrast between them.

Rhyme most often refers to *end rhyme*, where the final syllables of a line match one or more syllables with the same vowel complex or phoneme and the same rhythmic pattern in another line. Rhyme can also refer to *initial rhyme*, where the first syllables in the lines rhyme. Or it can indicate *internal rhyme*, where syllables in the middle of a line rhyme with each other, with the initial or final syllables of the line, or with syllables in other lines. All of these forms of rhyme are used for significant effect by Gerard Manley Hopkins in "God's Grandeur":

The world is charged with the grandeur of God.   *a*
  It *will flame out, like shining from shook* foil;   *b*
  It *gathers to a greatness, like the ooze of* oil   *b*
Crushed. Why do men then *now not reck his* rod?   *a*
Gen*erations* have trod, have trod, have trod;   *a*
  And *all is* seared *with trade;* bleared, smeared *with* toil;   *b*
  And wears man's sm*udge* and shares man's sm*ell: the* soil   *b*
Is bare now, nor can foot feel, being shod.   *a*

God and his *rod* of punishment are clearly related, and so are the industrial images of *foil* and *oil* through which Hopkins intimates God's grandeur. The *trod* of civilized man is inseparable from his being *shod*. Similarly, *seared, bleared,* and *smeared* all describe man's corrosive effect upon nature. *Toil* is the means by which the *soil* is laid bare.

Other kinds of repetitive sounds are closely related to rhyme and often have the same function. Hopkins "rhymes" phrases such as *have trod, have trod, have trod;* and *wears man's sm–* and *shares man's sm–*. These forms of internal rhyme, moreover, are supported by other complex repetitions of sounds. *Near rhyme* matches words such as *trod* and *trade;* and *bleared, wears,* and *bare. Alliteration* "rhymes" initial letters, as in "grandeur of God . . . *sh*ining from *sh*ook foil . . . gathers to a greatness . . . *o*oze *o*f *o*il . . . *r*eck his *r*od." By further emphasizing stressed syllables, alliteration as a form of rhyme clearly supports rhythm.

From this cooperation of rhyme and rhythm Hopkins is able to evolve a highly organic sound pattern for a poem that declares the organic and self-renewing power of nature that overcomes human destructiveness. The sestet of this innovative sonnet typically resolves the problem posed in the octet:

And for all this, nature is never spent;   *c*
  There lives the dearest freshness deep down things;   *d*
And though the last lights off the black West went   *c*
  Oh, morning, at the brown brink eastward, springs—   *d*
Because the Holy Ghost over the bent   *c*
  World broods with warm breast and with ah! bright wings.   *d*

("God's Grandeur," p. 200)

The rhyming of alliteration is further enriched here by a subtle pattern of *consonance,* or the repetition of consonant sounds that come at the end of a syllable: "dearest freshness . . . last . . . West . . . eastward . . . Ghost . . . breast." Furthermore, *assonance*, or the repetition of the same vowel sound in different consonant groups, "rhymes" the key phrase "the Holy Ghost over. . . ." The pervasive and organic sound patterns of Hopkins' poem all insist upon the unity and divine power implicit in nature; at the same time they insist upon the unity and spiritual integrity of the poem's experience. The style of the poem, as expressed through rhythm and rhyme, insists that the same thing cannot be said in any other way. Its style is its meaning.

STYLE AND DICTION

Rhyme and rhythm are easily recognized as significant patterns of language. But diction, the kind of language a poet uses, creates more subtle patterns that help to communicate a poem's experience.

Our descriptions of diction reflect a recognition of pattern. We say that the diction of Donne is colloquial, which means that it creates a recognizable pattern of conversational words and everyday expressions. We say that Pope's diction is elevated, or colloquial, or mock-heroic, depending on the extent to which Pope uses elegant or epic words, or conversational terms, or an ironic mixture of the two. We recognize related terms or patterns of diction in a poem, such as Donne's use of scientific and mathematical terms in "A Valediction: Forbidding Mourning" and Eliot's words for dampness, warmth, light, and animality in "The Love Song of J. Alfred Prufrock." These repetitive associative meanings typically provide a pattern, or context, from which the experience of the poem evolves.

For instance, Herrick's sensuous descriptions of women often employ scientific or religious diction not often associated with women. The effect of this diction is to express the speaker's admiration and to evoke a similar response from the listener:

Whenas in silks my Julia goes,
Then, then (methinks) how sweetly flows
That liquefaction of her clothes.

Next, when I cast mine eyes and see
That brave vibration each way free,
O how that glittering taketh me!

("Upon Julia's Clothes," p. 60)

The speaker obviously is aroused, but he seeks a "cool" medium for expressing his excitement. *Liquefaction* and *vibration* are chosen as scientific terms that describe the effects of light on her clothes as it is transmitted to his eye. Her sensuous beauty then is seen as an interdependence of her clothes themselves, the physical properties of light and its effects on the eye, and the response of her admirer.

Similarly, in Herrick's description of Anthea, the interplay of light and half-light becomes a way of graphing his response to her undressing in bed:

So looks Anthea when in bed she lies,
O'ercome, or half-betrayed by tiffanies,
Like to a twilight or that simp'ring dawn
That roses show, when misted o'er with lawn.
Twilight is yet, till that her lawns give way;
Which done, that dawn turns then to perfect day.

("To Anthea Lying in Bed," p. 61)

Explicit metaphors are established comparing Anthea to *twilight, dawn, roses,* and *perfect day,* but the military diction of *O'ercome* and *half-betrayed* also compares her implicitly to a victim of war. The same words imply that *tiffanies* can have human personality, just as *dawn* attracts the human attribute of *simp'ring.*

But the most important pattern of diction here refers to clothes: *tiffanies* and *lawn* are both diaphanous materials that permit the half-seeing (or "half-betraying") that both pleases and frustrates the speaker. Moreover, both words have religious connotations: *lawn* was a kind of lace used in a bishop's sleeves, and *tiffany* derives from *theophany,* which means "the shining through or manifestation of the god." The girl's name, *Anthea,* literally means "blossom," which supports her likeness to a rose, but the Greek root *-thea* also punningly likens her to the concept of godhead implied in *theo*phany. The purpose of these etymological puns and religious associations becomes clear in the course of the poem: The speaker responds to the roselike beauty of Anthea as though her warm sensuality were the light through which God manifests himself. Her emerging nakedness is implicitly an experience of religious revelation, a tearing away of the veil, an emergence of light from darkness.

Herrick uses patterns of diction to establish implicit metaphors. In mock-epic and burlesque poetry, on the other hand, contrasting patterns of diction establish ironic incongruities. Most readers are familiar with the processes of mock-heroic in Pope. Swift's "A Description of the Morning" and "A Description of a City Shower" likewise parody more limited epic motifs through patterns of diction and rhetoric. His narratives of "The Lady's Dressing Room" and "A Beautiful Young Nymph Going to Bed" similarly employ hilariously vulgar patterns of diction and rhetoric to create a mock-pastoral.

This use of diction to establish ironic incongruities is brilliantly modernized in Nemerov's satirical "Grace to Be Said at the Supermarket" (p. 294). Nemerov juxtaposes the language of religion (*grace*) with the everyday language of shopping (*supermarket*) in a way that underscores the contrast between them. He then complicates this incongruity by describing God and the wares of the supermarket in the language and concepts of mathematics (*Geometer, cubes, cylinder, ellipsoid*, etc.):

That God of ours, the Great Geometer,
Does something for us here, where He hath put
(if you want to put it that way) things in shape,
Compressing the little lambs in orderly cubes,
Making the roast a decent cylinder,
Fairing the tin ellipsoid of a ham,
Getting the luncheon meat anonymous
In squares and oblongs with the edges beveled
Or rounded (streamlined, maybe, for greater speed).

We read sequentially—a word, a phrase, a concept at a time. We absorb one idea; this creates expectations of the next idea, and then we must adjust the new idea to our expectations. The title of this poem has led us to expect a prayer, and it has implied an opposition of religion and everyday life. This opposition is reflected in the colloquial tone of "That God of ours," which differs radically in meaning from a pious introduction to prayer such as "Our God. . . ." Our expectations of prayer are partly satisfied by "the Great Geometer," which follows the usual formula for describing God at the beginning of a prayer by one or several qualifying phrases ("Our Father, who art in heaven . . ."). "The Great Geometer" is a more elevated phrase than "That God of ours," but it has already been qualified by the colloquial tone of the first phrase. Thus we sense in the diction alone the tone of irony that controls the poem.

Just as rhyme evolves patterns of repetition and significant variation, irony grows out of an ordering, then a re-ordering, of our expectations. The ironic tone of Nemerov's poem emerges from this dialectic of repetition and variation. The formal tone of a phrase like "the Great Geometer" is easily undercut by the double meaning of "put things in shape" and even further by the parenthetical colloquialism of "if you want to put it that way." These incongruities are developed then in the easy ironies of "orderly cubes" of lamb, "a decent cylinder" of roast, and "the tin ellipsoid of a ham." Each of these ironies reflects the speaker's playful and satiric doublevision of the supermarket's reduction of flesh and bone to technical abstractions and depersonalized, deanimalized physical objects. Through the image of the supermarket, of course, Nemerov is hinting at the dehumanizing and despiritualizing processes of contemporary society.

The ironic incongruities of Nemerov's diction are further reinforced by his manipulation of conventions of syntax and rhetoric. Each stanza is introduced by syntactical and rhetorical formulas that recall the Book of Common Prayer. Then these formulas are undercut by more colloquial patterns of speech. Again the poem begins by creating one set of expectations in the reader and then reverses them. The understanding of the poem is a matter of adjusting those expectations to what is actually said. In the second stanza, this parody of prayer-book rhetoric is complemented by parodies of Old Testament diction and allusion:

Praise Him, He hath conferred aesthetic distance
Upon our appetites, and on the bloody
Mess of our birthright, our unseemly need,
Imposed significant form. Through Him the brutes
Enter the pure Euclidean kingdom of number,
Free of their bulging and blood-swollen lives
They come to us holy, in cellophane
Transparencies, in the mystical body,

That we may look unflinchingly on death
As the greatest good, like a philosopher should.

(p. 294)

The final irony grows suddenly out of the juxtaposition of a pious homiletic cliché ("look unflinchingly on death") with the rhyming echo of an ungrammatical cigarette advertisement. The tone of moral exhortation is thus undercut by a kind of statement familiar in advertising, which we are by experience conditioned not to believe. In this way, our sense of the distinctness and mutual incongruity of the types of diction employed in Nemerov's poem has carried its ironic meaning.

STYLE AND IMITATIVE FORM

Pope's dictum that "the sound should be the echo of the sense" remains one of the most problematic concepts in the understanding of poetry. In the stream of sibilants that Herrick uses to suggest the rustling of Julia's clothes, or the sounds which suggest their flowing (*goes, flows, clothes*) we are reminded of treacherous clichés about hissing *s*'s and flowing *z*'s. Similarly we sense that Nemerov's parenthetical remark, "streamlined, maybe, for greater speed," implies through its sounds and rhythms a sense of easy motion. Conversely, the stately formality of "Praise Him . . ." is reflected in the heavy and nearly equal stresses on the words. This formal rhythm and sound then jars with the contrasting broken rhythms and informal internal rhyme in:

That we may look unflinchingly on death
As the greatest good, like a philosopher should.

The same concept of "imitative form" would lead us to regard phrases like "pure Euclidean kingdom" and "bulging and blood-swollen" as distinctly onomatopoeic; that is, their sound in some way imitates their meaning. The difficulty arises in attempts to state that a short *i* often goes with the idea of smallness or ephemerality, or that *ulg* and *ōl* suggest over-fullness and ugliness. Whereas these statements seem true for the phrases quoted above, they are certainly contradicted by similar phrases: e.g., short *i* in "big 'n thick," and *ulg* and *ōl* in "indulgent soul."

The range of sounds and rhythms in any language is very limited. Consequently, each sound and rhythm must carry a large number of possible meanings and a wide range of associations. Like conventional metrics, the conventional descriptions of imitative form— those familiar discoveries of hissing *s*'s and murmuring *m*'s—cannot do justice to the complexity of associations that sounds evoke. A poet's imitative skill will consist in drawing upon the right associations by creating an appropriate context. In other words, imitative form is possible only within the larger patterns that control a poem—its patterns of rhythm, rhyme, diction, and rhetoric—and it must be understood in relation to these patterns. When this is done, the conventional associations of sounds and rhythm reinforce the more definite patterns of style which create meaning.

METAPHOR

Because a poem attempts to communicate its experience through its style, knowing a poem requires a special way of apprehending the quality of that experience. Knowing a poem is not the same as knowing, for instance, that a chair is an artifact of a roughly predictable size and shape designed to be seen and sat upon. Knowing a poem is more like knowing a chair by acquaintance and use, often as we know other people:

A funny thing about a Chair:
You hardly ever think it's there.
To know a Chair is really it,
You sometimes have to go and sit.

("A Chair," p. 275)

Characteristically, *it* and *sit* are rhymed in a way that suggests a logical relationship between them. And in this poem Theodore Roethke is insisting that the *it-ness* of the chair cannot be adequately perceived except through the experience of *sitting* on it.

Another way of stating the logical relationships suggested by the many forms of rhyme is to say that they are metaphorical. That is, rhyme tends implicitly to equate or contrast things which sound alike. Rhythm likewise suggests implicit associations. The associative power of words or patterns of diction is similarly a means of creating implicit metaphor. All of the effective structural and linguistic features of poetry through which the experience of the reader meshes with the experience of the poem are, in effect, implicitly metaphorical.

Explicit metaphor more openly attempts to assimilate the experience of the reader to the experience of the poem. The basic purpose of comparisons is to say that A (which you do not know) is like B (which you do know or may have imagined). For instance, Herrick tells us that Julia (whom we don't know) is like a rose (whose general qualities we do know). This, of course, is only partial "knowing," but in respect to the more complex experiences that a poem attempts to communicate, it is, except for direct experience, the only means of knowing.

In order to communicate through metaphor, a speaker must assimilate an experience to something in his own memory or imagination. Then he asks his listener in turn to assimilate this equation to his own imagination. This tentative assimilation of mind and object is, I think, the root of metaphor. It is implicit, for instance, in Roethke's "Cuttings," where the gardener-poet communicates the experience of green shoots rising from plant cuttings:

One nub of growth
Nudges a sand-crumb loose,
Pokes through a musty sheath
Its pale tendrilous horn.

(p. 276)

Then in the sequel poem "Cuttings (later)," this implicit participation of both perceiver and plant in the process of rebirth becomes explicit:

I can hear, underground, that sucking and sobbing,
In my veins, in my bones I feel it,—
The small waters seeping upward,
The tight grains parting at last.
When sprouts break out,
Slippery as fish,
I quail, lean to beginnings, sheath-wet.

(p. 277)

Through metaphor, then, the speaker communicates both his perception of an expereince and the way in which he perceives it. Implicitly he asks the listener to participate in the same process of perception, by which each new experience is compared to and defined through an older experience. This process of comparison shapes our understanding of the new experience. It provides a frame, a context, or a concept through which an undefined experience may be understood. At the same time, the new experience necessarily modifies the frame of our old experiences. It is through this process that poetry can modify or transform our perception of things.

This innovative use of metaphor is particularly associated with John Donne, whose "The Good-Morrow," which celebrates the awakening of the self to the possibilities of a new experience, opens this selection of poems. In another famous poem, Donne transforms the highly traditional metaphor of the soul as the bride of Christ into a deliberately startling image: Since I am betrothed to Satan, your enemy, he begs God,

Divorce me, untie, or break that knot again;
Take me to you, imprison me, for I,
Except you enthrall me, never shall be free,
Nor ever chaste, except you ravish me.

("Holy Sonnet XIV," p. 55)

A man who sees himself as the female soul and God as a rapist requires from us a new way of perceiving things. This particular metaphor has led the speaker to a rediscovery of the wholeness of his personality, which responds to human love and divine love alike. At the same time, he has discovered in himself an attitude of spiritual and erotic submissiveness.

Donne is for English poetry the earliest model for this radical use of metaphor. The Donne tradition is renewed in the nineteenth century by Gerard Manley Hopkins, who discovers intimations of God's creative power in the ooze of oil ("God's Grandeur," p. 200) and of his beauty and diversity in brindled cows and speckled trout ("Pied Beauty," p. 202). For us, though, the great modern discoverer of radical metaphor is T. S. Eliot, who finds Prufrock's personality reflected in the yellow fog and labyrinthine streets of London, and in the evening "spread out against the sky/Like a patient etherised upon a table" (p. 239). Metaphor is for these poets the expression of a new perception, of an experience charged with new insight.

Metaphor usually expresses some degree of self-consciousness about its mode of perception. That is, it expresses an awareness of both the sameness and the difference of the things it compares. This is obviously true of negative metaphor, where a poet considers a comparison and then rejects it. A good example would be "Love's Alchemy" (p. 45), where Donne mocks the idealist who would confuse the music of the spheres with the "rude minstrelsy" of a wedding. This heightened awareness of sameness and difference simultaneously, moreover, is true of hyperbolic (or consciously exaggerated) equations, such as Donne's insistence that he and his mistress are, incredibly, the whole world ("The Sun Rising," p. 41). This hyperbole, which he uses in several poems, demonstrates a high degree of self-awareness, even in the act of celebrating his own strong feeling of love. This self-awareness also anticipates the lover's eventual and inevitable rediscovery of things as they usually are, uncharged with passion.

Metaphor, then, not only manifests perception; it also shows the speaker's consciousness of his mode and process of perception. In many poems, such as Donne's famous comparison of himself and his mistress to the legs of a compass ("A Valediction: Forbidding Mourning," pp. 149–150) or Marvell's precise and deliberate comparison of the soul to a drop of dew (pp. 169–170), metaphor and simile demonstrate progressive stages of the act of perception as the speaker thinks his way through the meaning of his experience. Or it may embody his reflection on and memory of that process of perception, such as Wordsworth so often gives us.

SYMBOL

The reality of metaphor, then, evolves from the conscious and deliberate perception of the equation of dissimilar things. Symbol, however, assumes a reality for itself which participates both in the object perceived and in the perceiving intellect. For the symbolist poet, the symbol is a real intellectual entity which mediates between the mind and the world of objects. For instance, in "Good Friday, 1613. Riding Westward," Donne assumes the reality of the east as symbol *and* scene of Christ's recurrent crucifixion and resurrection. If he were not riding toward the west, he reflects, he would be able to contemplate the crucifixion in the east:

There I should see a sun by rising set
And by that setting endless day beget.

(pp. 56–57)

This symbolic equation of the sun which rises in the east with the Son of God who died there is not, for Donne, a fiction or a fortunate pun. Christ was traditionally described as *Oriens*, the rising sun. And the setting and rising of the sun were familiar emblems for his death and resurrection. The fact that the sun is rising in the east makes Donne able to conceive of and communicate the reality of his spiritual relationship to God. Donne's seventeenth-century readers, moreover, assumed the reality of symbolic correspondences between the worlds of matter and spirit. For instance, God's power over all things corresponds to the primacy of the sun in the heavens, of the king in society, and of gold among the minerals. Thus the words *gold* and *golden* are often associated with God, the sun, and kings and reinforce the correspondences between them. For Donne, as for Shakespeare and Dante, the world was a poem of symbolic correspondences written by the hand of God. The poet's task lay in the discovery of these correspondences.

The concept of discovery is an important one. Since the symbol is assumed to participate in the reality it indicates, it acquires much of the diversity which belongs to reality; its meaning is not fixed. Just as real objects stand in many different relationships to each other, symbols also are able to express changing or evolving relationships between the mind and the world. For example, the sun in Donne's poem also gains significance through its eclipse at the crucifixion and its rising behind the speaker on this Good Friday when he travels toward the west.

Furthermore, since Donne believed that all of nature was a system of complex correspondences, he was free to "discover" new meanings for familiar symbols when they were viewed in new contexts. For instance, in "Good Friday," the sun implies also the more general light symbols associated with God and the light of redemptive grace which drives out the darkness of sin:

But that Christ on this cross did rise and fall,
Sin had eternally benighted all.

In the experience of the poem, the sun thus gains its literal reference, a cosmic theological reference, and a personal relevance for the speaker, who must turn back toward the east, *Oriens*, the rising sun, the Son of God, before the deformity of his guilt can be burned away. This traditional symbol thus becomes the center of an expanding circle of multidirectional references and meanings.

Donne's own century put an end to the belief in nature as a complex system of symbolic correspondences. The rationalism of the late seventeenth century reduced symbol to a decorative figure. A century later, however, the Romantics rediscovered the psychological validity of traditional symbols. In nature Wordsworth discovers forms and presences which, like Lucy herself, reflect his innermost attitudes. Similarly, Keats' nightingale and the figures on his Grecian urn justify their symbolic references through their ability to interpret the speaker's state of mind and feeling.

A clear example of the rediscovery of the validity of symbol is the poem "Spring and Fall: To a young child" by Hopkins, whose sensibility lies somewhere between the Romantics and the modern poets. The poem re-creates the experience of rediscovering the symbolic death of nature in the fall. The child Margaret seems to grieve for the trees themselves:

Márgarét, are you grieving
Over Goldengrove unleaving?
Leáves, like the things of man, you
With your fresh thoughts care for, can you?

It is the experience of youth to be intensely aware of decay and death. Hence the beauty of Goldengrove creates for Margaret the antithetical expectation of its imminent decay. The man of experience, in this case the speaker, distances himself from this pathos:

Áh! ás the heart grows older
It will come to such sights colder
By and by, nor spare a sigh
Though worlds of wanwood leafmeal lie.

Reason has created emotional distance from nature, but not from the fact of death:

And yet you will weep and know why.

What Margaret has learned is the symbolic correspondence of man and nature, of man's life and the tree of life:

Now no matter, child, the name:
Sórrow's spríngs áre the same.
Nor mouth had, no nor mind, expressed,
What heart heard of, ghost guessed:
It ís the blight man was born for,
It is Margaret you mourn for.

(p. 204)

The familiar symbol of the tree of life shedding its leaves which fall like the generations of men has thus been rediscovered as a way of conceptualizing the girl's attitude toward herself. Her achievement, like the poet's, has been to recognize and communicate the depth of pathos and the inevitability embodied in this rediscovery. Where the Romantic poet is still concerned with the *discovery* of symbol, the modern poet is self-consciously involved in its *creation*. Eliot and Yeats, particularly, are intensely conscious of the widespread collapse of traditional humanist and Christian values (and their symbols) in our century. Eliot is concerned with re-investing the old symbols with meaning—meaning drawn from the universals of psychology and anthropology and, after his conversion, from the universals of Christianity.

Yeats in particular is self-consciously dedicated to the deliberate creation of meaning and value through symbol and language. For Yeats the creation or re-creation of a symbol is the renewal of a means of knowledge otherwise lost. The poet, like the scientist and mathematician, evolves the concepts or symbols through which experience and the world of objects are understood. In "Lapis Lazuli," for instance, Yeats first develops an explicit theme appropriate to his apprehension of the approaching disasters of World War II—a concept of human tragedy and consequent renewal:

All things fall and are built again,
And those that build them again are gay.

Then he deliberately imposes this meaning on the Chinese carving on a piece of lapis lazuli that shows two ancient men and a servant climbing a mountain. The symbol becomes meaningful because of Yeats' imaginative interpretation of each detail:

Every discoloration of the stone,
Every accidental crack or dent,
Seems a water-course or an avalanche.

On the stone, as in Yeats' view of tragedy, each flaw or disaster is transformed into meaningful art:

There, on the mountain and the sky,
On all the tragic scene they stare.
One asks for mournful melodies;
Accomplished fingers begin to play.
Their eyes mid many wrinkles, their eyes,
Their ancient, glittering eyes, are gay.

(pp. 224–225)

Like his ancients, Yeats has created a contemporary meaning out of the disasters of his culture. Through art, through the creation of symbols, the mind has projected the reality of its forms upon the disorderly world of objects and experience. In the breakdown of old traditions of symbolic correspondences, he has found an opportunity to explore the capacity of the imagination for creating symbolic meanings.

RHETORICAL SITUATIONS: narrative

Like other forms of communication, poetry is a social phenomenon. It assumes a speaker and a listener. It is, in fact, a meeting, an encounter where language and form are the means of mediation. Like most social encounters, poetry adopts rules or built-in assumptions that govern what is to be communicated. Familiar examples of highly structured social encounters are the telephone conversation where you request information from a stranger; dinner-table conversations with the family; the banter that surrounds team sports; or the well-known patterns of first-date behavior. But since in a poem the speaker is usually not present, more complex and implicit rules of communication come into play, as they do in the writing of a letter.

These rules or built-in assumptions are, of course, very flexible, but they determine to a large extent what may be communicated. Taken together they define the genre, or type, of an individual statement or of an entire poem. The genre of a statement or of a poem determines our expectations of what may be said. We are able to understand what is actually said then by adjusting what we hear to our expectations.

In this way we are able to understand highly compressed statements, such as the beginning of the narrative in Eliot's poem "Sweeney Erect" (pp. 243–244):

Morning stirs the feet and hands
(Nausicaa and Polypheme).
Gesture of orang-outang
Rises from the sheets in steam.

This genre of statement leads us to expect the kind of sequential information usually available in an indicative sentence. In the larger sense of genre, the genre of the poem, it leads us to expect a descriptive or a narrative poem. Isolated from its context, however, the first line denies our expectations, because by itself it does not make sense. Eliot proceeds then to qualify it by another genre of statement, the parenthetical second line which stands in some kind of apposition to the first. Again, however, we must adjust our expectation to what is actually said. To what part of the first line does the parenthesis, "(Nausicaa and Polypheme)," stand in apposition? Normally we would reply, the nearest member, which in this case would be "feet and hands."

To make sense of this, we will have to recognize "feet and hands" as a genre of statement we had not anticipated: synecdoche, where the part stands for the whole. That is, "feet and hands" denote two persons, who are then identified by the parenthesis as Nausicaa, the Phaeacian girl who fell in love with Odysseus, and Polyphemus, the one-eyed giant who tried to kill him. Still, this does not make complete sense of the second line. The title of the poem has promised a statement about Sweeney, and Sweeney is explicitly introduced as one of the two persons in the bedroom later on. Thus we must again adjust our expectations of the parenthesis "(Nausicaa and Polypheme)" and recognize it as an implicit comparison of the girl on the bed to Nausicaa and of Sweeney to Polyphemus. Having seen this, we easily recognize the orang-outang rising from the sheets as Sweeney getting out of bed. It is not necessary to have a name for each of these genres of statement. We have learned them from our experience with language, and we usually recognize them, as here, spontaneously.

Moreover, because we know that sequential information about an event implies a narrative, we recognize this description of Sweeney rising from bed as the beginning of a narrative we expect to continue. Without this concept of the larger genre, narrative, that controls the poem, it would be difficult to understand the distorted description of the girl on the bed which follows:

This withered root of knots of hair
  Slitted below and gashed with eyes,
This oval O cropped out with teeth:
  The sickle motion from the thighs

Jackknifes upward at the knees
  Then straightens out from heel to hip
Pushing the framework of the bed
  And clawing at the pillow slip.

Because we expect narrative, we recognize the apparently discon-
nected images of the first three lines as part of a sequential narrative,
although the finite verbs are omitted. Thus we can tentatively reconstruct these two sentences by supplying the verbs: "This withered root . . . *is* slitted . . . This oval O *is* cropped out with
teeth." This procedure is justified by the remainder of the passage,
since Eliot himself provides action verbs for the next clause: "The
sickle motion . . . *Jackknifes* . . . Then *straightens*. . . ." In this
way we are able to reconstruct the two stanzas as a fairly complex
indicative sentence which is part of a narrative. What is actually
happening, however, becomes clear only several stanzas later when
Eliot describes the girl as "The epileptic on the bed."

What sort of narrative this may be is a more difficult question. The
narrator apparently stands outside the action, but the radical dis-
tortion of ordinary syntax here seems to reflect empathetically the
wild behavior of the epileptic. Moreover, from the comparison of
Sweeney and the girl to Polyphemus and Nausicaa we know that
the narrator is, in some way, commenting upon the actions he describes.

Furthermore, the allusion to Nausicaa and Polyphemus, and thus to
Homer's *Odyssey*, places the entire poem in relation to a more elabo-
rate form of narrative, the epic. Hence we must understand it partly
as straight narrative, and partly as an adaptation or parody of epic
narrative. This is made clear by the modified epic invocation which
introduces the poem, with its recollection of Odysseus' Aegean Sea:

> *Paint me a cavernous waste shore*
> *Cast in the unstilled Cyclades,*
> *Paint me the bold anfractuous rocks*
> *Faced by the snarled and yelping seas.*

Eliot's description also recalls the voluminous complaints of the
jilted women in Ovid's *Heroides*, especially the lament of Ariadne,
who was abandoned by Theseus on the shores of Naxos in the
Cyclades:

> *Display me Aeolus above*
> *Reviewing the insurgent gales*
> *Which tangle Ariadne's hair*
> *And swell with haste the perjured sails.*

The epic and Ovidian antecedents of Eliot's narrative, then, ask us to compare "The epileptic on the bed" to Ariadne and Nausicaa, and we are asked to compare "Sweeney addressed full length to shave/Broadbottomed, pink from nape to base," with Odysseus, Theseus, and Polyphemus. The obvious incongruity of these comparisons allows us to see that we are in the realm of a very special genre of narrative, the mock-heroic.

From this recognition results our perception of Eliot's ironic narrative tone. Eliot has, in fact, established an ironic dialectic between the simple narrative and its antecedents in myth and poetry. We listen, as it were, to two voices. This is the technique which Eliot explores in his cat comedies and which Pope perfected in "The Rape of the Lock." The poet has succeeded in creating a self-consciousness which both narrates and comments upon itself.

RHETORICAL SITUATIONS: lyric

A similar kind of complication is frequent in the lyric. Like the narrative voice, the lyric voice creates a consciousness both of itself and of its intended audience. The audience of narrative is clearly the reader or listener of the poem. The intended audience of lyric, however, may not include the reader. Instead the reader may simply overhear the speaker addressing someone else—a friend, a woman, or himself. Whereas narrative emphasizes the event, the lyric voice trains our awareness upon the speaker and his processes of thought. Narrative is controlled by time or by some sense of chronological sequence; in lyric, time is reshaped by the consciousness of the speaker. Whereas narrative establishes a setting primarily for its characters, lyric creates its setting chiefly for its speaker and his audience. In a word, lyric is implicitly dramatic.

This dramatic aspect of lyric is obvious in a poem such as Marvell's "To His Coy Mistress" (pp. 73–74), in which the speaker employs a three-part syllogistic argument in an attempt to seduce a woman. It is more complex in a poem like Marvell's "The Garden" (pp. 84–86) or Eliot's "Prufrock" (pp. 239–242), where the speaker seems to be talking to himself. Similar to the complex form of narrative that employs two or more voices, the lyric at its most introspective may become an interior dialectic, where inner voices seem to be carrying on a debate within the consciousness of the speaker.

In "La Figlia Che Piange," for instance, Eliot first creates the expectation of a normal dramatic situation. The speaker commands a girl to assume the melodramatic pose of a rejected woman:

Stand on the highest pavement of the stair—
Lean on a garden urn—
Weave, weave the sunlight in your hair—
Clasp your flowers to you with a pained surprise—
Fling them to the ground and turn
With a fugitive resentment in your eyes:
But weave, weave the sunlight in your hair.

This would seem to establish both a narrative and a dramatic situation with speaker and girl both present in the same place. But with the next stanza, this apparently simple dramatic situation is revealed, by a conditional "would," to be purely hypothetical:

　So I would have had him leave,
So I would have had her stand and grieve,
So he would have left
As the soul leaves the body torn and bruised,
As the mind deserts the body it has used.

The repetition of "I would have" and the alternation of "soul leaves the body" with "mind deserts the body" make it clear that the narrator is not describing an event, but instead imagining the alternative ways in which an event might have occurred. The change from "I would have . . . I would have" to "he would have" also begins to blur the distinction between "I" and "he," the narrator and the lover. This distinction becomes even vaguer in the remainder of the stanza, in which the speaker wishfully states his desire for a simpler, less painful leave-taking:

I should find
Some way incomparably light and deft,
Some way we both should understand,
Simple and faithless as a smile and shake of the hand.

Instead. of addressing the girl herself, then, he is speaking to her image in his mind. Instead of recalling an event, he is re-creating it. Instead of observing the parting of two other people, he has taken himself the man's part. In this way, the seemingly one-sided dramatic statement implied by the first stanza has been revealed as a dialectic that evolves in the mind of the speaker.

In the third stanza, the narrator finally gives us a clear piece of narrative:

> *She turned away, but with the autumn weather*
> *Compelled my imagination many days,*
> *Many days and many hours:*
> *Her hair over her arms and her arms full of flowers.*

And then he dissociates himself from the lovers, reducing their moment of passionate grief to a matter of vague aesthetic curiosity:

> *And I wonder how they should have been together!*
> *I should have lost a gesture and a pose.*
> *Sometimes these cogitations still amaze*
> *The troubled midnight and the noon's repose.*

(p. 238)

As the last lines make clear, the chief interest of the poem lies not in the two lovers, but in the troubled cogitations of the speaker. In effect, the poem traces these recurring meditations from his reconstruction of the parting, to his full empathy with the lovers, concluding with his Prufrock-like withdrawal from passionate involvement. The poem does not give us the lovers, but instead presents in its dialectic between fact and hypothesis, between commitment and noncommitment, the mind and character of the speaker.

RHETORICAL SITUATIONS: dramatic verse

The dramatic quality implicit in lyric becomes explicit in dramatic verse, in which two speakers are present. While clarifying the latent substructure of much poetry, dialogue also simplifies it and eliminates some of its tensions. In "The Blue Swallows" (pp. 300–301), for instance, Nemerov approaches the problem of epistemology, or the perception of reality, through a lyric meditation; in his dialogue "This, That, & the Other" (pp. 297–299), he deals with the same problem in an explicit debate.

Similarly, in "Crazy Jane Talks with the Bishop," Yeats once more approaches the problem of the relationship of the body and the soul, but he allows Jane to simplify the issues. The Bishop mocks her physical decay and exhorts her to the spiritual life:

I met the Bishop on the road
And much said he and I.
"Those breasts are flat and fallen now,
Those veins must soon be dry;
Live in a heavenly mansion,
Not in some foul sty."

Echoing the witches in *Macbeth*, Jane rejects this opposition of heaven and the body:

"Fair and foul are near of kin,
And fair needs foul," I cried.
"My friends are gone, but that's a truth
Nor grave nor bed denied,
Learned in bodily lowliness
And in the heart's pride."

Love is communicated through the body; and for Jane, only that which has been defiled may be made good:

"A woman can be proud and stiff
When on love intent;
But Love has pitched his mansion in
The place of excrement;
For nothing can be sole or whole
That has not been rent."

(p. 223)

Thus the dramatic form simplifies the process of dialectic and resolution by giving Jane the last word. Only our recognition that this dialogue is embodied in a narrative that Jane controls is able to preserve some of the tension of dialectic. Yeats has, in fact, shown us Jane giving herself the last word, and this qualifies our acceptance of what she says.

.   .   .

Out of these larger *rhetorical situations*—narrative, lyric, dramatic—grow the more specific genres of poetry: epic, mock-epic, romance, sonnet, ode, meditative poem, drama. These are the forms of poetry that the ancients most often use and that they expect their audience to understand implicitly, just as we understand implicitly the forms that govern speech and make communication possible in a letter or telephone conversation.

But in addition to these traditional genres, poets since the Romantic period have elaborated a series of highly particularized genres of statement, many of which are defined only by highly individual poems. Whereas the ancients were able to innovate by transforming traditional genres, the moderns often allow each poem to create its own genre. In the case of these modern innovative poems, the rules that govern communication are, to a large extent, reshaped by the poem itself or by similar poems written by the same poet.

Consequently the innovative modern poet—T. S. Eliot is an outstanding example—must create through his poems and his criticism an audience that can understand and appreciate what he has written. Since his innovations are in the realms of either traditional genres of poetry or conventional forms of speech, or both, he must create an awareness of these innovations. This he does through violence of language, through the associativeness of rhythm, rhyme, and diction, and through the mediative attributes of metaphor and symbol. Genre creates an awareness of itself and evolves its meaning through the medium of style.

INTERPRETATION

Since a poem is a voice speaking and a person listening, an act of mediation, it follows that a poem does not *mean* by itself. Its meaning is inseparable from the act of speaking and listening (or reading, which is both speaking and listening to ourselves). Moreover, since a poem communicates experience rather than simple information, its meaning depends in large part upon the reader's ability to participate in or fully understand the experience of another person. Because of the very real barriers between people and because of differences of time, education, and culture, the success of any poem is necessarily limited. Its meaning will depend in large part upon the reader's sensitivity, the depth and breadth of his experience, and his willingness to subordinate his own meanings and his own experiences to the poem's meanings and experiences.

But a good reader of poems, realizing to what extent meaning depends upon him, will attempt to distinguish between the poem's meanings and his own. The poem's meaning is hypothetical, of course, since it cannot be perceived intrinsically; it always requires a reader, who may impose his own meanings upon it. But it is a reasonable hypothesis that the poet intended some meaning, even if that meaning was vague, ambiguous, or only half-understood. He may have meant the poem to have no meaning, to be instead a sounding-board for the reader's feelings. But that too is a kind of meaning.

It will prove valuable, then, to distinguish a poem's *meaning* from the reader's *understanding* of it, even if in experience these two prove ultimately inseparable. The point is that a pursuit of the poem's meaning can improve and enrich the reader's understanding. Without this pursuit, the reader remains within a narrowly subjective, solipsistic world where all poems are static mirrors of his own mind.

Interpretations of a poem's meaning should be limited to the elements of language which can be discussed with some degree of objectivity: the conventional meanings of words, metaphors, symbols, and the use of rhetoric. With a good dictionary and a wide experience of reading poetry, a careful reader can provide interpretations of these elements that are demonstrably more plausible than other interpretations. Analysis of the relationship of style (which includes rhythm, rhyme, sound, and diction) to meaning should remain more tentative. The personal relevance of a poem and its evaluation fall largely within the realm of the *understanding* of its readers.

The usefulness—and the limits—of the interpretation of a poem's meaning can be demonstrated by comparing two readings of the first two stanzas of Donne's "A Valediction: Forbidding Mourning":

As virtuous men pass mildly away
  And whisper to their souls to go,
Whilst some of their sad friends do say,
  "The breath goes now," and some say, "No":

So let us melt and make no noise,
  No tear-floods nor sigh-tempests move;
'Twere profanation of our joys
  To tell the laity our love.

(pp. 49–50)

The new reader often responds, "The man is dying. He is speaking to a woman, perhaps his mistress or his wife, urging decorum and silence between them as he dies." The scholarly reader immediately replies, "Oh no. Donne is leaving his wife to go to France with Sir Robert Drury in 1611, as Izaak Walton tells us in his *Life of Donne*. These stanzas simply compare Donne's separation from his wife to the parting of a man from his friends at death, or the parting of the soul ('breath') from his body."

Neither the new reader nor the scholar is completely wrong in this case. The new reader errs chiefly in overlooking the poem's first word, "As," which implies a comparison: "*As* virtuous men pass mildly away . . . *So* let us melt." But the scholar commits the more serious error of valuing Walton's external testimony more than the poem's internal details. Walton only gives us the *occasion* on which the poem was written, which is quite different from the poem's *meaning*. As often happens, biographical and historical information here distorts rather than improves understanding, because it has been placed before an interpretation of the poem's meaning.

The new reader's response is, in fact, much closer to the poem's meaning. In these two stanzas, the speaker does not draw a clear distinction between "pass mildly away" and "So let us melt." Although these phrases are framed as a comparison, the meaning of "melt" is not specified as "part." Only in the poem's last line, where the speaker says that his journey will be a circle ("and make me end where I begun"), does it become clear that he is not dying. But even here, the image of the unbroken circle confirms "melt" rather than such a paraphrase as "part." *Melting*, like the circle, implies change and motion, but not separation. The speaker, in effect, does not distinguish "melt" from "pass away" because he finds his experience indistinguishable from dying. And this is the experience to which the new reader genuinely responds.

More specifically, the first stanza describes the process of death, not death itself. The situation is at the point where the friends are unsure whether the breath has left the body or not. It is this intermediate state which reflects the speaker's own experience of leaving a woman. He is going but, as he will explain, he is also remaining with her. Their united souls "endure not yet/A breach, but an expansion,/Like gold to airy thinness beat." It is this ambivalent state that he attempts to convey through the image of the dying man, through the idea of gold beaten out to a great expanse, and through the image of the compass which, in moving, describes the circle of perfection. The reader's uncertainty about the exact nature of this "melting" reflects the speaker's refusal to admit it as a real separation and his consequent attempts to describe it in other terms.

The interpretation of the first two stanzas, then, depends largely on the meaning of the word *melt*. The principle that the same thing cannot be said in different ways is important here: *melt* does not mean *part*, a word that is not used in the poem. *Melt* is qualified by other words, *pass away*, *go*, and by the notions of dying, trepidation of the spheres, beaten gold, and the circle of perfection, but *melt* does not mean any of these things exactly. Instead it points toward, attempts to communicate, the same experience that they attempt to convey. And as the speaker insists, this is not a parting or a separation of substances, but a liquefaction and extension (*melting*), an expansion (*like gold*), and a completion and perfection (*circle*) of the interrelationship of the lovers.

These meanings are verifiable within the context of the poem. They are supported by the conventions of Donne's language and imagery, and they are reinforced by his rhetoric and style. They can be seen to be more plausible than the response of the new reader or the external meaning supplied by the scholar. These meanings only lay the groundwork, however, for the reader's *understanding* of the poem, which will depend upon his response to this experience and to Donne's strategy for communicating it. Moreover, his evaluation of the poem will, in large measure, reflect his ability to understand and participate in this experience, and Donne's ability to communicate it to him. The process of interpretation and understanding, like the poem itself, ends in a reaffirmation of the distinctiveness of the experiences and perceptions of both speaker and listener, and of the poem's unique act of mediation between them.

THE POEMS

JOHN DONNE
(1572–1631)

THE GOOD-MORROW

I wonder, by my troth, what thou and I
Did, till we loved? Were we not weaned till then?
But sucked on country pleasures, childishly?
Or snorted we in the seven sleepers' den?
'Twas so. But this, all pleasures fancies be.   5
If ever any beauty I did see,
Which I desired and got, 'twas but a dream of thee.

And now good morrow to our waking souls,
Which watch not one another out of fear;
For love, all love of other sights controls,   10
And makes one little room an everywhere.
Let sea-discoverers to new worlds have gone;
Let maps to others, worlds on worlds have shown;
Let us possess one world; each hath one and is one.

My face in thine eye, thine in mine appears,   15
And true plain hearts do in the faces rest.
Where can we find two better hemispheres
Without sharp North, without declining West?
Whatever dies was not mixed equally;

If our two loves be one, or thou and I   20
Love so alike that none do slacken, none can die.

---

4. *seven sleepers' den:* According to legend, seven Christian youths of
Ephesus fell asleep after being sealed in a cave by their persecutors. Two
hundred years later they awoke to find a world converted to Christianity.
5. *but:* except for.   **19.** According to medieval doctrine, all mixed substances
containing contrary elements are subject to decay.

SONG

Go and catch a falling star,
   Get with child a mandrake root,
Tell me where all past years are,
   Or who cleft the Devil's foot;
Teach me to hear mermaids singing,   5
Or to keep off envy's stinging,
      And find
      What wind
Serves to advance an honest mind.

If thou beest born to strange sights,   10
   Things invisible to see,
Ride ten thousand days and nights,
   Till age snow white hairs on thee;
Thou, when thou return'st, wilt tell me
All strange wonders that befell thee,   15
      And swear
      Nowhere
Lives a woman true and fair.

If thou find'st one, let me know;
   Such a pilgrimage were sweet;   20
Yet do not, I would not go,
   Though at next door we might meet;
Though she were true when you met her,
And last till you write your letter,
      Yet she   25
      Will be
False, ere I come, to two or three.

2. *mandrake root:* thought to resemble the human form, either male or
female, according to the number of branches.

THE SUN RISING

Busy old fool, unruly sun,
Why dost thou thus
Through windows and through curtains call on us?
Must to thy motions lovers' seasons run?
Saucy pedantic wretch, go chide   5
Late schoolboys and sour prentices;
Go tell court-huntsmen that the King will ride;
Call country ants to harvest offices;
Love, all alike, no season knows nor clime,
Nor hours, days, months, which are the rags of time.   10

Thy beams so reverend and strong
Why shouldst thou think?
I could eclipse and cloud them with a wink,
But that I would not lose her sight so long.
If her eyes have not blinded thine,   15
Look, and tomorrow late, tell me,
Whether both the Indias of spice and mine
Be where thou left'st them, or lie here with me.
Ask for those kings whom thou saw'st yesterday,
And thou shalt hear, all here in one bed lay.   20

She is all states, and all princes, I.
Nothing else is.
Princes do but play us; compared to this,
All honor's mimic; all wealth, alchemy.
Thou, sun, art half as happy as we,   25
In that the world's contracted thus;
Thine age asks ease, and since thy duties be
To warm the world, that's done in warming us.
Shine here to us, and thou art everywhere;
This bed thy center is, these walls, thy sphere.   30

17. *Indias . . . mine:* the East (spice) and West (mine) Indies.

THE INDIFFERENT

I can love both fair and brown,
Her whom abundance melts, and her whom want betrays,
Her who loves loneness best, and her who masques and plays,
Her whom the country formed, and whom the town,
Her who believes, and her who tries,   5
Her who still weeps with spongy eyes,
And her who is dry cork and never cries;
I can love her and her and you and you;
I can love any, so she be not true.

Will no other vice content you?   10
Will it not serve your turn to do as did your mothers?
Or have you all old vices spent and now would find out others?
Or doth a fear that men are true torment you?
Oh we are not, be not you so.
Let me, and do you, twenty know.   15
Rob me, but bind me not, and let me go.
Must I, who came to travail thorough you,
Grow your fixed subject, because you are true?

Venus heard me sigh this song,
And by Love's sweetest part, Variety, she swore   20
She heard not this till now; and that it should be so no more.
She went, examined, and returned ere long,
And said, "Alas, some two or three
Poor heretics in love there be,
Which think to stablish dangerous constancy.   25
But I have told them, 'Since you will be true,
You shall be true to them who are false to you.' "

17. *thorough:* through.

THE CANONIZATION

For God's sake hold your tongue, and let me love,
   Or chide my palsy, or my gout,
My five gray hairs, or ruined fortune flout;
    With wealth your state, your mind with arts improve,
      Take you a course, get you a place,   5
      Observe his honor, or his grace;
Or the King's real, or his stamped face
   Contemplate; what you will, approve,
   So you will let me love.

Alas, alas, who's injured by my love?   10
   What merchant's ships have my sighs drowned?
Who says my tears have overflowed his ground?
   When did my colds a forward spring remove?
      When did the heats which my veins fill
      Add one more to the plaguy bill?   15
Soldiers find wars, and lawyers find out still
   Litigious men, which quarrels move,
   Though she and I do love.

Call us what you will, we are made such by love;
   Call her one, me another fly;   20
We are tapers too, and at our own cost die.
   And we in us find the Eagle and the Dove.
      The Phoenix riddle hath more wit
      By us; we two, being one, are it.
So to one neutral thing both sexes fit,   25
   We die and rise the same and prove
   Mysterious by this love.

---

15. *plaguy bill:* an official list of those who had died of the plague. **22.** *the Eagle . . . Dove:* proverbial types of the predator and his prey. **23.** *Phoenix:* a mythical bird. Only one exists, and it is either sexless or bisexual. Every five hundred years it flies to Thebes in Egypt, bursts into flame, and then is reborn from its ashes.

We can die by it, if not live by love,
   And if unfit for tombs and hearse
Our legend be, it will be fit for verse;   30
   And if no piece of chronicle we prove,
     We'll build in sonnets pretty rooms;
     As well a well wrought urn becomes
The greatest ashes, as half-acre tombs.
   And by these hymns, all shall approve   35
   Us canonized for love:

And thus invoke us: "You whom reverend love
   Made one another's hermitage;
You, to whom love was peace, that now is rage;
   Who did the whole world's soul extract and drove   40
     Into the glasses of your eyes,
     So made such mirrors and such spies
That they did all to you epitomize,
   Countries, towns, courts: Beg from above
   A pattern of your love!"   45

40. *extract:* i.e., by chemical distillation. Some versions read *contract.* **41.** *glasses:* vessels for distillation; also, the pupils of the eyes seen either as transparent glass or as mirrors.

LOVE'S ALCHEMY

Some that have deeper digged love's mine than I,
Say where his centric happiness doth lie:
    I have loved, and got, and told,
But should I love, get, tell, till I were old,
I should not find that hidden mystery.   5
    Oh, 'tis imposture all:
And as no chemic yet th'elixir got,
    But glorifies his pregnant pot,
    If by the way to him befall
Some odoriferous thing or medicinal,   10
    So lovers dream a rich and long delight,
    But get a winter-seeming summer's night.

Our ease, our thrift, our honor, and our day,
Shall we for this vain bubble's shadow pay?
    Ends love in this, that my man,   15
Can be as happy as I can, if he can
Endure the short scorn of a bridegroom's play?
    That loving wretch that swears,
'Tis not the bodies marry, but the minds,
    Which he in her angelic finds,
    Would swear as justly that he hears   20
In that day's rude hoarse minstrelsy the spheres.
    Hope not for mind in women; at their best
    Sweetness and wit, they are but mummy possessed.

22. *spheres:* in Ptolemaic astronomy, the spheres described by the orbits of the planets. Their motion was said to create a music of celestial harmony.

THE FLEA

Mark but this flea, and mark in this
How little that which thou deny'st me is:
It sucked me first and now sucks thee,
And in this flea our two bloods mingled be;
Thou know'st that this cannot be said   5
A sin, nor shame, nor loss of maidenhead,
 Yet this enjoys before it woo,
 And pampered swells with one blood made of two,
 And this, alas, is more than we would do.

Oh stay, three lives in one flea spare,   10
Where we almost, yea more than married are:
This flea is you and I, and this
Our marriage bed and marriage temple is;
Though parents grudge, and you, we are met,
And cloistered in these living walls of jet.   15
 Though use make you apt to kill me,
 Let not to that, self-murder added be,
 And sacrilege, three sins in killing three.

Cruel and sudden, hast thou since
Purpled thy nail in blood of innocence?   20
Wherein could this flea guilty be,
Except in that drop which it sucked from thee?
Yet thou triumph'st and say'st that thou
Find'st not thyself nor me the weaker now.
 'Tis true. Then learn how false fears be: 25
 Just so much honor, when thou yield'st to me,
 Will waste as this flea's death took life from thee.

A NOCTURNAL UPON SAINT LUCY'S DAY, BEING THE SHORTEST DAY

'Tis the year's midnight, and it is the day's,
Lucy's, who scarce seven hours herself unmasks.
   The sun is spent, and now his flasks
    Send forth light squibs, no constant rays;
      The world's whole sap is sunk: 5
The general balm th'hydroptic earth hath drunk,
Whither, as to the bed's-feet, life is shrunk,
Dead and interred; yet all these seem to laugh
Compared with me, who am their epitaph.

Study me then, you who shall lovers be   10
At the next world, that is, at the next spring:
   For I am every dead thing,
    In whom love wrought new alchemy.
      For his art did express
A quintessence even from nothingness,   15
From dull privations, and lean emptiness:
He ruined me, and I am re-begot
Of absence, darkness, death: things which are not.

All others from all things draw all that's good,
Life, soul, form, spirit, whence they being have;   20
   I, by love's limbeck, am the grave
    Of all that's nothing. Oft a flood
      Have we two wept and so
Drowned the whole world, us two; oft did we grow
To be two chaoses, when we did show   25
Care to ought else; and often absences
Withdrew our souls and made us carcasses.

But I am by her death (which word wrongs her),
Of the first nothing, the elixir grown;
   Were I a man, that I were one,
    I needs must know; I should prefer,   30
      If I were any beast,

Saint Lucy's Day: December 13. According to the Julian calendar, it had the fewest hours of sunlight of any day in the year. **6.** hydroptic: swollen with fluids, as in the disease dropsy. **21.** limbeck: an alembic, a vessel used for distilling and purifying chemicals.

Some ends, some means; yea plants, yea stones detest
And love; all, all some properties invest;
If I an ordinary nothing were,   35
As shadow, a light and body must be here.

But I am none; nor will my sun renew.
You lovers for whose sake the lesser sun
  At this time to the Goat is run
   To fetch new lust and give it you,   40
    Enjoy your summer all;
Since she enjoys her long night's festival,
Let me prepare towards her, and let me call
This hour her vigil and her eve, since this
Both the year's and the day's deep midnight is.   45

39. *Goat:* the zodiacal sign of Capricorn, which the sun entered December 13 in the Julian calendar.

A VALEDICTION: FORBIDDING MOURNING

As virtuous men pass mildly away
   And whisper to their souls to go,
Whilst some of their sad friends do say,
   "The breath goes now," and some say, "No":

So let us melt and make no noise,   5
   No tear-floods nor sigh-tempests move;
'Twere profanation of our joys
   To tell the laity our love.

Moving of th'earth brings harms and fears;
   Men reckon what it did and meant.
But trepidation of the spheres,   10
   Though greater far, is innocent.

Dull sublunary lovers' love
   (Whose soul is sense) cannot admit
Absence, because it doth remove
   Those things which elemented it.   15

But we by a love so much refined
   That our selves know not what it is,
Inter-assured of the mind,
   Care less eyes, lips, and hands to miss.   20

Our two souls, therefore, which are one,
   Though I must go, endure not yet
A breach, but an expansion,
   Like gold to airy thinness beat.

If they be two, they are two so   25
   As stiff twin compasses are two:
Thy soul, the fixed foot, makes no show
   To move, but doth, if the other do.

---

9. *Moving . . . earth:* an earthquake.   12. *trepidation . . . spheres:* an os-
cillation in the planetary orbits, by which Ptolemaic astronomers attempted
to explain the apparent irregular motions of the planets (actually caused by
the motion of the earth's axis).

And though it in the center sit,
   Yet when the other far doth roam,   30
It leans and hearkens after it,
   And grows erect as that comes home.

Such wilt thou be to me, who must
   Like th'other foot, obliquely run;
Thy firmness makes my circle just   35
   And makes me end where I begun.

THE BLOSSOM

Little think'st thou, poor flower,
  Whom I have watched six or seven days,
And seen thy birth, and seen what every hour
Gave to thy growth, thee to this height to raise,
And now dost laugh and triumph on this bough: 5
    Little think'st thou
That it will freeze anon, and that I shall
Tomorrow find thee fallen, or not at all.

Little think'st thou, poor heart,
  That labor'st yet to nestle thee,
And think'st by hovering here to get a part   10
In a forbidden or forbidding tree,
And hope'st her stiffness by long siege to bow:
    Little think'st thou
That thou tomorrow, ere that sun doth wake,
Must with this sun and me a journey take.   15

But thou which lov'st to be
  Subtle to plague thyself wilt say,
"Alas, if you must go, what's that to me?
Here lies my business, and here I will stay:
You go to friends whose love and means present   20
    Various content
To your eyes, ears, and tongue, and every part.
If then your body go, what need you a heart?"

Well then, stay here; but know,
  When thou hast stayed and done thy most,   25
A naked thinking heart that makes no show
Is to a woman but a kind of ghost;
How shall she know my heart; or having none,
    Know thee for one?
Practice may make her know some other part,   30
But take my word, she doth not know a heart.

Meet me at London then
  Twenty days hence, and thou shalt see
Me fresher and more fat by being with men   35
Than if I had stayed still with her and thee.
For God's sake, if you can, be you so too:
  I would give you
There to another friend, whom we shall find
As glad to have my body as my mind.   40

ELEGY XIX: TO HIS MISTRESS GOING TO BED

Come, Madam, come, all rest my powers defy;
Until I labor, I in labor lie.
The foe oft-times having the foe in sight
Is tired with standing though he never fight.
Off with that girdle, like heaven's zone glittering,   5
But a far fairer world encompassing.
Unpin that spangled breastplate, which you wear
That the eyes of busy fools may be stopped there.
Unlace yourself, for that harmonious chime
Tells me from you that now it is bedtime.   10
Off with that happy busk which I envy,
That still can be and still can stand so nigh.
Your gown going off such beauteous state reveals,
As when from flow'ry meads th' hill's shadow steals.
Off with that wiry coronet and show   15
The hairy diadem which on you doth grow;
Now off with those shoes, and then safely tread
In this love's hallowed temple, this soft bed.
In such white robes heaven's angels used to be
Received by men. Thou, angel, bring'st with thee   20
A heaven like Mahomet's paradise; and though
Ill spirits walk in white, we easily know
By this these angels from an evil sprite:
Those set our hairs, but these our flesh upright.
   Licence my roving hands and let them go   25
Before, behind, between, above, below.
O my America! my new-found-land,
My kingdom, safeliest when with one man manned,
My mine of precious stones, my empery,
How blest am I in this discovering thee!   30
To enter in these bonds is to be free;
Then where my hand is set, my seal shall be.
   Full nakedness! All joys are due to thee:
As souls unbodied, bodies unclothed must be
To taste whole joys. Gems which you women use   35

11. *busk:* a corset. **21.** *Mahomet's paradise:* represented as a heaven of sensual pleasure.

Are like Atlanta's balls, cast in men's views,
That when a fool's eye lighteth on a gem,
His earthly soul may covet theirs, not them.
Like pictures, or like books' gay coverings made
For lay-men, are all women thus arrayed;   40
Themselves are mystic books, which only we
(Whom their imputed grace will dignify)
Must see revealed. Then since that I may know,
As liberally as to a midwife show
Thyself: cast all, yea, this white linen hence,   45
There is no penance due to innocence.
    To teach thee, I am naked first; why then
What need'st thou have more covering than a man?

---

36. *Atlanta's balls:* Hippomenes defeated Atlanta in a foot race by throwing three golden apples in her path, which she stopped to pick up. **42.** *imputed grace:* the theological doctrine that divine grace is conferred upon those who have faith in what they cannot see directly.

HOLY SONNET X

Death, be not proud, though some have called thee
Mighty and dreadful, for thou art not so.
For those whom thou think'st thou dost overthrow
Die not, poor death, nor yet canst thou kill me.
From rest and sleep, which but thy pictures be,   5
Much pleasure; then from thee, much more must flow;
And soonest our best men with thee do go,
Rest of their bones, and soul's delivery.
Thou art slave to fate, chance, kings, and desperate men,
And dost with poison, war, and sickness dwell,   10
And poppy or charms can make us sleep as well,
And better than thy stroke; why swell'st thou then?
One short sleep past, we wake eternally,
And death shall be no more; death, thou shalt die.

HOLY SONNET XIV

Batter my heart, three-personed God; for you
As yet but knock, breathe, shine, and seek to mend;
That I may rise and stand, o'erthrow me and bend
Your force to break, blow, burn, and make me new.
I, like an usurped town, to another due,   5
Labor to admit you, but oh, to no end.
Reason your viceroy in me, me should defend,
But is captived and proves weak or untrue.
Yet dearly I love you and would be loved fain,
But am betrothed unto your enemy.   10
Divorce me, untie, or break that knot again;
Take me to you, imprison me, for I,
Except you enthrall me, never shall be free,
Nor ever chaste, except you ravish me.

GOOD FRIDAY, 1613. RIDING WESTWARD

Let man's soul be a sphere, and then in this
The intelligence that moves, devotion is;
And as the other spheres, by being grown
Subject to foreign motions, lose their own,
And being by others hurried every day,   5
Scarce in a year their natural form obey:
Pleasure or business, so, our souls admit
For their first mover, and are whirled by it.
Hence is't that I am carried towards the West
This day when my soul's form bends toward the East.   10
There I should see a sun by rising set
And by that setting endless day beget;
But that Christ on this cross did rise and fall,
Sin had eternally benighted all.
Yet dare I almost be glad I do not see   15
That spectacle of too much weight for me.
Who sees God's face, that is self life, must die;
What a death were it then to see God die?
It made his own lieutenant Nature shrink;
It made his footstool crack and the sun wink.   20
Could I behold those hands which span the poles
And tune all spheres at once pierced with those holes?
Could I behold that endless height which is
Zenith to us and our antipodes
Humbled below us? or that blood which is   25
The seat of all our souls, if not of his,
Made dirt of dust, or that flesh which was worn
By God for his apparel ragg'd and torn?
If on these things I durst not look, durst I
Upon his miserable mother cast mine eye,   30
Who was God's partner here and furnished thus
Half of that sacrifice which ransomed us?
Though these things, as I ride, be from mine eye,
They are present yet unto my memory,
For that looks towards them; and thou look'st towards me, 35
O Saviour, as thou hang'st upon the tree;

2. *intelligence:* Each of the Ptolemaic spheres was thought to be controlled by an angelic intelligence, or spirit.   **20.** *footstool:* the earth. See Isaiah 66:1.

I turn my back to thee but to receive
Corrections, till thy mercies bid thee leave.
O think me worth thine anger, punish me,
Burn off my rusts and my deformity;
Restore thine image so much by thy grace
That thou may'st know me, and I'll turn my face.

HYMN TO GOD MY GOD, IN MY SICKNESS

Since I am coming to that holy room
   Where with thy choir of saints for evermore
I shall be made thy music; as I come
   I tune the instrument here at the door
   And what I must do then think here before;   5

Whilst my physicians by their love are grown
   Cosmographers, and I their map, who lie
Flat on this bed, that by them may be shown
   That this is my south-west discovery
   Per fretum febris, by these straits to die;   10

I joy that in these straits I see my West;
   For though their currents yield return to none,
What shall my West hurt me? As West and East
   In all flat maps (and I am one) are one,
   So death doth touch the Resurrection.   15

Is the Pacific Sea my home? Or are
   The eastern riches? Is Jerusalem?
Anyan, and Magellan, and Gibraltar,
   All straits, and none but straits are ways to them,
   Whether where Japhet dwelt, or Cham, or Sem.   20

We think that Paradise and Calvary,
   Christ's Cross, and Adam's tree, stood in one place;
Look, Lord, and find both Adams met in me;
   As the first Adam's sweat surrounds my face,
   May the last Adam's blood my soul embrace.   25

So in his purple wrapped, receive me, Lord;
   By these his thorns give me his other crown;
And as to others' souls I preached thy word,
   Be this my text, my sermon to mine own,
   Therefore that he may raise the Lord throws down.   30

---

10. *per . . . febris:* through the strait of fever. *Fretum* also means "raging heat." **20.** *Japhet . . . Sem:* Noah's sons. Japhet inherited Europe; Ham (Cham), Africa; and Shem (Sem), Asia. **23.** *both Adams:* Because of Adam, man dies; but in Christ, the "second Adam," man is given new life. See I Corinthians 15:20–22 and 15:45–57.

ROBERT HERRICK
(1591–1674)

TO THE VIRGINS, TO MAKE MUCH OF TIME

Gather ye rosebuds while ye may,
   Old Time is still a-flying:
And this same flower that smiles today,
   Tomorrow will be dying.

The glorious lamp of heaven, the Sun,   5
   The higher he's a-getting;
The sooner will his race be run,
   And nearer he's to setting.

That age is best, which is the first,
   When youth and blood are warmer;   10
But being spent, the worse, and worst
   Times still succeed the former.

Then be not coy, but use your time;
   And while ye may, go marry:
For having lost but once your prime,
   You may forever tarry.   15

DELIGHT IN DISORDER

A sweet disorder in the dress
Kindles in clothes a wantonness:
A lawn about the shoulders thrown
Into a fine distraction,
An erring lace, which here and there   5
Enthralls the crimson stomacher,
A cuff neglectful, and thereby
Ribbons to flow confusedly,
A winning wave (deserving note)
In the tempestuous petticoat,   10
A careless shoestring, in whose tie
I see a wild civility,
Do more bewitch me than when art
Is too precise in every part.

3. *lawn:* a fine lace.

TO ANTHEA LYING IN BED

So looks Anthea when in bed she lies,
O'ercome, or half-betrayed by tiffanies,
Like to a twilight or that simp'ring dawn
That roses show, when misted o'er with lawn.
Twilight is yet, till that her lawns give way;   5
Which done, that dawn turns then to perfect day.

2. *tiffanies:* a translucent or diaphanous material.   4. *lawn:* a fine lace.

UPON JULIA'S CLOTHES

Whenas in silks my Julia goes,
Then, then (methinks) how sweetly flows
That liquefaction of her clothes.

Next, when I cast mine eyes and see
That brave vibration each way free,
O how that glittering taketh me!

5

UPON JULIA'S VOICE

So smooth, so sweet, so silv'ry is thy voice,
As, could they hear, the damned would make no noise,
But listen to thee (walking in thy chamber)
Melting melodious words to lutes of amber.

CORINNA'S GOING A-MAYING

Get up, get up for shame, the blooming morn
Upon her wings presents the god unshorn.
    See how Aurora throws her fair
    Fresh-quilted colors through the air.
    Get up, sweet slug-a-bed, and see   5
    The dew-bespangling herb and tree.
Each flower has wept and bowed toward the East
Above an hour since; yet you not dressed,
    Nay! not so much as out of bed?
    When all the birds have matins said,   10
    And sung their thankful hymns: 'tis sin,
    Nay, profanation, to keep in,
Whenas a thousand virgins on this day
Spring, sooner than the lark, to fetch in May.

Rise and put on your foliage and be seen   15
To come forth like the springtime, fresh and green
    And sweet as Flora. Take no care
    For jewels for your gown or hair;
    Fear not, the leaves will strew
    Gems in abundance upon you.   20
Besides, the childhood of the day has kept,
Against you come, some orient pearls unwept;
    Come, and receive them while the light
    Hangs on the dew-locks of the night.
    And Titan on the eastern hill   25
    Retires himself, or else stands still
Till you come forth. Wash, dress, be brief in praying:
Few beads are best, when once we go a-Maying.

Come, my Corinna, come; and coming, mark
How each field turns a street; each street a park   30
    Made green and trimmed with trees; see how
    Devotion gives each house a bough
    Or branch; each porch, each door, ere this,
    An ark, a tabernacle is,

---

2. *the god:* Phoebus, the sun. **3.** *Aurora:* the dawn. **10.** *matins:* morning prayer. **14.** *May:* hawthorn blossoms. **25.** *Titan:* the sun.

Made up of white-thorn neatly interwove, 35
As if here were those cooler shades of love.
　　Can such delights be in the street,
　　And open fields, and we not see't?
　　Come, we'll abroad; and let's obey
　　The proclamation made for May, 40
And sin no more, as we have done, by staying;
But my Corinna, come, let's go a-Maying.

There's not a budding boy or girl this day
But is got up and gone to bring in May.
　　A deal of youth ere this is come 45
　　Back and with white-thorn laden home.
　　Some have dispatched their cakes and cream,
　　Before that we have left to dream;
And some have wept, and wooed, and plighted troth,
And chose their priest, ere we can cast off sloth. 50
　　Many a green-gown has been given;
　　Many a kiss, both odd and even;
　　Many a glance too has been sent
　　From out the eye, love's firmament;
Many a jest told of the keys betraying 55
This night, and locks picked, yet we're not a-Maying.

Come, let us go, while we are in our prime;
And take the harmless folly of the time.
　　We shall grow old apace and die
　　Before we know our liberty.
　　Our life is short; and our days run 60
　　As fast away as does the sun:
And as a vapor or a drop of rain
Once lost, can ne'er be found again,
　　So when or you or I are made
　　A fable, song, or fleeting shade, 65
　　All love, all liking, all delight
　　Lies drowned with us in endless night.
Then while time serves, and we are but decaying,
Come, my Corinna, come, let's go a-Maying. 70

GEORGE HERBERT
(1593–1633)

THE ALTAR

A broken A L T A R, Lord, thy servant rears,
Made of a heart; and cemented with tears;
   Whose parts are as thy hand did frame;
    No workman's tool hath touched the same.
       A H E A R T alone   5
       Is such a stone,
       As nothing but
       Thy power doth cut.
       Wherefore each part
       Of my hard heart   10
       Meets in this frame
       To praise thy name;
   That if I chance to hold my peace,
   These stones to praise thee may not cease.
Oh, let thy blessed SACRIFICE be mine,   15
And sanctify this ALTAR to be thine.

EASTER WINGS

Lord, who createdst man in wealth and store,
   Though foolishly he lost the same,
      Decaying more and more
         Till he became
           Most poor;   5
           With thee
         Oh, let me rise
      As larks, harmoniously,
   And sing this day thy victories;
Then shall the fall further the flight in me.   10

My tender age in sorrow did begin;
   And still with sicknesses and shame
      Thou didst so punish sin,
         That I became
           Most thin.   15
           With thee
         Let me combine,
   And feel this day thy victory;
  For if I imp my wing on thine,
Affliction shall advance the flight in me.   20

THE WINDOWS

Lord, how can man preach thy eternal word?
    He is a brittle crazy glass;
Yet in thy temple thou dost him afford
    This glorious and transcendent place,
    To be a window, through thy grace.   5

But when thou dost anneal in glass thy story,
    Making thy life to shine within
The holy preachers, then the light and glory
    More rev'rend grows and more doth win,
    Which else shows wat'rish, bleak, and thin.   10

Doctrine and life, colors and light, in one
    When they combine and mingle, bring
A strong regard and awe; but speech alone
    Doth vanish like a flaring thing
    And in the ear, not conscience, ring.   15

6. *anneal:* fix the colors by heating.

THE BUNCH OF GRAPES

Joy, I did lock thee up, but some bad man
    Hath let thee out again;
And now, methinks, I am where I began
    Sev'n years ago: one vogue and vein,
    One air of thoughts usurps my brain.   5
I did toward Canaan draw; but now I am
Brought back to the Red Sea, the sea of shame.

For as the Jews of old by God's command
    Traveled and saw no town;
So now each Christian hath his journeys spanned,   10
    Their story pens and sets us down.
    A single deed is small renown.
God's works are wide and let in future times;
His ancient justice overflows our crimes.

Then have we too our guardian fires and clouds;   15
    Our scripture-dew drops fast:
We have our sands and serpents, tents and shrouds;
    Alas! our murmurings come not last.
    But where's the cluster? where's the taste
Of mine inheritance? Lord, if I must borrow,   20
Let me as well take up their joy, as sorrow.

But can he want the grape, who hath the wine?
    I have their fruit and more.
Blessed be God, who prospered Noah's vine,
    And made it bring forth grapes good store.   25
    But much more him I must adore,
Who of the law's sour juice sweet wine did make,
Ev'n God himself, being pressed for my sake.

6. *Canaan:* the Promised Land. The speaker imagines himself wandering in
the wilderness like the Israelites. **19ff.** *the cluster:* the huge cluster of
grapes brought back from Canaan to the Israelites in the wilderness (see
Numbers 13:17–24). Herbert sees it as a symbolic anticipation of the role of
Christ in the life of the faithful Christian. **27.** *law's sour juice . . . sweet
wine:* the traditional Pauline opposition of the Law of the Old Testament to
the promise of forgiveness given in the New Testament.

THE COLLAR

I struck the board, and cried: No more.
                    I will abroad.
What? shall I ever sigh and pine?
My lines and life are free, free as the road,
    Loose as the wind, as large as store.   5
        Shall I be still in suit?
Have I no harvest but a thorn
To let me blood, and not restore
What I have lost with cordial fruit?
                    Sure there was wine   10
    Before my sighs did dry it: there was corn
        Before my tears did drown it.
Is the year only lost to me?
    Have I no bays to crown it?
No flowers, no garlands gay? all blasted?   15
                    All wasted?
    Not so, my heart: but there is fruit,
            And thou hast hands.
        Recover all thy sigh-blown age
On double pleasures; leave thy cold dispute   20
Of what is fit and not. Forsake thy cage,
                    Thy rope of sands,
Which petty thoughts have made, and made to thee
    Good cable, to enforce and draw,
            And be thy law,   25
While thou didst wink and wouldst not see.
            Away; take heed;
            I will abroad.
Call in thy death's head there; tie up thy fears.
        He that forbears   30
    To suit and serve his need
        Deserves his load.
But as I raved and grew more fierce and wild
        At every word,
    Methoughts I heard one calling, Child;   35
        And I replied, My Lord.

9. *cordial:* from the heart; hence, heartfelt and sincere. In the noun form, a cordial is a medicinal drink that invigorates the heart. **14.** *bays:* triumphal garland.

ANDREW MARVELL
(1621–1678)

ON A DROP OF DEW

See how the orient dew,
Shed from the bosom of the morn
    Into the blowing roses,
Yet careless of its mansion new,
For the clear region where 'twas born   5
    Round in its self encloses;
    And in its little globe's extent
Frames as it can its native element.
    How it the purple flow'r does slight,
        Scarce touching where it lies,
    But gazing back upon the skies   10
        Shines with a mournful light,
            Like its own tear,
Because so long divided from the sphere.
    Restless it rolls and unsecure,   15
        Trembling lest it grow impure,
    Till the warm sun pity its pain
And to the skies exhale it back again.
        So the soul, that drop, that ray
Of the clear fountain of eternal day,   20
Could it within the human flow'r be seen,
    Rememb'ring still its former height,
    Shuns the sweet leaves and blossoms green;
    And, recollecting its own light,
Does in its pure and circling thoughts express   25
The greater heaven in an heaven less.
    In how coy a figure wound,
    Every way it turns away;
    So the world excluding round,
    Yet receiving in the day.   30
    Dark beneath but bright above;
    Here disdaining, there in love.
How loose and easy hence to go,
How girt and ready to ascend.

Moving but on a point below,
   It all about does upwards bend.
Such did the manna's sacred dew distill;
White and entire, though congealed and chill.
Congealed on earth: but does, dissolving, run
Into the glories of th' almighty sun.

35

40

BERMUDAS

Where the remote Bermudas ride
In th' ocean's bosom unespied,
From a small boat that rowed along
The list'ning winds received this song:
    What should we do but sing his praise 5
That led us through the wat'ry maze,
Unto an isle so long unknown
And yet far kinder than our own?
Where he the huge sea-monsters wracks,
That lift the deep upon their backs. 10
He lands us on a grassy stage
Safe from the storms and prelate's rage.
He gave us this eternal spring
Which here enamels every thing;
And sends the fowls to us in care, 15
On daily visits through the air.
He hangs in shades the orange bright,
Like golden lamps in a green night,
And does in the pomegranates close
Jewels more rich than Ormus shows. 20
He makes the figs our mouths to meet
And throws the melons at our feet,
But apples plants of such a price,
No tree could ever bear them twice.
With cedars, chosen by his hand 25
From Lebanon, he stores the land,
And makes the hollow seas that roar
Proclaim the ambergris on shore.
He cast (of which we rather boast)
The Gospel's pearl upon our coast. 30
And in these rocks for us did frame
A temple, where to sound his name.
Oh let our voice his praise exalt
Till it arrive at heaven's vault,
Which thence (perhaps) rebounding, may 35

12. *prelate's rage:* The singers are Puritans fleeing the judicial power of the
Anglican bishops, or prelates.

Echo beyond the Mexique Bay.
Thus sung they in the English boat
An holy and a cheerful note,
And all the way to guide their chime,
With falling oars they kept the time.   40

TO HIS COY MISTRESS

Had we but world enough and time,
This coyness, lady, were no crime.
We would sit down and think which way
To walk and pass our long love's day.
Thou by the Indian Ganges' side   5
Shouldst rubies find; I by the tide
Of Humber would complain. I would
Love you ten years before the flood:
And you should, if you please, refuse
Till the conversion of the Jews.   10
My vegetable love should grow
Vaster than empires and more slow.
An hundred years should go to praise
Thine eyes and on thy forehead gaze.
Two hundred to adore each breast,   15
But thirty thousand to the rest.
An age at least to every part,
And the last age should show your heart.
For, lady, you deserve this state;
Nor would I love at lower rate.   20
  But at my back I always hear
Time's winged chariot hurrying near;
And yonder all before us lie
Deserts of vast eternity.
Thy beauty shall no more be found;   25
Nor in thy marble vault shall sound
My echoing song; then worms shall try
That long preserved virginity,
And your quaint honor turn to dust,
And into ashes all my lust.   30
The grave's a fine and private place,
But none, I think, do there embrace.
  Now, therefore, while the youthful hue
Sits on thy skin like morning dew,
And while thy willing soul transpires   35
At every pore with instant fires,

8–10. *flood . . . Jews:* Noah's flood marks a beginning; the conversion of the Jews was said to come just before the end of the world. **19.** *state:* pomp and ceremony.

Now let us sport us while we may;
And now, like am'rous birds of prey,
Rather at once our time devour,
Than languish in his slow-chap't pow'r.   40
Let us roll all our strength and all
Our sweetness up into one ball;
And tear our pleasures with rough strife
Thorough the iron gates of life.
Thus, though we cannot make our sun   45
Stand still, yet we will make him run.

40. *slow-chap't:* slowly devoured by Time's chaps, or jaws. **44.** *thorough:* through.

THE DEFINITION OF LOVE

I
My love is of a birth as rare
As 'tis for object strange and high:
It was begotten by despair
Upon impossibility.

II
Magnanimous despair alone   5
Could show me so divine a thing,
Where feeble hope could ne'er have flown
But vainly flapped its tinsel wing.

III
And yet I quickly might arrive
Where my extended soul is fixed,   10
But Fate does iron wedges drive
And always crowds itself betwixt.

IV
For Fate with jealous eye does see
Two perfect loves; nor lets them close:
Their union would her ruin be,   15
And her tyrannic pow'r depose.

V
And therefore her decrees of steel
Us as the distant poles have placed,
(Though love's whole world on us doth wheel)
Not by themselves to be embraced;   20

VI
Unless the giddy heaven fall,
And earth some new convulsion tear;
And, us to join, the world should all
Be cramped into a planisphere.

18. *poles:* In the Ptolemaic system of astronomy, the poles of the earth's axis extended to the spheres of the fixed stars.

VII

As lines, so loves oblique may well   25
Themselves in every angle greet:
But ours so truly parallel,
Though infinite, can never meet.

VIII

Therefore the love which us doth bind,
But Fate so enviously debars,   30
Is the conjunction of the mind
And opposition of the stars.

31–32. conjunction . . . opposition: astrological terms for positive and negative influences of the planets, as determined by their relative positions in
space.

THE MOWER AGAINST GARDENS

Luxurious man, to bring his vice in use,
   Did after him the world seduce,
And from the fields the flow'rs and plants allure,
   Where nature was most plain and pure.
He first enclosed within the garden's square   5
   A dead and standing pool of air;
And a more luscious earth for them did knead,
   Which stupified them while it fed.
The pink grew then as double as his mind;
   The nutriment did change the kind.   10
With strange perfumes he did the roses taint;
   And flow'rs themselves were taught to paint.
The tulip white did for complexion seek,
   And learned to interline its cheek;
Its onion root they then so high did hold,   15
   That one was for a meadow sold.
Another world was searched, through oceans new,
   To find the marvel of Peru.
And yet these rarities might be allowed
   To man, that sov'reign thing and proud,   20
Had he not dealt between the bark and tree,
   Forbidden mixtures there to see.
No plant now knew the stock from which it came;
   He grafts upon the wild the tame,
That the uncertain and adult'rate fruit   25
   Might put the palate in dispute.
His green seraglio has its eunuchs too;
   Lest any tyrant him outdo;
And in the cherry he does nature vex,
   To procreate without a sex.   30
'Tis all enforced, the fountain and the grot,
   While the sweet fields do lie forgot,
Where willing nature does to all dispense
   A wild and fragrant innocence;

2. *after him:* after the fall of man and the loss of Eden. **12.** *paint:* use cosmetics.

And fauns and fairies do the meadows till 35
    More by their presence than their skill.
Their statues, polished by some ancient hand,
    May to adorn the gardens stand;
But howsoe'er the figures do excel,
    The gods themselves with us do dwell. 40

DAMON THE MOWER

I

Hark how the mower Damon sung,
With love of Juliana stung!
While ev'ry thing did seem to paint
The scene more fit for his complaint.
Like her fair eyes the day was fair,   5
But scorching like his am'rous care;
Sharp like his scythe his sorrow was,
And withered like his hopes the grass.

II

"Oh what unusual heats are here,
Which thus our sunburned meadows sear!   10
The grasshopper its pipe gives o'er
And hamstringed frogs can dance no more.
But in the brook the green frog wades,
And grasshoppers seek out the shades.
Only the snake, that kept within,   15
Now glitters in its second skin.

III

"This heat the sun could never raise,
Nor Dog Star so inflames the days.
It from an higher beauty grow'th,
Which burns the fields and mower both,   20
Which made the Dog and makes the sun
Hotter than his own Phaeton.
Not July causeth these extremes,
But Juliana's scorching beams.

18; 21. *Dog Star; the Dog:* Sirius, the Dog Star, said to be responsible for
the scorching heat of August. **22.** *Phaeton:* the son of Apollo. He wrecked
the chariot of the sun and scorched the earth.

IV

"Tell me where I may pass the fires   25
Of the hot day, or hot desires.
To what cool cave shall I descend,
Or to what gelid fountain bend?
Alas! I look for ease in vain,
When remedies themselves complain.   30
No moisture but my ears do rest,
Nor cold but in her icy breast.

V

"How long wilt thou, fair shepherdess,
Esteem me, and my presents less?
To thee the harmless snake I bring,   35
Disarmed of its teeth and sting.
To thee chameleons changing-hue,
And oak leaves tipped with honey dew.
Yet thou ungrateful hast not sought
Nor what they are, nor who them brought.   40

VI

"I am the mower Damon, known
Through all the meadows I have mown.
On me the morn her dew distills
Before her darling daffodils.
And, if at noon my toil me heat,   45
The sun himself licks off my sweat;
While, going home, the ev'ning sweet
In cowslip-water bathes my feet.

VII

"What though the piping shepherd stock
The plains with an unnumbered flock,   50
This scythe of mine discovers wide
More ground than all his sheep do hide.
With this the golden fleece I shear
Of all these closes ev'ry year;
And though in wool more poor than they,   55
Yet am I richer far in hay.

54. *closes:* enclosed meadows.

VIII

"Nor am I so deformed to sight,
If in my scythe I looked right;
In which I see my picture done,
As in a crescent moon the sun.
The deathless fairies take me oft
To lead them in their dances soft;
And when I tune myself to sing,
About me they contract their ring.

60

IX

"How happy might I still have mowed,
Had not love here his thistles sowed!
But now I all the day complain,
Joining my labor to my pain;
And with my scythe cut down the grass,
Yet still my grief is where it was;
But when the iron blunter grows,
Sighing I whet my scythe and woes."

65

70

X

While thus he threw his elbow round,
Depopulating all the ground,
And with his whistling scythe does cut
Each stroke between the earth and root,
The edged steel by careless chance
Did into his own ankle glance;
And there among the grass fell down,
By his own scythe the mower mown.

75

80

XI

"Alas!" said he, "these hurts are slight
To those that die by love's despite.
With shepherds-purse and clowns-all-heal,
The blood I stanch and wound I seal.
Only for him no cure is found
Whom Juliana's eyes do wound.
'Tis death alone that this must do,
For death thou art a mower too."

85

THE MOWER TO THE GLO-WORMS

I

Ye living lamps, by whose dear light
The nightingale does sit so late,
And studying all the summer night,
Her matchless songs does meditate;

II

Ye country comets that portend   5
No war nor prince's funeral,
Shining unto no higher end
Than to presage the grasses' fall;

III

Ye glo-worms, whose officious flame
To wand'ring mowers shows the way,   10
That in the night have lost their aim,
And after foolish fires do stray;

IV

Your courteous lights in vain you waste
Since Juliana here is come,
For she my mind hath so displaced   15
That I shall never find my home.

---

12. *foolish fires:* the *ignis fatuus,* or will o' the wisp, a wandering light said to lead travelers astray in the night.

THE MOWER'S SONG

I

My mind was once the true survey
Of all these meadows fresh and gay,
And in the greenness of the grass
Did see its hopes as in a glass;
When Juliana came, and she,   5
What I do to the grass, does to my thoughts and me.

II

But these, while I with sorrow pine,
Grew more luxuriant still and fine,
That not one blade of grass you spied,
But had a flower on either side;   10
When Juliana came, and she,
What I do to the grass, does to my thoughts and me.

III

Unthankful meadows, could you so
A fellowship so true forego,
And in your gaudy May-games meet,   15
While I lay trodden under feet?
When Juliana came, and she,
What I do to the grass, does to my thoughts and me.

IV

But what you in compassion ought,
Shall now by my revenge be wrought;   20
And flow'rs and grass and I and all,
Will in one common ruin fall.
For Juliana comes, and she,
What I do to the grass, does to my thoughts and me.

V

And thus, ye meadows, which have been   25
Companions of my thoughts more green,
Shall now the heraldry become
With which I shall adorn my tomb;
For Juliana comes, and she,
What I do to the grass, does to my thoughts and me.   30

THE GARDEN

I

How vainly men themselves amaze
To win the palm, the oak or bays;
And their incessant labors see
Crowned from some single herb or tree,
Whose short and narrow verged shade   5
Does prudently their toils upbraid;
While all flow'rs and all trees do close
To weave the garlands of repose.

II

Fair quiet, have I found thee here,
And innocence thy sister dear!   10
Mistaken long, I sought you then
In busy companies of men.
Your sacred plants, if here below,
Only among the plants will grow.
Society is all but rude,   15
To this delicious solitude.

III

No white nor red was ever seen
So am'rous as this lovely green.
Fond lovers, cruel as their flame,
Cut in these trees their mistress' name.   20
Little, alas, they know or heed
How far these beauties hers exceed!
Fair trees! wheres'e'er your barks I wound,
No name shall but your own be found.

IV

When we have run our passion's heat,   25
Love hither makes his best retreat.
The gods, that mortal beauty chase,
Still in a tree did end their race.

---

1. *amaze:* bewilder. **2.** *palm . . . oak . . . bays:* triumphal garlands celebrating peace, conquest, and poetry, respectively. **5.** *verged:* bordered.
17. *white . . . red:* as in a woman's complexion.

Apollo hunted Daphne so,
Only that she might laurel grow.   30
And Pan did after Syrinx speed,
Not as a nymph, but for a reed.

V

What wond'rous life in this I lead!
Ripe apples drop about my head;
The luscious clusters of the vine   35
Upon my mouth do crush their wine;
The nectarine and curious peach
Into my hands themselves do reach;
Stumbling on melons as I pass,
Ensnared with flow'rs, I fall on grass.   40

VI

Meanwhile the mind, from pleasure less,
Withdraws into its happiness;
The mind, that ocean where each kind
Does straight its own resemblance find;
Yet it creates, transcending these,   45
Far other worlds and other seas;
Annihilating all that's made
To a green thought in a green shade.

VII

Here at the fountain's sliding foot,
Or at some fruit tree's mossy root,   50
Casting the body's vest aside,
My soul into the boughs does glide;
There like a bird it sits and sings,
Then whets and combs its silver wings;
And till prepared for longer flight,   55
Waves in its plumes the various light.

29–32. *Apollo . . . Daphne . . . Pan . . . Syrinx:* To avoid rape by Apollo, Daphne was transformed into a laurel, a symbol of poetry; fleeing the advances of Pan, Syrinx was turned into a reed, from which Pan made his flute.

VIII

Such was that happy garden-state,
While man there walked without a mate:
After a place so pure and sweet,
What other help could yet be meet!   60
But 'twas beyond a mortal's share
To wander solitary there:
Two paradises 'twere in one
To live in paradise alone.

IX

How well the skillful gard'ner drew   65
Of flow'rs and herbs this dial new;
Where from above the milder sun
Does through a fragrant Zodiac run;
And as it works th' industrious bee
Computes its time as well as we.   70
How could such sweet and wholesome hours
Be reckoned but with herbs and flow'rs!

---

57. *garden-state:* Eden. **60.** *help . . . meet:* i.e., woman, made by God to be a meet, or appropriate, help to man. See Genesis 2:18.

JOHN MILTON
(1608–1674)

AT A SOLEMN MUSIC

Blest pair of Sirens, pledges of heav'n's joy,
Sphere-born harmonious sisters, Voice and Verse,
Wed your divine sounds, and mixed power employ
Dead things with inbreathed sense able to pierce,
And to our high-raised fantasy present   5
That undisturbed song of pure concent,
Aye sung before the sapphire-colored throne
To him that sits thereon,
With saintly shout and solemn jubilee,
Where the bright seraphim in burning row   10
Their loud uplifted angel-trumpets blow,
And the cherubic host in thousand choirs
Touch their immortal harps of golden wires,
With those just spirits that wear victorious palms,
Hymns devout and holy psalms   15
Singing everlastingly;
That we on earth with undiscording voice
May rightly answer that melodious noise;
As once we did, till disproportioned sin
Jarred against Nature's chime, and with harsh din   20
Broke the fair music that all creatures made
To their great Lord, whose love their motion swayed
In perfect diapason, whilst they stood
In first obedience and their state of good.
O may we soon again renew that song,   25
And keep in tune with heav'n, till God ere long
To his celestial consort us unite,
To live with him, and sing in endless morn of light.

6. *concent:* harmony.

SONNET XIX

When I consider how my light is spent,
    Ere half my days, in this dark world and wide,
    And that one talent which is death to hide
    Lodged with me useless, though my soul more bent
To serve therewith my maker, and present   5
    My true account, lest he returning chide;
    "Doth God exact day-labor, light denied?"
    I fondly ask. But Patience, to prevent
That murmur, soon replies: "God doth not need
    Either man's work or his own gifts; who best   10
    Bear his mild yoke, they serve him best. His state
Is kingly: thousands at his bidding speed,
    And post o'er land and ocean without rest;
    They also serve who only stand and wait."

3. *talent:* In the parable of the talents (Matthew 25:14–30), the servant who buried the talent (literally, a unit of money) that his master gave him was rebuked for not making use of it.

SONNET XVIII: ON THE LATE MASSACRE IN PIEDMONT

Avenge, O Lord, thy slaughtered saints, whose bones
    Lie scattered on the Alpine mountains cold,
    Ev'n them who kept thy truth so pure of old
    When all our fathers worshiped stocks and stones;
Forget not; in thy book record their groans   5
    Who were thy sheep, and in their ancient fold
    Slain by the bloody Piedmontese that rolled
    Mother with infant down the rocks. Their moans
The vales redoubled to the hills, and they
    To heav'n. Their martyred blood and ashes sow   10
    O'er all th' Italian fields, where still doth sway
The triple tyrant, that from these may grow
    A hundredfold, who, having learnt thy way,
    Early may fly the Babylonian woe.

On . . . Piedmont: On April 24, 1655, Italian troops massacred the Protestant sect of Waldensians in Piedmont. **12.** *triple:* the pope's triple crown. **14.** *Babylonian woe:* the captivity of the Jews in Babylon; metaphorically, the enslavement of the Church.

LYCIDAS

Yet once more, O ye laurels, and once more,
Ye myrtles brown, with ivy never sere,
I come to pluck your berries harsh and crude,
And with forced fingers rude
Shatter your leaves before the mellowing year. 5
Bitter constraint, and sad occasion dear,
Compels me to disturb your season due;
For Lycidas is dead, dead ere his prime,
Young Lycidas, and hath not left his peer.
Who would not sing for Lycidas? He knew 10
Himself to sing, and build the lofty rhyme.
He must not float upon his wat'ry bier
Unwept, and welter to the parching wind,
Without the meed of some melodious tear.

    Begin then, sisters of the sacred well 15
That from beneath the seat of Jove doth spring,
Begin, and somewhat loudly sweep the string.
Hence with denial vain and coy excuse;
So may some gentle muse
With lucky words favor my destined urn, 20
And as he passes turn,
And bid fair peace be to my sable shroud.
For we were nursed upon the self-same hill,
Fed the same flock, by fountain, shade, and rill.

    Together both, ere the high lawns appeared 25
Under the opening eyelids of the morn,
We drove afield, and both together heard
What time the gray-fly winds her sultry horn,
Batt'ning our flocks with the fresh dews of night,
Oft till the star that rose, at ev'ning, bright 30
Toward heav'n's descent had sloped his westering wheel.
Meanwhile the rural ditties were not mute,
Tempered to th' oaten flute;
Rough satyrs danced, and fauns with clov'n heel
From the glad sound would not be absent long, 35

---

8. *Lycidas:* a shepherd drowned in the sea. He is represented by "the un-couth swain" (l. 186) as a poet, scholar, and candidate for the priesthood.
15. *sisters . . . well:* the muses, who drew their inspiration from the Pierian spring at the base of Mt. Olympus ("the seat of Jove").

And old Damoetas loved to hear our song.
   But O the heavy change, now thou art gone,
Now thou art gone, and never must return!
Thee, shepherd, thee the woods and desert caves,
With wild thyme and the gadding vine o'ergrown,   40
And all their echoes mourn.
The willows and the hazel copses green
Shall now no more be seen
Fanning their joyous leaves to thy soft lays.
As killing as the canker to the rose,   45
Or taint-worm to the weanling herds that graze,
Or frost to flowers, that their gay wardrobe wear,
When first the white-thorn blows;
Such, Lycidas, thy loss to shepherd's ear.
   Where were ye, nymphs, when the remorseless deep   50
Closed o'er the head of your loved Lycidas?
For neither were ye playing on the steep
Where your old bards, the famous druids, lie,
Nor on the shaggy top of Mona high,
Nor yet where Deva spreads her wizard stream.   55
Ay me, I fondly dream,
Had ye been there!—for what could that have done?
What could the muse herself that Orpheus bore,
The muse herself, for her enchanting son
Whom universal nature did lament,   60
When by the rout that made the hideous roar
His gory visage down the stream was sent,
Down the swift Hebrus to the Lesbian shore?
   Alas! what boots it with uncessant care
To tend the homely slighted shepherd's trade,   65
And strictly meditate the thankless muse?
Were it not better done as others use,
To sport with Amaryllis in the shade,
Or with the tangles of Neaera's hair?
Fame is the spur that the clear spirit doth raise   70
(That last infirmity of noble mind)

58–63. *What . . . shore:* Orpheus, the son of the muse Calliope, was a priest of Dionysus. His poetry and his death drew a sympathetic response from nature ("enchanting," "lament"). He was torn to pieces by Thracian women; his body floated down the Hebrus River to the shore of the island of Lesbos.

To scorn delights, and live laborious days;
But the fair guerdon when we hope to find,
And think to burst out into sudden blaze,
Comes the blind Fury with th'abhorred shears,   75
And slits the thin-spun life. "But not the praise,"
Phoebus replied, and touched my trembling ears:
"Fame is no plant that grows on mortal soil,
Nor in the glistering foil
Set off to th' world, nor in broad rumor lies,   80
But lives and spreads aloft by those pure eyes
And perfect witness of all-judging Jove;
As he pronounces lastly on each deed,
Of so much fame in heav'n expect thy meed."

   O fountain Arethuse, and thou honored flood,   85
Smooth-sliding Mincius, crowned with vocal reeds,
That strain I heard was of a higher mood.
But now my oat proceeds,
And listens to the herald of the sea
That came in Neptune's plea.   90
He asked the waves, and asked the felon winds,
"What hard mishap hath doomed this gentle swain?"
And questioned every gust of rugged wings
That blows from off each beaked promontory;
They knew not of his story,   95
And sage Hippotades their answer brings,
That not a blast was from his dungeon strayed;
The air was calm, and on the level brine
Sleek Panope with her all sisters played.
It was that fatal and perfidious bark,   100
Built in th' eclipse, and rigged with curses dark,
That sunk so low that sacred head of thine.

   Next Camus, reverend sire, went footing slow,
His mantle hairy, and his bonnet sedge,
Inwrought with figures dim, and on the edge   105
Like to that sanguine flower inscribed with woe.

85–86. *Arethuse . . . Mincius:* rivers associated with pastoral poetry.
88. *oat:* oaten flute.   **89.** *herald:* Triton.   **96.** *Hippotades:* Aeolus, god of
the wind.   **103.** *Camus:* the river Cam, associated with Cambridge University.
106. *that . . . flower:* the hyacinth, said to have sprung from the blood of
a young man. On its petals, it is said, are inscribed the letters "Ai," the
Greek sound of mourning ("woe").

"Ah, who hath reft," quoth he, "my dearest pledge?"
Last came, and last did go,
The Pilot of the Galilean lake;
Two massy keys he bore of metals twain   110
(The golden opes, the iron shuts amain).
He shook his mitred locks, and stern bespake:
"How well could I have spared for thee, young swain,
Enow of such as for their bellies' sake
Creep and intrude and climb into the fold!   115
Of other care they little reck'ning make
Than how to scramble at the shearers' feast,
And shove away the worthy bidden guest.
Blind mouths! that scarce themselves know how to hold
A sheep-hook, or have learned aught else the least   120
That to the faithful herdman's art belongs!
What recks it them? What need they? They are sped;
And when they list, their lean and flashy songs
Grate on their scrannel pipes of wretched straw;
The hungry sheep look up, and are not fed,   125
But swol'n with wind, and the rank mist they draw,
Rot inwardly, and foul contagion spread;
Besides what the grim wolf with privy paw
Daily devours apace, and nothing said;
But that two-handed engine at the door   130
Stands ready to smite once, and smite no more."
    Return, Alpheus, the dread voice is past
That shrunk thy streams; return, Sicilian muse,
And call the vales, and bid them hither cast
Their bells and flow'rets of a thousand hues.   135
Ye valleys low where the mild whispers use
Of shades and wanton winds and gushing brooks,
On whose fresh lap the swart star sparely looks,
Throw hither all your quaint enameled eyes,
That on the green turf suck the honeyed show'rs,   140
And purple all the ground with vernal flow'rs.

107. *pledge:* child or disciple. 109. *Pilot:* Saint Peter, the fishermen of Galilee, who bears the keys of Heaven. 122. *recks:* profits; *sped:* prospered. 124. *scrannel:* thin and harsh. 130. *that . . . engine:* a cryptic prophecy of divine retribution. 132–133. *Alpheus . . . muse:* a river in Arcadia, associated, like the "Sicilian muse," with pastoral poetry. 138. *swart star:* Sirius, the Dog Star, associated with the drought of late summer.

Bring the rathe primrose that forsaken dies,
The tufted crowtoe, and pale jessamine,
The white pink, and the pansy freaked with jet,
The glowing violet,   145
The musk-rose, and the well-attired woodbine,
With cowslips wan that hang the pensive head,
And every flower that sad embroidery wears.
Bid amaranthus all his beauty shed,
And daffadillies fill their cups with tears,   150
To strew the laureate hearse where Lycid lies.
For so to interpose a little ease,
Let our frail thoughts dally with false surmise.
Ay me! whilst thee the shores and sounding seas
Wash far away, where'er thy bones are hurled,   155
Whether beyond the stormy Hebrides,
Where thou perhaps under the whelming tide
Visit'st the bottom of the monstrous world;
Or whether thou, to our moist vows denied,
Sleep'st by the fable of Bellerus old,   160
Where the great Vision of the guarded mount
Looks toward Namancos and Bayona's hold:
Look homeward, Angel, now, and melt with ruth;
And, O ye dolphins, waft the hapless youth.
        Weep no more, woeful shepherds, weep no more,   165
For Lycidas, your sorrow, is not dead,
Sunk though he be beneath the wat'ry floor;
So sinks the day-star in the ocean bed,
And yet anon repairs his drooping head,
And tricks his beams, and with new-spangled ore   170
Flames in the forehead of the morning sky:
So Lycidas sunk low, but mounted high,
Through the dear might of him that walked the waves,
Where, other groves and other streams along,
With nectar pure his oozy locks he laves,   175
And hears the unexpressive nuptial song
In the blest kingdoms meek of joy and love.

---

142. *rathe:* early.   **160.** *Bellerus:* a giant from whom Land's End, at the tip of
Cornwall, was thought to have got its Roman name, Bellerium. **161–163.**
Where . . . Angel: "The great Vision" is the archangel Michael, who is
imagined upon Saint Michael's Mount in Cornwall, looking toward Spain
("Namancos and Bayona's hold").

There entertain him all the saints above,
In solemn troops and sweet societies
That sing, and singing in their glory move,   180
And wipe the tears for ever from his eyes.
Now, Lycidas, the shepherds weep no more;
Henceforth thou art the Genius of the shore,
In thy large recompense, and shalt be good
To all that wander in that perilous flood.   185

    Thus sang the uncouth swain to th' oaks and rills,
While the still morn went out with sandals gray;
He touched the tender stops of various quills,
With eager thought warbling his Doric lay.
And now the sun had stretched out all the hills,   190
And now was dropped into the western bay;
At last he rose, and twitched his mantle blue:
Tomorrow to fresh woods and pastures new.

---

183. *Genius:* tutelary god.   **189.** *Doric:* thought to be the original language of Greek pastoral.

JOHN DRYDEN
(1631–1700)

A SONG FOR SAINT CECILIA'S DAY, 1687

I

From harmony, from heav'nly harmony,
    This universal frame began.
    When nature underneath a heap
      Of jarring atoms lay
    And could not heave her head, 5
The tuneful voice was heard from high,
    "Arise, ye more than dead."
Then cold and hot and moist and dry
In order to their stations leap
    And music's pow'r obey. 10
From harmony, from heav'nly harmony,
    This universal frame began:
    From harmony to harmony
Through all the compass of the notes it ran,
The diapason closing full in man. 15

II

What passion cannot music raise and quell!
    When Jubal struck the corded shell
    His list'ning brethren stood around
    And wond'ring on their faces fell
    To worship that celestial sound. 20
Less than a god they thought there could not dwell
    Within the hollow of that shell
    That spoke so sweetly and so well.
What passion cannot music raise and quell!

Saint Cecilia: the patron saint of music. She was credited with the invention of the organ. **8.** *Then . . . dry:* the attributes of the four elements—earth, fire, water, and air. **17.** *Jubal:* said in Genesis 4:21 to be the "father of such as handle the harp and organ."

III

    The trumpet's loud clangor 25
      Excites us to arms
    With shrill notes of anger
      And mortal alarms.
    The double double double beat
      Of the thund'ring drum 30
    Cries, "Hark! the foes come;
Charge! charge! 'tis too late to retreat!"

IV

    The soft complaining flute
    In dying notes discovers
    The woes of hopeless lovers, 35
Whose dirge is whispered by the warbling lute.

V

    Sharp violins proclaim
Their jealous pangs and desperation,
Fury, frantic indignation,
Depth of pains and height of passion 40
    For the fair, disdainful dame.

VI

    But oh! what art can teach
    What human voice can reach
The sacred organ's praise?
Notes inspiring holy love, 45
Notes that wing their heav'nly ways
    To mend the choirs above.

VII

Orpheus could lead the savage race;
And trees unrooted left their place
    Sequacious of the lyre. 50
But bright Cecilia raised the wonder high'r:
When to her organ vocal breath was giv'n,
An angel heard and straight appeared
    Mistaking earth for heaven.

48–50. *Orpheus:* said to be able to move nature in cosmic sympathy with the sound of his lyre.

GRAND CHORUS

As from the pow'r of sacred lays 55
  The spheres began to move,
And sung the great Creator's praise
  To all the bless'd above;
So when the last and dreadful hour
This crumbling pageant shall devour, 60
The trumpet shall be heard on high,
The dead shall live, the living die,
And music shall untune the sky.

55–56. cf. Milton's "At a Solemn Music," p. 87.

JONATHAN SWIFT
(1667–1745)

A DESCRIPTION OF THE MORNING

Now hardly here and there a hackney-coach
Appearing, showed the ruddy morn's approach.
Now Betty from her master's bed had flown,
And softly stole to discompose her own.
The slipshod 'prentice from his master's door   5
Had pared the dirt and sprinkled round the floor.
Now Moll had whirled her mop with dext'rous airs,
Prepared to scrub the entry and the stairs.
The youth with broomy stumps began to trace
The kennel-edge where wheels had worn the place.   10
The small-coal man was heard with cadence deep,
'Till drowned in shriller notes of chimney-sweep.
Duns at his Lordship's gate began to meet,
And brick-dust Moll had screamed through half the street.
The turnkey now his flock returning sees,   15
Duly let out a-nights to steal for fees.
The watchful bailiffs take their silent stands,
And schoolboys lag with satchels in their hands.

10. *kennel-edge:* gutter.   13. *duns:* bill collectors.   14. *brick-dust:* probably
a scouring powder that she sells.   15. *turnkey:* jailer.   16. *fees:* for priv-
ileges in prison.   17. *bailiffs:* agents of the law, here apparently in wait for
insolvent debtors.

A DESCRIPTION OF A CITY SHOWER

Careful observers may foretell the hour
(By sure prognostics) when to dread a show'r:
While rain depends, the pensive cat gives o'er
Her frolics and pursues her tail no more.
Returning home at night, you'll find the sink   5
Strike your offended sense with double stink.
If you be wise, then go not far to dine,
You'll spend in coach-hire more than save in wine.
A coming show'r your shooting corns presage,
Old aches throb, your hollow tooth will rage.   10
Saunt'ring in coffee-house is Dulman seen;
He damns the climate and complains of spleen.

Meanwhile the south rising with dabbled wings,
A sable cloud a-thwart the welkin flings,
That swilled more liquor than it could contain,   15
And like a drunkard gives it up again.
Brisk Susan whips her linen from the rope
While the first drizzling show'r is borne aslope,
Such is that sprinkling which some careless quean
Flirts on you from her mop, but not so clean.   20
You fly, invoke the gods; then turning, stop
To rail; she singing, still whirls on her mop.
Not yet the dust had shunned th' unequal strife,
But aided by the wind fought still for life;
And wafted with its foe by violent gust,   25
'Twas doubtful which was rain and which was dust.
Ah! where must needy poet seek for aid,
When dust and rain at once his coat invade;
His only coat, where dust confused with rain,
Roughen the nap, and leave a mingled stain.   30

---

3. *depends:* hangs back, delays. **5.** *sink:* sewer. **12.** *spleen:* a splenetic, or irritable, condition said to be aggravated by damp weather. **14.** *welkin:* poetic diction for *sky*. **18.** *is borne aslope:* is carried in a slanting, downward direction. **19.** *quean:* slut. **20.** *Flirts:* flicks.

Now in contiguous drops the flood comes down,
Threat'ning with deluge this devoted town.
To shops in crowds the dagged females fly,
Pretend to cheapen goods, but nothing buy.
The templar spruce, while ev'ry spout's a-broach, 35
Stays till 'tis fair, yet seems to call a coach.
The tucked-up seamstress walks with hasty strides,
While streams run down her oiled umbrella's sides.
Here various kinds by various fortunes led,
Commence acquaintance underneath a shed. 40
Triumphant Tories and desponding Whigs,
Forget their feuds and join to save their wigs.
Boxed in a chair the beau impatient sits,
While spouts run clatt'ring o'er the roof by fits;
And ever and anon with frightful din 45
The leather sounds; he trembles from within.
So when Troy chair-men bore the wooden steed,
Pregnant with Greeks, impatient to be freed,
(Those bully Greeks, who, as the moderns do,
Instead of paying chair-men, run them thro'.) 50
Laoco'n struck the outside with his spear,
And each imprisoned hero quaked for fear.

Now from all parts the swelling kennels flow,
And bear their trophies with them as they go:
Filth of all hues and odors seem to tell 55
What street they sailed from by their sight and smell.
They, as each torrent drives, with rapid force
From Smithfield, or St. Pulchre's shape their course,
And in huge confluent join at Snow-Hill Ridge,
Fall from the conduit prone to Holborn Bridge. 60
Sweeping from butchers' stalls, dung, guts, and blood,
Drowned puppies, stinking sprats, all drenched in mud,
Dead cats and turnip-tops come tumbling down the flood.

32. *deluge:* as in Noah's flood. *devoted:* pious.   **33.** *dagged:* daggled, splattered with mud.   **34.** *cheapen:* bargain for.   **35.** *templar:* barrister or lawyer. **43.** *chair:* sedan chair, an elegant conveyance.   **51–52.** In Book II of the *Aeneid*, the priest Laocoön tries to show the Trojans that the wooden horse is hollow by throwing a spear at it.   **53.** *kennels:* gutters.

THE PROGRESS OF BEAUTY

When first Diana leaves her bed
Vapors and steams her looks disgrace;
A frowzy dirty colored red
Sits on her cloudy wrinkled face.

But by degrees when mounted high   5
Her artificial face appears
Down from her window in the sky,
Her spots are gone, her visage clears.

'Twixt earthly females and the moon
All parallels exactly run;   10
If Celia should appear too soon,
Alas, the nymph would be undone.

To see her from her pillow rise
All reeking in a cloudy steam,
Cracked lips, foul teeth, and gummy eyes,   15
Poor Strephon, how would he blaspheme!

The soot or powder which was wont
To make her hair look black as jet,
Falls from her tresses on her front,
A mingled mass of dirt and sweat.   20

Three colors, black and red and white,
So graceful in their proper place,
Remove them to a diff'rent light
They form a frightful hideous face;

For instance, when the lily slips   25
Into the precincts of the rose,
And takes possession of the lips,
Leaving the purple to the nose.

So Celia went entire to bed,
All her complexions safe and sound,   30
But when she rose, the black and red
Though still in sight, had changed their ground.

Progress: triumphal procession, as of a queen. **1.** *Diana:* the moon.

The black, which would not be confined,
A more inferior station seeks,
Leaving the fiery red behind, 35
And mingles in her muddy cheeks.

The paint by perspiration cracks,
And falls in rivulets of sweat;
On either side you see the tracks,
While at her chin the confluent's met. 40

A skillful housewife thus her thumb
With spittle while she spins anoints,
And thus the brown meanders come
In trickling streams betwixt her joints.

But Celia can with ease reduce 45
By help of pencil, paint and brush
Each color to its place and use,
And teach her cheeks again to blush.

She knows her early self no more,
But filled with admiration stands, 50
As other painters oft adore
The workmanship of their own hands.

Thus after four important hours
Celia's the wonder of her sex;
Say, which among the heav'nly pow'rs 55
Could cause such wonderful effects?

Venus, indulgent to her kind,
Gave women all their hearts could wish
When first she taught them where to find
White lead and Lusitanian dish. 60

Love with white lead cements his wings;
White lead was sent us to repair
Two brightest, brittlest earthly things,
A lady's face and chinaware.

37. *paint:* cosmetics.

She ventures now to lift the sash,
The window is her proper sphere;
Ah, lovely nymph, be not too rash,
Nor let the beaux approach too near.   65

Take pattern by your sister star;
Delude at once and bless our sight;
When you are seen, be seen from far,   70
And chiefly choose to shine by night.

In the pell-mell when passing by,
Keep up the glasses of your chair,
Then each transported fop will cry,   75
"G-d d--n me Jack, she's wondrous fair."

But art no longer can prevail
When the materials all are gone;
The best mechanic hand must fail
Where nothing's left to work upon.   80

Matter, as wise logicians say,
Cannot without a form subsist,
And form, say I, as well as they,
Must fail if matter brings no grist.

And this is fair Diana's case;   85
For all astrologers maintain
Each night a bit drops off her face
When mortals say she's in her wane.

While Partridge wisely shows the cause
Efficient of the moon's decay,   90
That Cancer with his pois'nous claws
Attacks her in the Milky Way;

---

73. *pell-mell:* probably Pall Mall, an elegant avenue in London; also, a jostling crowd. 74. *chair:* sedan chair. 89. *Partridge:* John Partridge (1644–1715), a ridiculous astrologer.

But Gadbury in art profound
From her pale cheeks pretends to show
That swain Endymion is not sound,   95
Or else, that Mercury's her foe.

But let the cause be what it will,
In half a month she looks so thin
That Flamstead can with all his skill
See but her forehead and her chin.   100

Yet as she wastes, she grows discreet,
Till midnight never shows her head;
So rotting Celia strolls the street
When sober folks are all a-bed.

For sure if this be Luna's fate,   105
Poor Celia, but of mortal race,
In vain expects a longer date
To the materials of her face.

When mercury her tresses mows
To think of oil and soot is vain;   110
No painting can restore a nose,
Nor will her teeth return again.

Two balls of glass may serve for eyes,
White lead can plaster up a cleft,
But these, alas, are poor supplies   115
If neither cheeks nor lips be left.

Ye pow'rs who over love preside,
Since mortal beauties drop so soon,
If you would have us well supplied,
Send us new nymphs with each new moon.   120

---

93. *Gadbury: John Gadbury* (1627–1704), an astrologer suspected at one time of treason. **95.** *Endymion:* Diana's (or the moon's) lover. **96.** *Mercury:* either the influence of the planet; or the god, who was reputed to be a malicious gossip; or the metal, which was used as a cure for venereal disease. **99.** *Flamstead:* John Flamstead (1646–1719), a respected astronomer and a friend of Newton. **105.** *Luna's:* the moon's, or Diana's.

THE LADY'S DRESSING ROOM

Five hours (and who can do it less in?)
By haughty Celia spent in dressing;
The goddess from her chamber issues,
Arrayed in lace, brocades and tissues.
Strephon, who found the room was void, 5
And Betty otherwise employed,
Stole in and took a strict survey
Of all the litter as it lay;
Whereof, to make the matter clear,
An inventory follows here. 10

And first a dirty smock appeared,
Beneath the armpits well besmeared.
Strephon, the rogue, displayed it wide,
And turned it round on every side.
On such a point few words are best,
And Strephon bids us guess the rest; 15
But swears how damnably men lie,
In calling Celia sweet and cleanly.

Now listen while he next produces,
The various combs for various uses,
Filled up with dirt so closely fixed, 20
No brush could force a way betwixt.
A paste of composition rare,
Sweat, dandruff, powder, lead and hair;
A forehead cloth with oil upon't
To smooth the wrinkles on her front; 25
Here alum flour to stop the steams
Exhaled from sour unsavory streams;
There night-gloves made of Tripsy's hide,
Bequeathed by Tripsy when she died,
With puppy water, beauty's help, 30
Distilled from Tripsy's darling whelp;
Here gallipots and vials placed,
Some filled with washes, some with paste,
Some with pomatum, paints and slops, 35

25. *front:* forehead. **33.** *gallipots:* apothecary jars. **34–35.** *washes . . . slops:* astringents and cosmetics.

And ointments good for scabby chops.
Hard by a filthy basin stands,
Fouled with the scouring of her hands;
The basin takes whatever comes:
The scrapings of her teeth and gums,   40
A nasty compound of all hues,
For here she spits and there she spews.

But oh! it turned poor Strephon's bowels,
When he beheld and smelt the towels,
Begummed, bemattered, and beslimed   45
With dirt and sweat and ear-wax grimed.
No object Strephon's eye escapes;
Here petticoats in frowzy heaps;
Nor be the handkerchiefs forgot
All varnished o'er with snuff and snot.   50
The stockings why should I expose,
Stained with the marks of stinking toes;
Or greasy coifs and pinners reeking,
Which Celia slept at least a week in?
A pair of tweezers next he found   55
To pluck her brows in arches round,
Or hairs that sink the forehead low,
Or on her chin like bristles grow.

The virtues we must not let pass,
Of Celia's magnifying glass.   60
When frightened Strephon cast his eye on't,
It showed the visage of a giant.
A glass that can to sight disclose,
The smallest worm in Celia's nose,
And faithfully direct her nail   65
To squeeze it out from head to tail;
For catch it nicely by the head,
It must come out alive or dead.

Why, Strephon, will you tell the rest?
And must you needs describe the chest?   70
That careless wench! no creature warn her
To move it out from yonder corner;
But leave it standing full in sight

36. *chops:* jaws. **53.** *coifs:* caps; *pinners:* slips or dressing gowns.

For you to exercise your spite.
In vain the workman showed his wit   75
With rings and hinges counterfeit
To make it seem in this disguise,
A cabinet to vulgar eyes;
For Strephon ventured to look in,
Resolved to go through thick and thin;   80
He lifts the lid, there needs no more,
He smelt it all the time before.
As from within Pandora's box
When Epimetheus oped the locks
A sudden universal crew   85
Of human evils upwards flew;
He still was comforted to find
That Hope at last remained behind;
So Strephon, lifting up the lid,
To view what in the chest was hid.   90
The vapors flew from out the vent,
But Strephon, cautious, never meant
The bottom of the pan to grope
And foul his hands in search of Hope.
O never may such vile machine   95
Be once in Celia's chamber seen!
O may she better learn to keep
"Those secrets of the hoary deep!"

    As mutton cutlets, prime of meat,
Which though with art you salt and beat,   100
As laws of cookery require,
And toast them at the clearest fire;
If from adown the hopeful chops
The fat upon a cinder drops,
To stinking smoke it turns the flame,   105
Pois'ning the flesh from whence it came;
And up exhales a greasy stench,
For which you curse the careless wench;
So things which must not be expressed,
When plumped into the reeking chest   110
Send up an excremental smell
To taint the parts from whence they fell;
The petticoats and gown perfume,
Which waft a stink round every room.

Thus finishing his grand survey, 115
Disgusted Strephon stole away
Repeating in his amorous fits,
Oh! Celia, Celia, Celia sh---!

But Vengeance, goddess never sleeping,
Soon punished Strephon for his peeping; 120
His foul imagination links
Each dame he sees with all her stinks:
And if unsav'ry odors fly,
Conceives a lady standing by.
All women his description fits, 125
And both ideas jump like wits,
By vicious fancy coupled fast,
And still appearing in contrast.
I pity wretched Strephon blind
To all the charms of female kind; 130
Should I the Queen of Love refuse,
Because she rose from stinking ooze?
To him that looks behind the scene,
Satira's but some pocky quean.

When Celia in her glory shows, 135
If Strephon would but stop his nose
(Who now so impiously blasphemes
Her ointments, daubs, and paints and creams,
Her washes, slops, and every clout,
With which he makes so foul a rout) 140
He soon would learn to think like me
And bless his ravished sight to see
Such order from confusion sprung,
Such gaudy tulips raised from dung.

---

134. *Satira:* probably a woman who satirizes other women; also a personification of satirical poetry; *pocky quean:* a slut scarred by small-pox.

A BEAUTIFUL YOUNG NYMPH GOING TO BED

Corinna, pride of Drury Lane,
For whom no shepherd sighs in vain;
Never did Covent Garden boast
So bright a battered, strolling toast;
No drunken rake to pick her up,   5
No cellar where on tick to sup;
Returning at the midnight hour;
Four stories climbing to her bow'r;
Then seated on a three-legg'd chair,
Takes off her artificial hair: 10
Now picking out a crystal eye,
She wipes it clean and lays it by.
Her eyebrows from a mouse's hide,
Stuck on with art on either side,
Pulls off with care and first displays 'em,   15
Then in a play-book smoothly lays 'em.
Now dextrously her plumpers draws,
That serves to fill her hollow jaws.
Untwists a wire and from her gums
A set of teeth completely comes.   20
Pulls out the rags contrived to prop
Her flabby dugs, and down they drop.
Proceeding on, the lovely goddess
Unlaces next her steel-ribbed bodice;
Which by the operator's skill,   25
Press down the lumps, the hollows fill.
Up goes her hand and off she slips
The bolsters that supply her hips.
With gentlest touch she next explores
Her shankers, issues, running sores,   30
Effects of many a sad disaster;
And then to each applies a plaster.
But must, before she goes to bed,
Rub off the daubs of white and red;
And smooth the furrows in her front,   35
With greasy paper stuck upon't.
She takes a bolus ere she sleeps;

---

4. *toast:* a woman famous for being toasted at men's drinking parties.
5. *rake:* a playboy. **6.** *on tick:* on credit. **30.** *shankers:* cankers, or open
sores. **35.** *front:* forehead. **37.** *bolus:* a large pill.

And then between two blankets creeps.
With pains of love tormented lies;
Or if she chance to close her eyes,   40
Of Bridewell and the Compter dreams,
And feels the lash and faintly screams;
Or by a faithless bully drawn,
At some hedge-tavern lies in pawn;
Or to Jamaica seems transported,   45
Alone and by no planter courted;
Or near Fleet Ditch's oozy brinks,
Surrounded with a hundred stinks,
Belated, seems on watch to lie,
And snap some cully passing by;   50
Or, struck with fear, her fancy runs
On watchmen, constables and duns,
From whom she meets with frequent rubs;
But never from religious clubs,
Whose favor she is sure to find,   55
Because she pays 'em all in kind.
   Corinna wakes. A dreadful sight!
Behold the ruins of the night!
A wicked rat her plaster stole,
Half ate, and dragged it to his hole.   60
The crystal eye, alas, was missed;
And Puss had on her plumpers p--sed.
A pigeon picked her issue-peas;
And Shock her tresses filled with fleas.
   The nymph, though in this mangled plight,   65
Must ev'ry morn her limbs unite.
But how shall I describe her arts
To recollect the scattered parts?
Or show the anguish, toil and pain,
Of gath'ring up herself again?   70
The bashful muse will never bear
In such a scene to interfere.
Corinna in the morning dizened,
Who sees, will spew; who smells, be poisoned.

41. *Bridewell . . . Compter:* London prisons. **44.** *hedge-tavern:* a low-class tavern. **45.** *transported:* criminals were often shipped to the colonies to serve virtually as slaves. **50.** *cully:* a sucker. **52.** *duns:* bill collectors. **63.** *issue-peas:* peas or granules placed in a wound or venereal sore to keep up irritation and, thus, drainage. **73.** *dizened:* arrayed.

ON HIS OWN DEAFNESS

Deaf, giddy, helpless, left alone,
To all my friends a burthen grown,
No more I hear my church's bell,
Than if it rang out for my knell:

At thunder now no more I start,   5
Than at the rumbling of a cart:
Nay, what's incredible, alack!
I hardly hear a woman's clack.

ALEXANDER POPE
(1688–1744)

ENGRAVED ON THE COLLAR OF A DOG WHICH I GAVE TO HIS ROYAL HIGHNESS

I am his Highness' dog at Kew;
Pray tell me, sir, whose dog are you?

TWO OR THREE; OR, A RECEIPT TO MAKE A CUCKOLD

Two or three visits, and two or three bows,
Two or three civil things, two or three vows,
Two or three kisses, with two or three sighs,
Two or three Jesus's—and let me dies—
Two or three squeezes, and two or three touses,
With two or three thousand pound lost at their houses,
Can never fail cuckolding two or three spouses.

5. *touses:* romps.

Lines from **THE ART OF SINKING IN POETRY**

Who knocks at the door?
For whom thus rudely pleads my loud-tongued gate,
That he may enter? . . .

Shut the door.
The wooden guardian of our privacy
Quick on its axle turn. . . .

Bring my clothes.
Bring me what Nature, tailor to the bear,
To Man himself denied: She gave me cold,
But would not give me clothes. . . .

Light the fire.
Bring forth some remnant of Promethean theft,
Quick to expand th'inclement air congealed
By Boreas' rude breath. . . .

Snuff the candle.
Yon luminary amputation needs;
Thus shall you save its half-extinguished life.

Uncork the bottle, and chip the bread.
Apply thine engine to the spongy door,
Set Bacchus from his glassy prison free,
And strip white Ceres of her nut-brown coat.

THE RAPE OF THE LOCK

Nolueram, Belinda, tuos violare capillos;
Sed juvat, hoc precibus me tribuisse tuis.
　　　　　—Martial, *Epigrams* xii. 84.

CANTO I

What dire offense from amorous causes springs,
What mighty contests rise from trivial things,
I sing—This verse to CARYLL, Muse! is due;
This, even Belinda may vouchsafe to view:
Slight is the subject, but not so the praise,　　　　　5
If she inspire, and he approve my lays.
　　Say what strange motive, goddess! could compel
A well-bred lord t'assault a gentle belle?
Oh say what stranger cause, yet unexplored,
Could make a gentle belle reject a lord?　　　　　10
In tasks so bold, can little men engage,
And in soft bosoms dwells such mighty rage?
　　Sol through white curtains shot a tim'rous ray,
And oped those eyes that must eclipse the day;
Now lap-dogs give themselves the rousing shake,　　　　　15
And sleepless lovers, just at twelve, awake:
Thrice rung the bell, the slipper knocked the ground,
And the pressed watch returned a silver sound.
Belinda still her downy pillow pressed;
Her guardian sylph prolonged the balmy rest.　　　　　20
'Twas he had summoned to her silent bed
The morning dream that hovered o'er her head;
A youth more glittering than a birth-night beau,
(That even in slumber caused her cheek to glow)
Seemed to her ear his winning lips to lay,　　　　　25
And thus in whispers said, or seemed to say.
　　"Fairest of mortals, thou distinguished care
Of thousand bright inhabitants of air!

Nolueram . . . tuis: "I was unwilling to violate your locks, Belinda, but I am
delighted to grant this to your requests." **3.** *Caryll:* John Caryll, a friend of
Pope's, at whose request the poem was written in hopes of improving relations
between the families of Arabella Fermor and Lord Petre, who had fallen out
over the incident on which the poem's narrative is based. **18.** *pressed . . .*
sound: Pressing the stem makes the watch sound the hour. **23.** *birth-night*
beau: a young man dressed for a royal birthday.

If e'er one vision touched thy infant thought,
Of all the nurse and all the priest have taught;   30
Of airy elves by moonlight shadows seen,
The silver token, and the circled green,
Or virgins visited by angel powers,
With golden crowns and wreaths of heavenly flowers;
Hear and believe! thy own importance know,   35
Nor bound thy narrow views to things below.
Some secret truths, from learned pride concealed,
To maids alone and children are revealed:
What though no credit doubting wits may give?
The fair and innocent shall still believe.   40
Know, then, unnumbered spirits round thee fly,
The light militia of the lower sky;
These, though unseen, are ever on the wing,
Hang o'er the box, and hover round the Ring.
Think what an equipage thou hast in air,   45
And view with scorn two pages and a chair.
As now your own, our beings were of old,
And once enclosed in woman's beauteous mold;
Thence, by a soft transition, we repair
From earthly vehicles to these of air.   50
Think not, when woman's transient breath is fled,
That all her vanities at once are dead;
Succeeding vanities she still regards,
And though she plays no more, o'erlooks the cards.
Her joy in gilded chariots, when alive,   55
And love of omber, after death survive.
For when the fair in all their pride expire,
To their first elements their souls retire:
The sprites of fiery termagants in flame
Mount up, and take a salamander's name.   60
Soft yielding minds to water glide away,
And sip, with nymphs, their elemental tea.
The graver prude sinks downward to a gnome,
In search of mischief still on earth to roam.
The light coquettes in sylphs aloft repair,   65
And sport and flutter in the fields of air.

---

32. *silver token:* coin left by the fairies; *circled green:* a fairy-ring on the grass. **44.** *box:* at the theater; *Ring:* carriage-drive in Hyde Park. **46.** *chair:* sedan chair. **56.** *omber:* a card game, from Spanish *hombre.*

"Know farther yet; whoever fair and chaste
Rejects mankind, is by some sylph embraced:
For spirits, freed from mortal laws, with ease
Assume what sexes and what shapes they please.   70
What guards the purity of melting maids,
In courtly balls, and midnight masquerades,
Safe from the treacherous friend, the daring spark,
The glance by day, the whisper in the dark,
When kind occasion prompts their warm desires,   75
When music softens, and when dancing fires?
'Tis but their sylph, the wise celestials know,
Though honor is the word with men below.
   "Some nymphs there are, too conscious of their face,
For life predestined to the gnomes' embrace.   80
These swell their prospects and exalt their pride,
When offers are disdained, and love denied.
Then gay ideas crowd the vacant brain,
While peers, and dukes, and all their sweeping train,
And garters, stars, and coronets appear,   85
And in soft sounds, 'Your Grace' salutes their ear.
'Tis these that early taint the female soul,
Instruct the eyes of young coquettes to roll,
Teach infant cheeks a bidden blush to know,
And little hearts to flutter at a beau.   90
   "Oft when the world imagine women stray,
The sylphs through mystic mazes guide their way,
Through all the giddy circle they pursue,
And old impertinence expel by new.
What tender maid but must a victim fall   95
To one man's treat, but for another's ball?
When Florio speaks, what virgin could withstand,
If gentle Damon did not squeeze her hand?
With varying vanities, from every part,
They shift the moving toyshop of their heart;   100
Where wigs with wigs, with sword-knots sword-knots strive,
Beaux banish beaux, and coaches coaches drive.
This erring mortals levity may call,
Oh blind to truth! the sylphs contrive it all.
   "Of these am I, who thy protection claim,   105
A watchful sprite, and Ariel is my name.

73. *spark:* man of fashion.

Late, as I ranged the crystal wilds of air,
In the clear mirror of thy ruling star
I saw, alas! some dread event impend,
Ere to the main this morning sun descend,   110
But heaven reveals not what, or how, or where:
Warned by the sylph, oh pious maid, beware!
This to disclose is all thy guardian can:
Beware of all, but most beware of man!"
    He said; when Shock, who thought she slept too long,   115
Leapt up, and waked his mistress with his tongue.
'Twas then, Belinda, if report say true,
Thy eyes first opened on a billet-doux;
Wounds, charms, and ardors, were no sooner read,
But all the vision vanished from thy head.   120
    And now, unveiled, the toilet stands displayed,
Each silver vase in mystic order laid.
First, robed in white, the nymph intent adores,
With head uncovered, the cosmetic powers.
A heavenly image in the glass appears,   125
To that she bends, to that her eyes she rears;
Th' inferior priestess, at her altar's side,
Trembling, begins the sacred rites of pride.
Unnumbered treasures ope at once, and here
The various offerings of the world appear;   130
From each she nicely culls with curious toil,
And decks the goddess with the glittering spoil.
This casket India's glowing gems unlocks,
And all Arabia breathes from yonder box.
The tortoise here and elephant unite,   135
Transformed to combs, the speckled and the white.
Here files of pins extend their shining rows,
Puffs, powders, patches, bibles, billet-doux.
Now awful beauty puts on all its arms;
The fair each moment rises in her charms,   140
Repairs her smiles, awakens every grace,
And calls forth all the wonders of her face;
Sees by degrees a purer blush arise,
And keener lightnings quicken in her eyes.

---

138. *patches:* bits of black silk used to cover pimples or to make "beauty spots."

The busy sylphs surround their darling care;   145
These set the head, and those divide the hair,
Some fold the sleeve, while others plait the gown;
And Betty's praised for labors not her own.

CANTO II

Not with more glories, in th' ethereal plain,
The sun first rises o'er the purpled main,
Than, issuing forth, the rival of his beams
Launched on the bosom of the silver Thames.
Fair nymphs, and well-dressed youths around her shone,   5
But every eye was fixed on her alone.
On her white breast a sparkling cross she wore,
Which Jews might kiss, and infidels adore.
Her lively looks a sprightly mind disclose,
Quick as her eyes, and as unfixed as those: 10
Favors to none, to all she smiles extends;
Oft she rejects, but never once offends.
Bright as the sun, her eyes the gazers strike,
And, like the sun, they shine on all alike.
Yet graceful ease, and sweetness void of pride,   15
Might hide her faults, if belles had faults to hide:
If to her share some female errors fall,
Look on her face, and you'll forget 'em all.
    This nymph, to the destruction of mankind,
Nourished two locks, which graceful hung behind   20
In equal curls, and well conspired to deck
With shining ringlets the smooth ivory neck.
Love in these labyrinths his slaves detains,
And mighty hearts are held in slender chains.
With hairy springes we the birds betray,   25
Slight lines of hair surprise the finny prey,
Fair tresses man's imperial race ensnare,
And beauty draws us with a single hair.
    Th' adventurous baron the bright locks admired;
He saw, he wished, and to the prize aspired.   30
Resolved to win, he meditates the way,
By force to ravish, or by fraud betray;
For when success a lover's toil attends,
Few ask, if fraud or force attained his ends.
    For this, ere Phoebus rose, he had implored   35
Propitious Heaven, and every power adored,

But chiefly Love—to Love an altar built,
Of twelve vast French romances, neatly gilt.
There lay three garters, half a pair of gloves;
And all the trophies of his former loves.   40
With tender billet-doux he lights the pyre,
And breathes three amorous sighs to raise the fire.
Then prostrate falls, and begs with ardent eyes
Soon to obtain, and long possess the prize:
The powers gave ear, and granted half his prayer,   45
The rest, the winds dispersed in empty air.

   But now secure the painted vessel glides,
The sunbeams trembling on the floating tides,
While melting music steals upon the sky,
And softened sounds along the waters die;   50
Smooth flow the waves, the zephyrs gently play,
Belinda smiled, and all the world was gay.
All but the sylph—with careful thoughts oppressed,
Th' impending woe sat heavy on his breast.
He summons straight his denizens of air;   55
The lucid squadrons round the sails repair:
Soft o'er the shrouds aërial whispers breathe,
That seemed but zephyrs to the train beneath.
Some to the sun their insect-wings unfold,
Waft on the breeze, or sink in clouds of gold;   60
Transparent forms, too fine for mortal sight,
Their fluid bodies half dissolved in light.
Loose to the wind their airy garments flew,
Thin glittering textures of the filmy dew,
Dipped in the richest tincture of the skies,   65
Where light disports in ever-mingling dyes,
While every beam new transient colors flings,
Colors that change whene'er they wave their wings.
Amid the circle, on the gilded mast,
Superior by the head, was Ariel placed;   70
His purple pinions opening to the sun,
He raised his azure wand, and thus begun.
   "Ye sylphs and sylphids, to your chief give ear,
Fays, fairies, genii, elves, and daemons, hear!
Ye know the spheres and various tasks assigned   75
By laws eternal to th' aërial kind.
Some in the fields of purest ether play,
And bask and whiten in the blaze of day.

Some guide the course of wandering orbs on high,
Or roll the planets through the boundless sky.   80
Some less refined, beneath the moon's pale light,
Pursue the stars that shoot athwart the night,
Or suck the mists in grosser air below,
Or dip their pinions in the painted bow,
Or brew fierce tempests on the wintry main,   85
Or o'er the glebe distill the kindly rain.
Others on earth o'er human race preside,
Watch all their ways, and all their actions guide:
Of these the chief the care of nations own,
And guard with arms divine the British throne.   90
   "Our humbler province is to tend the fair,
Not a less pleasing, though less glorious care;
To save the powder from too rude a gale,
Nor let th' imprisoned essences exhale;
To draw fresh colors from the vernal flowers;   95
To steal from rainbows ere they drop in showers
A brighter wash; to curl their waving hairs,
Assist their blushes, and inspire their airs;
Nay oft, in dreams, invention we bestow,
To change a flounce, or add a furbelow.   100
   "This day, black omens threat the brightest fair
That e'er deserved a watchful spirit's care;
Some dire disaster, or by force, or slight;
But what, or where, the Fates have wrapped in night.
Whether the nymph shall break Diana's law,   105
Or some frail china jar receive a flaw;
Or stain her honor, or her new brocade,
Forget her prayers, or miss a masquerade;
Or lose her heart, or necklace, at a ball;
Or whether Heaven has doomed that Shock must fall.   110
Haste, then, ye spirits! to your charge repair:
The fluttering fan be Zephyretta's care;
The drops to thee, Brillante, we consign;
And, Momentilla, let the watch be thine;
Do thou, Crispissa, tend her favorite lock;   115
Ariel himself shall be the guard of Shock.

---

86. *glebe:* arable land.   **113.** *drops:* pendant earrings.

"To fifty chosen sylphs, of special note,
We trust th' important charge, the petticoat:
Oft have we known that sevenfold fence to fail,
Though stiff with hoops, and armed with ribs of whale;   120
Form a strong line about the silver bound,
And guard the wide circumference around.
   "Whatever spirit, careless of his charge,
His post neglects, or leaves the fair at large,
Shall feel sharp vengeance soon o'ertake his sins,   125
Be stopped in vials, or transfixed with pins;
Or plunged in lakes of bitter washes lie,
Or wedged whole ages in a bodkin's eye:
Gums and pomatums shall his flight restrain,
While clogged he beats his silken wings in vain;   130
Or alum styptics with contracting power
Shrink his thin essence like a rivelled flower:
Or, as Ixion fixed, the wretch shall feel
The giddy motion of the whirling mill,
In fumes of burning chocolate shall glow,   135
And tremble at the sea that froths below!"
  He spoke; the spirits from the sails descend;
Some, orb in orb, around the nymph extend;
Some thread the mazy ringlets of her hair;
Some hang upon the pendants of her ear;   140
With beating hearts the dire event they wait,
Anxious, and trembling for the birth of Fate.

CANTO III

Close by those meads, for ever crowned with flowers,
Where Thames with pride surveys his rising towers,
There stands a structure of majestic frame,
Which from the neighboring Hampton takes its name.
Here Britain's statesmen oft the fall foredoom   5
Of foreign tyrants, and of nymphs at home;
Here thou, great ANNA! whom three realms obey,
Dost sometimes counsel take—and sometimes tea.

---

132. *rivelled:* shrivelled. **133.** *Ixion:* For attempting to seduce Hera, Ixion was condemned by Zeus to be bound to a burning wheel which rolled endlessly through the sky. **7.** *Anna . . . obey:* Queen Anne (1665–1714), ruler of England, Scotland, and Ireland.

Hither the heroes and the nymphs resort,
To taste awhile the pleasures of a court;   10
In various talk th' instructive hours they passed,
Who gave the ball, or paid the visit last;
One speaks the glory of the British Queen,
And one describes a charming Indian screen;
A third interprets motions, looks, and eyes;   15
At every word a reputation dies.
Snuff, or the fan, supply each pause of chat,
With singing, laughing, ogling, and all that.

Meanwhile, declining from the noon of day,
The sun obliquely shoots his burning ray;   20
The hungry judges soon the sentence sign,
And wretches hang that jurymen may dine;
The merchant from th' exchange returns in peace,
And the long labors of the toilet cease.
Belinda now, whom thirst of fame invites,   25
Burns to encounter two adventurous knights,
At ombre singly to decide their doom;
And swells her breast with conquests yet to come.
Straight the three bands prepare in arms to join,
Each band the number of the sacred nine.   30
Soon as she spreads her hand, th' aërial guard
Descend, and sit on each important card:
First Ariel perched upon a Matadore,
Then each, according to the rank they bore;
For sylphs, yet mindful of their ancient race,   35
Are, as when women, wondrous fond of place.

Behold, four Kings in majesty revered,
With hoary whiskers and a forky beard;
And four fair Queens whose hands sustain a flower,
Th' expressive emblem of their softer power;   40
Four Knaves in garbs succinct, a trusty band,
Caps on their heads, and halberds in their hand;
And particolored troops, a shining train,
Draw forth to combat on the velvet plain.

The skillful nymph reviews her force with care;   45
"Let Spades be trumps!" she said, and trumps they were.

---

30. *nine:* each player held nine cards.   **33.** *Matadore:* the three highest cards
in ombre, according to the trump suit, were called matadors. Belinda's matadors are Spadillio, the ace of spades; Manillio, the two of spades; and Basto,
the ace of clubs.

Now move to war her sable Matadores,
In show like leaders of the swarthy Moors.
Spadillio first, unconquerable lord!
Led off two captive trumps, and swept the board.   50
As many more Manillio forced to yield,
And marched a victor from the verdant field.
Him Basto followed, but his fate more hard
Gained but one trump and one plebeian card.
With his broad saber next, a chief in years,   55
The hoary Majesty of Spades appears,
Puts forth one manly leg, to sight revealed;
The rest, his many-colored robe concealed.
The rebel Knave, who dares his prince engage,
Proves the just victim of his royal rage.   60
Even mighty Pam, that kings and queens o'erthrew
And mowed down armies in the fights of Loo,
Sad chance of war! now destitute of aid,
Falls undistinguished by the victor Spade!

    Thus far both armies to Belinda yield;   65
Now to the baron fate inclines the field.
His warlike Amazon her host invades,
Th' imperial consort of the crown of Spades.
The Club's black tyrant first her victim died,
Spite of his haughty mien, and barbarous pride: 70
What boots the regal circle on his head,
His giant limbs, in state unwieldy spread;
That long behind he trails his pompous robe,
And, of all monarchs, only grasps the globe?

    The baron now his Diamonds pours apace;   75
Th' embroidered King who shows but half his face,
And his refulgent Queen, with powers combined,
Of broken troops an easy conquest find.
Clubs, Diamonds, Hearts, in wild disorder seen,
With throngs promiscuous strow the level green.   80
Thus when dispersed a routed army runs,
Of Asia's troops, and Afric's sable sons,
With like confusion different nations fly,
Of various habit, and of various dye,

61–62. *Pam . . . Loo:* the jack, or knave, of clubs, the strongest card in the game of loo.

The pierced battalions disunited fall,   85
In heaps on heaps; one fate o'erwhelms them all.
    The Knave of Diamonds tries his wily arts,
And wins (oh shameful chance!) the Queen of Hearts.
At this, the blood the virgin's cheek forsook,
A livid paleness spreads o'er all her look;   90
She sees, and trembles at th' approaching ill,
Just in the jaws of ruin, and codille.
And now (as oft in some distempered state)
On one nice trick depends the general fate.
An Ace of Hearts steps forth: the King unseen   95
Lurked in her hand, and mourned his captive Queen.
He springs to vengeance with an eager pace,
And falls like thunder on the prostrate Ace.
The nymph exulting fills with shouts the sky;
The walls, the woods, and long canals reply.   100
    Oh thoughtless mortals! ever blind to fate,
Too soon dejected, and too soon elate!
Sudden, these honors shall be snatched away,
And cursed for ever this victorious day.
    For lo! the board with cups and spoons is crowned,   105
The berries crackle, and the mill turns round;
On shining altars of Japan they raise
The silver lamp; the fiery spirits blaze.
From silver spouts the grateful liquors glide,
While China's earth receives the smoking tide.   110
At once they gratify their scent and taste,
And frequent cups prolong the rich repast.
Straight hover round the fair her airy band;
Some, as she sipped, the fuming liquor fanned,
Some o'er her lap their careful plumes displayed,   115
Trembling, and conscious of the rich brocade.
Coffee (which makes the politician wise,
And see through all things with his half-shut eyes)
Sent up in vapors to the baron's brain
New stratagems, the radiant lock to gain.   120
Ah cease, rash youth! desist ere 'tis too late,
Fear the just gods, and think of Scylla's fate!

---

92. *codille:* defeat.   **106.** *berries:* coffee beans; *mill:* coffee grinder.   **107.** *altars of Japan:* lacquered tables.

Changed to a bird, and sent to flit in air,
She dearly pays for Nisus' injured hair!
  But when to mischief mortals bend their will,   125
How soon they find fit instruments of ill!
Just then, Clarissa drew with tempting grace
A two-edged weapon from her shining case;
So ladies in romance assist their knight,
Present the spear, and arm him for the fight.   130
He takes the gift with reverence and extends
The little engine on his fingers' ends;
This just behind Belinda's neck he spread,
As o'er the fragrant steams she bends her head.
Swift to the lock a thousand sprites repair,   135
A thousand wings, by turns, blow back the hair;
And thrice they twitched the diamond in her ear;
Thrice she looked back, and thrice the foe drew near.
Just in that instant, anxious Ariel sought
The close recesses of the virgin's thought;   140
As on the nosegay in her breast reclined,
He watched th' ideas rising in her mind,
Sudden he viewed, in spite of all her art,
An earthly lover lurking at her heart.
Amazed, confused, he found his power expired,   145
Resigned to fate, and with a sigh retired.
  The peer now spreads the glittering forfex wide,
T'enclose the lock; now joins it, to divide.
Even then, before the fatal engine closed,
A wretched sylph too fondly interposed;   150
Fate urged the shears, and cut the sylph in twain,
(But airy substance soon unites again)
The meeting points the sacred hair dissever
From the fair head, for ever, and for ever!
  Then flashed the living lightning from her eyes,   155
And screams of horror rend th' affrighted skies.
Not louder shrieks to pitying Heaven are cast,
When husbands or when lap-dogs breathe their last;
Or when rich China vessels, fallen from high,
In glittering dust and painted fragments lie!   160
  "Let wreaths of triumph now my temples twine"
(The victor cried) "the glorious prize is mine!
While fish in streams, or birds delight in air,
Or in a coach and six the British fair,

As long as *Atalantis* shall be read, 165
Or the small pillow grace a lady's bed,
While visits shall be paid on solemn days,
When numerous wax lights in bright order blaze,
While nymphs take treats, or assignations give,
So long my honor, name, and praise shall live! 170
　"What time would spare, from steel receives its date,
And monuments, like men, submit to fate!
Steel could the labor of the gods destroy,
And strike to dust th' imperial towers of Troy;
Steel could the works of mortal pride confound, 175
And hew triumphal arches to the ground.
What wonder then, fair nymph! thy hairs should feel
The conquering force of unresisted steel?"

CANTO IV

But anxious cares the pensive nymph oppressed,
And secret passions labored in her breast.
Not youthful kings in battle seized alive,
Not scornful virgins who their charms survive,
Not ardent lovers robbed of all their bliss, 5
Not ancient ladies when refused a kiss,
Not tyrants fierce that unrepenting die,
Not Cynthia when her manteau's pinned awry,
E'er felt such rage, resentment, and despair,
As thou, sad virgin! for thy ravished hair. 10
　For, that sad moment, when the sylphs withdrew,
And Ariel weeping from Belinda flew,
Umbriel, a dusky, melancholy sprite,
As ever sullied the fair face of light,
Down to the central earth, his proper scene, 15
Repaired to search the gloomy Cave of Spleen.
　Swift on his sooty pinions flits the gnome,
And in a vapor reached the dismal dome.
No cheerful breeze this sullen region knows,
The dreaded east is all the wind that blows. 20
Here in a grotto, sheltered close from air,

---

165. *Atalantis:* a contemporary novel filled with gossip and scandal.
16. *Spleen:* one of the four bodily humors; the source of bad temper and malice.

And screened in shades from day's detested glare,
She sighs for ever on her pensive bed,
Pain at her side, and Megrim at her head.

    Two handmaids wait the throne: alike in place, 25
But differing far in figure and in face.
Here stood Ill Nature like an ancient maid,
Her wrinkled form in black and white arrayed;
With store of prayers, for mornings, nights, and noons,
Her hand is filled; her bosom, with lampoons. 30

    There Affectation, with a sickly mien,
Shows in her cheek the roses of eighteen,
Practiced to lisp, and hang the head aside,
Faints into airs, and languishes with pride,
On the rich quilt sinks with becoming woe, 35
Wrapped in a gown, for sickness, and for show.
The fair ones feel such maladies as these,
When each new nightdress gives a new disease.

    A constant vapor o'er the palace flies;
Strange phantoms rising as the mists arise; 40
Dreadful, as hermit's dreams in haunted shades,
Or bright, as visions of expiring maids.
Now glaring fiends, and snakes on rolling spires,
Pale specters, gaping tombs, and purple fires:
Now lakes of liquid gold, Elysian scenes, 45
And crystal domes, and angels in machines.

    Unnumbered throngs on every side are seen
Of bodies changed to various forms by Spleen.
Here living teapots stand, one arm held out,
One bent; the handle this, and that the spout: 50
A pipkin there, like Homer's tripod walks;
Here sighs a jar, and there a goose pie talks;
Men prove with child, as powerful fancy works,
And maids, turned bottles, call aloud for corks.

    Safe passed the gnome through this fantastic band, 55
A branch of healing spleenwort in his hand.
Then thus addressed the power: "Hail, wayward Queen!
Who rule the sex to fifty from fifteen:

---

24. *Megrim:* migraine. **43.** *spires:* coils. **51.** *pipkin . . . walks:* an earth-enware pot, which here walks like one of Hephaestos's self-propelled tripods, or three-legged stools, in *Iliad* XVIII.368 ff.

Parent of vapors, and of female wit,
Who give th' hysteric or poetic fit,   60
On various tempers act by various ways,
Make some take physic, others scribble plays;
Who cause the proud their visits to delay,
And send the godly in a pet to pray.
A nymph there is, that all thy power disdains,   65
And thousands more in equal mirth maintains.
But oh! if e'er thy gnome could spoil a grace,
Or raise a pimple on a beauteous face,
Like citron waters matrons' cheeks inflame,
Or change complexions at a losing game;   70
If e'er with airy horns I planted heads,
Or rumpled petticoats, or tumbled beds,
Or caused suspicion when no soul was rude,
Or discomposed the headdress of a prude,
Or e'er to costive lap dog gave disease,   75
Which not the tears of brightest eyes could ease:
Hear me, and touch Belinda with chagrin;
That single act gives half the world the spleen."
    The Goddess with a discontented air
Seems to reject him, though she grants his prayer.   80
A wondrous bag with both her hands she binds,
Like that where once Ulysses held the winds;
There she collects the force of female lungs,
Sighs, sobs, and passions, and the war of tongues.
A vial next she fills with fainting fears,   85
Soft sorrows, melting griefs, and flowing tears.
The gnome rejoicing bears her gifts away,
Spreads his black wings, and slowly mounts to day.
    Sunk in Thalestris' arms the nymph he found,
Her eyes dejected and her hair unbound.   90
Full o'er their heads the swelling bag he rent,
And all the furies issued at the vent.
Belinda burns with more than mortal ire,
And fierce Thalestris fans the rising fire.
"Oh wretched maid!" she spread her hands, and cried,   95

---

59. *vapors:* affected emotional depression.   **62.** *physic:* remedies; medicine.
69. *citron waters:* brandy flavored with lemon peel, thought to be good for
the complexion.   **71.** *horns:* the sign of the cuckold.   **75.** *costive:* con-
stipated.   **89.** *Thalestris:* a girl named for a queen of the Amazons.

(While Hampton's echoes, "Wretched maid!" replied)
"Was it for this you took such constant care
The bodkin, comb, and essence to prepare?
For this your locks in paper durance bound,
For this with torturing irons wreathed around?   100
For this with fillets strained your tender head,
And bravely bore the double loads of lead?
Gods! shall the ravisher display your hair,
While the fops envy and the ladies stare!
Honor forbid! at whose unrivaled shrine   105
Ease, pleasure, virtue, all our sex resign.
Methinks already I your tears survey,
Already hear the horrid things they say,
Already see you a degraded toast,
And all your honor in a whisper lost!   110
How shall I, then, your helpless fame defend?
'Twill then be infamy to seem your friend!
And shall this prize, th' inestimable prize,
Exposed through crystal to the gazing eyes,
And heightened by the diamond's circling rays,   115
On that rapacious hand for ever blaze?
Sooner shall grass in Hyde Park Circus grow,
And wits take lodgings in the sound of Bow;
Sooner let earth, air, sea, to chaos fall,
Men, monkeys, lap dogs, parrots, perish all!"   120
    She said; then raging to Sir Plume repairs,
And bids her beau demand the precious hairs:
(Sir Plume, of amber snuffbox justly vain,
And the nice conduct of a clouded cane)
With earnest eyes, and round unthinking face,   125
He first the snuffbox opened, then the case,
And thus broke out—"My Lord, why, what the devil?
Z—ds! damn the lock! 'fore Gad, you must be civil!
Plague on't! 'tis past a jest—nay prithee, pox!
Give her the hair"—he spoke, and rapped his box.   130
    "It grieves me much" (replied the peer again)
"Who speaks so well should ever speak in vain;

99–102. *For . . . lead:* The hair was wound on curling irons, fastened with papers, fillets (bands), and strips of lead.   109. *toast:* a woman toasted at a men's drinking party.   118. *And . . . Bow:* within sound of the bells of St. Mary-le-Bow, then an unfashionable district of London.

But by this lock, this sacred lock, I swear,
(Which never more shall join its parted hair;
Which never more its honors shall renew,   135
Clipped from the lovely head where late it grew)
That while my nostrils draw the vital air,
This hand, which won it, shall for ever wear."
He spoke, and speaking, in proud triumph spread
The long-contended honors of her head.   140
    But Umbriel, hateful gnome! forbears not so;
He breaks the vial whence the sorrows flow.
Then see! the nymph in beauteous grief appears,
Her eyes half-languishing, half-drowned in tears;
On her heaved bosom hung her drooping head,   145
Which, with a sigh, she raised; and thus she said:
    "For ever cursed be this detested day,
Which snatched my best, my favorite curl away!
Happy! ah ten times happy had I been,
If Hampton Court these eyes had never seen!   150
Yet am I not the first mistaken maid,
By love of courts to numerous ills betrayed.
Oh had I rather unadmired remained
In some lone isle, or distant northern land;
Where the gilt chariot never marks the way,   155
Where none learn omber, none e'er taste bohea!
There kept my charms concealed from mortal eye,
Like roses that in deserts bloom and die.
What moved my mind with youthful lords to roam?
Oh had I stayed, and said my prayers at home!   160
'Twas this the morning omens seemed to tell:
Thrice from my trembling hand the patchbox fell;
The tottering china shook without a wind;
Nay, Poll sat mute, and Shock was most unkind!
A sylph too warned me of the threats of fate,   165
In mystic visions, now believed too late!
See the poor remnants of these slighted hairs!
My hands shall rend what even thy rapine spares:
These, in two sable ringlets taught to break,
Once gave new beauties to the snowy neck;   170
The sister-lock now sits uncouth, alone,
And in its fellow's fate foresees its own;

156. *bohea:* a kind of black tea.

Uncurled it hangs, the fatal shears demands,
And tempts once more thy sacrilegious hands.
Oh hadst thou, cruel! been content to seize 175
Hairs less in sight, or any hairs but these!"

CANTO V

She said; the pitying audience melt in tears.
But fate and Jove had stopped the baron's ears.
In vain Thalestris with reproach assails,
For who can move when fair Belinda fails?
Not half so fixed the Trojan could remain, 5
While Anna begged and Dido raged in vain.
Then grave Clarissa graceful waved her fan;
Silence ensued, and thus the nymph began:
    "Say, why are beauties praised and honored most,
The wise man's passion, and the vain man's toast? 10
Why decked with all that land and sea afford,
Why angels called, and angel-like adored?
Why round our coaches crowd the white-gloved beaux,
Why bows the side-box from its immost rows?
How vain are all these glories, all our pains, 15
Unless good sense preserve what beauty gains:
That men may say, when we the front-box grace,
'Behold the first in virtue as in face!'
Oh! if to dance all night, and dress all day,
Charmed the smallpox, or chased old age away, 20
Who would not scorn what housewife's cares produce,
Or who would learn one earthly thing of use?
To patch, nay ogle, might become a saint,
Nor could it sure be such a sin to paint.
But since, alas! frail beauty must decay, 25
Curled or uncurled, since locks will turn to gray;
Since painted, or not painted, all shall fade,
And she who scorns a man, must die a maid;
What then remains, but well our power to use,
And keep good humor still whate'er we lose? 30
And trust me, dear! good humor can prevail,
When airs, and flights, and screams, and scolding fail.

5–6. *Not . . . vain:* Although Aeneas loved Dido, he left her in spite of her threats and the pleas of her sister Anna, in order to follow his higher destiny to found the city of Rome (see *Aeneid* IV).

Beauties in vain their pretty eyes may roll;
Charms strike the sight, but merit wins the soul."
  So spoke the dame, but no applause ensued; 35
Belinda frowned, Thalestris called her prude.
"To arms, to arms!" the fierce virago cries,
And swift as lightning to the combat flies.
All side in parties, and begin th' attack;
Fans clap, silks rustle, and tough whalebones crack; 40
Heroes' and heroines' shouts confusedly rise,
And bass and treble voices strike the skies.
No common weapons in their hands are found;
Like gods they fight, nor dread a mortal wound.
  So when bold Homer makes the gods engage, 45
And heavenly breasts with human passions rage;
'Gainst Pallas, Mars; Latona, Hermes arms;
And all Olympus rings with loud alarms;
Jove's thunder roars, Heaven trembles all around;
Blue Neptune storms, the bellowing deeps resound; 50
Earth shakes her nodding towers, the ground gives way,
And the pale ghosts start at the flash of day!
  Triumphant Umbriel on a sconce's height
Clapped his glad wings, and sat to view the fight:
Propped on their bodkin spears, the sprites survey 55
The growing combat, or assist the fray.
  While through the press enraged Thalestris flies,
And scatters deaths around from both her eyes,
A beau and witling perished in the throng;
One died in metaphor, and one in song. 60
"Oh cruel nymph! a living death I bear,"
Cried Dapperwit, and sunk beside his chair.
A mournful glance Sir Fopling upwards cast,
"Those eyes are made so killing"—was his last.
Thus on Meander's flowery margin lies 65
Th' expiring swan, and as he sings he dies.
  When bold Sir Plume had drawn Clarissa down,
Chloe stepped in, and killed him with a frown;
She smiled to see the doughty hero slain,
But at her smile, the beau revived again. 70
  Now Jove suspends his golden scales in air,
Weighs the men's wits against the lady's hair;
The doubtful beam long nods from side to side;
At length the wits mount up, the hairs subside.

See fierce Belinda on the baron flies,　　　　　　　　75
With more than usual lightning in her eyes;
Nor feared the chief th' unequal fight to try,
Who sought no more than on his foe to die.
But this bold lord with manly strength endued,
She with one finger and a thumb subdued:　　　　　80
Just where the breath of life his nostrils drew,
A charge of snuff the wily virgin threw;
The gnomes direct, to every atom just,
The pungent grains of titillating dust.
Sudden, with starting tears each eye o'erflows,　　85
And the high dome re-echoes to his nose.
　"Now meet thy fate," incensed Belinda cried,
And drew a deadly bodkin from her side.
(The same, his ancient personage to deck,
Her great-great-grandsire wore about his neck,　　90
In three seal rings; which after, melted down,
Formed a vast buckle for his widow's gown:
Her infant grandame's whistle next it grew,
The bells she jingled, and the whistle blew;
Then in a bodkin graced her mother's hairs,　　　95
Which long she wore, and now Belinda wears.)
　"Boast not my fall" (he cried) "insulting foe!
Thou by some other shalt be laid as low.
Nor think, to die dejects my lofty mind;
All that I dread is leaving you behind!　　　　　100
Rather than so, ah let me still survive,
And burn in Cupid's flames—but burn alive."
　"Restore the lock!" she cries; and all around
"Restore the lock!" the vaulted roofs rebound.
Not fierce Othello in so loud a strain　　　　　105
Roared for the handkerchief that caused his pain.
But see how oft ambitious aims are crossed,
And chiefs contend till all the prize is lost!
The lock, obtained with guilt, and kept with pain,
In every place is sought, but sought in vain:　　110
With such a prize no mortal must be blest,
So Heaven decrees! with Heaven who can contest?

105–106. *Not . . . pain:* Othello views Desdemona's supposed gift of her handkerchief to Cassio as a sign of loss of chastity.

Some thought it mounted to the lunar sphere,
Since all things lost on earth are treasured there.
There heroes' wits are kept in ponderous vases, 115
And beaux' in snuff-boxes and tweezer-cases.
There broken vows, and deathbed alms are found,
And lovers' hearts with ends of ribbon bound,
The courtier's promises, and sick man's prayers,
The smiles of harlots, and the tears of heirs, 120
Cages for gnats, and chains to yoke a flea,
Dried butterflies, and tomes of casuistry.
　　But trust the Muse—she saw it upward rise,
Though marked by none but quick, poetic eyes:
(So Rome's great founder to the heavens withdrew, 125
To Proculus alone confessed in view)
A sudden star, it shot through liquid air,
And drew behind a radiant trail of hair.
Not Berenice's locks first rose so bright,
The heavens bespangling with disheveled light. 130
The sylphs behold it kindling as it flies,
And pleased pursue its progress through the skies.
　　This the beau monde shall from the Mall survey,
And hail with music its propitious ray.
This the blest lover shall for Venus take, 135
And send up vows from Rosamonda's Lake.
This Partridge soon shall view in cloudless skies,
When next he looks through Galileo's eyes;
And hence th' egregious wizard shall foredoom
The fate of Louis, and the fall of Rome. 140
　　Then cease, bright nymph! to mourn thy ravished hair,
Which adds new glory to the shining sphere!
Not all the tresses that fair head can boast
Shall draw such envy as the lock you lost.

113–122. In Canto XXXIV of Ariosto's *Orlando Furioso* (stanzas 68 ff.), Astol-fo flies in a winged hippogriff to the moon and finds there whatever has been lost on earth, including Orlando's sanity. **125–126.** Romulus was taken to heaven in a cloud, but later appeared to Proculus, a senator. **129–130.** Bere-nice had promised Venus a lock of her hair if her husband returned home safely; it became the constellation *Coma Berenice.* **133.** *beau monde:* the fashionable world; *the Mall:* a fashionable walk in St. James's Park. **136.** *Rosamonda's Lake:* also in St. James's Park. **137–140.** *This . . . Rome:* John Partridge (1644–1715), an astrologer who each year predicted the down-fall of the Pope and the King of France. **138.** *Galileo's eyes:* the telescope.

For, after all the murders of your eye,
When, after millions slain, yourself shall die;
When those fair suns shall set, as set they must,
And all those tresses shall be laid in dust,
This lock, the Muse shall consecrate to fame,
And midst the stars inscribe Belinda's name.

CHRISTOPHER SMART
(1722–1771)

OF JEOFFRY, HIS CAT

For I will consider my cat Jeoffry.

For he is the servant of the living God, duly and daily serving him.

For at the first glance of the glory of God in the east he worships in his way.

For is this done by wreathing his body seven times round with elegant quickness.

For then he leaps up to catch the musk, which is the blessing of God upon his prayer.   5

For he rolls upon prank to work it in.

For having done duty and received blessing he begins to consider himself.

For this he performs in ten degrees.

For first he looks upon his forepaws to see if they are clean.

For secondly he kicks up behind to clear away there.   10

For thirdly he works it upon stretch with the forepaws extended.

For fourthly he sharpens his paws by wood.

For fifthly he washes himself.

For sixthly he rolls upon wash.

For seventhly he fleas himself, that he may not be interrupted upon the beat.   15

For eighthly he rubs himself against a post.

For ninthly he looks up for his instructions.

For tenthly he goes in quest of food.

For having considered God and himself he will consider his neighbor.

For if he meets another cat he will kiss her in kindness.   20

For when he takes his prey he plays with it to give it chance.

For one mouse in seven escapes by his dallying.

For when his day's work is done his business more properly begins.

For he keeps the Lord's watch in the night against the adversary.

For he counteracts the powers of darkness by his electrical skin
and glaring eyes. 25

For he counteracts the Devil, who is death, by brisking about
the life.

For in his morning orisons he loves the sun and the sun loves
him.

For he is of the tribe of Tiger.

For the Cherub Cat is a term of the Angel Tiger.

For he has the subtlety and hissing of a serpent, which in
goodness he suppresses. 30

For he will not do destruction, if he is well-fed, neither will he
spit without provocation.

For he purrs in thankfulness, when God tells him he's a good cat.

For he is an instrument for the children to learn benevolence
upon.

For every house is incomplete without him and a blessing is
lacking in the spirit.

For the Lord commanded Moses concerning the cats at the
departure of the children of Israel from Egypt. 35

For every family had one cat at least in the bag.

For the English cats are the best in Europe.

For he is the cleanest in the use of his forepaws of any quadrupede.

For the dexterity of his defense is an instance of the love of
God to him exceedingly.

For he is the quickest to his mark of any creature. 40

For he is tenacious of his point.

For he is a mixture of gravity and waggery.

For he knows that God is his Savior.

For there is nothing sweeter than his peace when at rest.

For there is nothing brisker than his life when in motion. 45

For he is of the Lord's poor and so indeed is he called by
benevolence perpetually—Poor Jeoffry! poor Jeoffry! the
rat has bit thy throat.

For I bless the name of the Lord Jesus that Jeoffry is better.

For the divine spirit comes about his body to sustain it in
complete cat.

For his tongue is exceeding pure so that it has in purity what it
wants in music.

For he is docile and can learn certain things. 50

For he can set up with gravity, which is patience upon appro-
bation.

For he can fetch and carry, which is patience in employment.

For he can jump over a stick, which is patience upon proof positive.

For he can spraggle upon waggle at the word of command.

For he can jump from an eminence into his master's bosom. 55

For he can catch the cork and toss it again.

For he is hated by the hypocrite and miser.

For the former is afraid of detection.

For the latter refuses the charge.

For he camels his back to bear the first notion of business. 60

For he is good to think on, if a man would express himself neatly.

For he made a great figure in Egypt for his signal services.

For he killed the Icneumon-rat very pernicious by land.

For his ears are so acute that they sting again.

For from this proceeds the passing quickness of his attention. 65

For by stroking of him I have found out electricity.

For I perceived God's light about him both wax and fire.

For the electrical fire is the spiritual substance, which God sends from heaven to sustain the bodies both of man and beast.

For God has blessed him in the variety of his movements.

For, though he cannot fly, he is an excellent clamberer. 70

For his motions upon the face of the earth are more than any other quadrupede.

For he can tread to all the measures upon the music.

For he can swim for life.

For he can creep.

WILLIAM BLAKE
(1757–1827)

THE LITTLE BLACK BOY

My mother bore me in the southern wild,
And I am black, but O! my soul is white;
White as an angel is the English child:
But I am black as if bereaved of light.

My mother taught me underneath a tree   5
And sitting down before the heat of day,
She took me on her lap and kissed me,
And pointing to the east began to say.

"Look on the rising sun: there God does live
And gives his light, and gives his heat away.   10
And flowers and trees and beasts and men receive
Comfort in morning, joy in the noon day.

"And we are put on earth a little space,
That we may learn to bear the beams of love,
And these black bodies and this sun-burnt face   15
Is but a cloud, and like a shady grove.

"For when our souls have learned the heat to bear,
The cloud will vanish; we shall hear his voice,
Saying: 'Come out from the grove, my love and care,
And round my golden tent like lambs rejoice.' "   20

Thus did my mother say and kissed me,
And thus I say to little English boy.
When I from black and he from white cloud free,
And round the tent of God like lambs we joy:

I'll shade him from the heat till he can bear   25
To lean in joy upon our father's knee.
And then I'll stand and stroke his silver hair,
And be like him and he will then love me.

THE CHIMNEY SWEEPER

When my mother died I was very young,
And my father sold me while yet my tongue
Could scarcely cry " 'weep 'weep 'weep 'weep."
So your chimneys I sweep and in soot I sleep.

There's little Tom Dacre, who cried when his head, 5
That curled like a lamb's back, was shaved, so I said:
"Hush, Tom, never mind it, for when your head's bare,
You know that the soot cannot spoil your white hair."

And so he was quiet, and that very night,
As Tom was a-sleeping, he had such a sight, 10
That thousands of sweepers, Dick, Joe, Ned, and Jack,
Were all of them locked up in coffins of black.

And by came an angel who had a bright key,
And he opened the coffins and set them all free.
Then down a green plain leaping, laughing, they run 15
And wash in a river and shine in the sun.

Then naked and white, all their bags left behind,
They rise upon clouds, and sport in the wind.
And the angel told Tom if he'd be a good boy,
He'd have God for his father and never want joy. 20

And so Tom awoke and we rose in the dark
And got with our bags and our brushes to work.
Though the morning was cold, Tom was happy and warm,
So if all do their duty, they need not fear harm.

THE CLOD AND THE PEBBLE

"Love seeketh not itself to please,
Nor for itself hath any care;
But for another gives its ease,
And builds a Heaven in Hell's despair."

   So sang a little Clod of Clay, 5
   Trodden with the cattle's feet:
   But a Pebble of the brook,
   Warbled out these meters meet:

"Love seeketh only Self to please,
To bind another to its delight;
Joys in another's loss of ease, 10
And builds a Hell in Heaven's despite."

I SAW A CHAPEL ALL OF GOLD

I saw a chapel all of gold
That none did dare to enter in;
And many weeping stood without
Weeping, mourning, worshiping.

I saw a serpent rise between 5
The white pillars of the door;
And he forced and forced and forced
Down the golden hinges tore.

And along the pavement sweet
Set with pearls and rubies bright 10
All his slimy length he drew,
Till upon the altar white,

Vomiting his poison out,
On the bread and on the wine:
So I turned into a sty 15
And laid me down among the swine.

LONDON

I wander through each chartered street,
Near where the chartered Thames does flow,
And mark in every face I meet
Marks of weakness, marks of woe.

In every cry of every man,   5
In every infant's cry of fear,
In every voice, in every ban,
The mind-forged manacles I hear.

How the chimney-sweeper's cry
Every black'ning church appalls,   10
And the hapless soldier's sigh
Runs in blood down palace walls.

But most through midnight streets I hear
How the youthful harlot's curse
Blasts the new-born infant's tear   15
And blights with plagues the marriage hearse.

MOCK ON, MOCK ON, VOLTAIRE, ROUSSEAU

Mock on, mock on, Voltaire, Rousseau;
Mock on, mock on; 'tis all in vain:
You throw the sand against the wind,
And the wind blows it back again.

And every sand becomes a gem   5
Reflected in the beams divine;
Blown back they blind the mocking eye,
But still in Israel's paths they shine.

The atoms of Democritus
And Newton's particles of light   10
Are sands upon the Red Sea shore,
Where Israel's tents do shine so bright.

A POISON TREE

I was angry with my friend;
I told my wrath, my wrath did end.
I was angry with my foe:
I told it not, my wrath did grow.

And I watered it in fears,   5
Night and morning with my tears:
And I sunned it with smiles,
And with soft deceitful wiles.

And it grew both day and night,
Till it bore an apple bright.   10
And my foe beheld it shine.
And he knew that it was mine.

And into my garden stole,
When the night had veiled the pole;
In the morning glad I see;   15
My foe outstretched beneath the tree.

14. *pole:* the sky; specifically, the North Pole.

SAMUEL TAYLOR COLERIDGE
(1772–1834)

KUBLA KHAN

In Xanadu did Kubla Khan
A stately pleasure-dome decree:
Where Alph, the sacred river, ran
Through caverns measureless to man
   Down to a sunless sea. 5
So twice five miles of fertile ground
With walls and towers were girdled round:
And there were gardens bright with sinuous rills,
Where blossomed many an incense-bearing tree;
And here were forests ancient as the hills, 10
Enfolding sunny spots of greenery.

But oh! that deep romantic chasm which slanted
Down the green hill athwart a cedarn cover!
A savage place! as holy and enchanted
As e'er beneath a waning moon was haunted 15
By woman wailing for her demon-lover!
And from this chasm, with ceaseless turmoil seething,
As if this earth in fast thick pants were breathing,
A mighty fountain momently was forced:
Amid whose swift half-intermitted burst 20
Huge fragments vaulted like rebounding hail,
Or chaffy grain beneath the thresher's flail:
And 'mid these dancing rocks at once and ever
It flung up momently the sacred river.
Five miles meandering with a mazy motion 25
Through wood and dale the sacred river ran,
Then reached the caverns measureless to man,
And sank in tumult to a lifeless ocean:
And 'mid this tumult Kubla heard from far
Ancestral voices prophesying war! 30
   The shadow of the dome of pleasure
   Floated midway on the waves;
   Where was heard the mingled measure
   From the fountain and the caves.

It was a miracle of rare device, 35
A sunny pleasure-dome with caves of ice!

    A damsel with a dulcimer
    In a vision once I saw:
    It was an Abyssinian maid,
    And on her dulcimer she played, 40
    Singing of Mount Abora.
    Could I revive within me
    Her symphony and song,
    To such a deep delight 'twould win me,
That with music loud and long, 45
I would build that dome in air,
That sunny dome! those caves of ice!
And all who heard should see them there,
And all should cry, "Beware! Beware!
His flashing eyes, his floating hair! 50
Weave a circle round him thrice,
And close your eyes with holy dread,
For he on honey-dew hath fed,
And drunk the milk of Paradise."

WORK WITHOUT HOPE

All Nature seems at work. Slugs leave their lair—
The bees are stirring—birds are on the wing—
And Winter slumbering in the open air,
Wears on his smiling face a dream of Spring!
And I the while, the sole unbusy thing,   5
Nor honey make, nor pair, nor build, nor sing.

 Yet well I ken the banks where amaranths blow,
Have traced the fount whence streams of nectar flow.
Bloom, O ye amaranths! bloom for whom ye may,
For me ye bloom not! Glide, rich streams, away!   10
With lips unbrightened, wreathless brow, I stroll:
And would you learn the spells that drowse my soul?
Work without Hope draws nectar in a sieve,
And Hope without an object cannot live.

WILLIAM WORDSWORTH
(1770–1850)

STRANGE FITS OF PASSION I HAVE KNOWN

Strange fits of passion I have known,
And I will dare to tell,
But in the lover's ear alone,
What once to me befell.

When she I loved was strong and gay   5
And like a rose in June,
I to her cottage bent my way,
Beneath the evening moon.

Upon the moon I fixed my eye,
All over the wide lea;   10
My horse trudged on, and we drew nigh
Those paths so dear to me.

And now we reached the orchard plot,
And, as we climbed the hill,
Towards the roof of Lucy's cot   15
The moon descended still.

In one of those sweet dreams I slept,
Kind Nature's gentlest boon!
And, all the while, my eyes I kept
On the descending moon.   20

My horse moved on; hoof after hoof
He raised and never stopped:
When down behind the cottage roof
At once the planet dropped.

What fond and wayward thoughts will slide   25
Into a lover's head—
"O mercy!" to myself I cried,
"If Lucy should be dead!"

SHE DWELT AMONG TH' UNTRODDEN WAYS

She dwelt among th' untrodden ways
    Beside the springs of Dove,
A maid whom there were none to praise
    And very few to love.

A violet by a mossy stone   5
    Half hidden from the eye!
—Fair as a star when only one
    Is shining in the sky!

She lived unknown, and few could know
    When Lucy ceased to be;   10
But she is in her grave, and Oh!
    The difference to me.

I TRAVELED AMONG UNKNOWN MEN

I traveled among unknown men,
    In lands beyond the sea;
Nor England! did I know till then
    What love I bore to thee.

'Tis past, that melancholy dream!   5
    Nor will I quit thy shore
A second time; for still I seem
    To love thee more and more.

Among thy mountains did I feel
    The joy of my desire;   10
And she I cherished turned her wheel
    Beside an English fire.

Thy morning showed, thy nights concealed
    The bowers where Lucy played;
And thine is, too, the last green field   15
    Which Lucy's eyes surveyed!

THREE YEARS SHE GREW IN SUN AND SHOWER

Three years she grew in sun and shower,
Then Nature said, "A lovelier flower
On earth was never sown;
This child I to myself will take,
She shall be mine, and I will make   5
A lady of my own.

"Myself will to my darling be
Both law and impulse, and with me
The girl in rock and plain,
In earth and heaven, in glade and bower,   10
Shall feel an overseeing power
To kindle or restrain.

"She shall be sportive as the fawn
That wild with glee across the lawn
Or up the mountain springs,   15
And hers shall be the breathing balm,
And hers the silence and the calm
Of mute insensate things.

"The floating clouds their state shall lend
To her, for her the willow bend,   20
Nor shall she fail to see
Even in the motions of the storm
A beauty that shall mold her form
By silent sympathy.

"The stars of midnight shall be dear   25
To her, and she shall lean her ear
In many a secret place
Where rivulets dance their wayward round,
And beauty born of murmuring sound
Shall pass into her face.   30

"And vital feelings of delight
Shall rear her form to stately height,
Her virgin bosom swell;
Such thoughts to Lucy I will give
While she and I together live   35
Here in this happy dell."

Thus Nature spake—the work was done—
How soon my Lucy's race was run!
She died and left to me
This heath, this calm and quiet scene,
The memory of what has been,
And never more will be.

40

A SLUMBER DID MY SPIRIT SEAL

A slumber did my spirit seal,
  I had no human fears:
She seemed a thing that could not feel
  The touch of earthly years.

No motion has she now, no force;   5
  She neither hears nor sees,
Rolled round in earth's diurnal course
  With rocks and stones and trees!

IT IS A BEAUTEOUS EVENING, CALM AND FREE

It is a beauteous evening, calm and free;
The holy time is quiet as a nun
Breathless with adoration; the broad sun
Is sinking down in its tranquillity;
The gentleness of heaven is on the sea: 5
Listen! the mighty Being is awake
And doth with his eternal motion make
A sound like thunder—everlastingly.
Dear child! dear girl! that walkest with me here,
If thou appear'st untouched by solemn thought,   10
Thy nature is not therefore less divine:
Thou liest in Abraham's bosom all the year;
And worship'st at the Temple's inner shrine,
God being with thee when we know it not.

COMPOSED UPON WESTMINSTER BRIDGE

Earth has not any thing to show more fair:
Dull would he be of soul who could pass by
A sight so touching in its majesty:
This city now doth like a garment wear
The beauty of the morning; silent, bare,   5
Ships, towers, domes, theaters, and temples lie
Open unto the fields, and to the sky;
All bright and glittering in the smokeless air.
Never did sun more beautifully steep
In his first splendor valley, rock, or hill;   10
Ne'er saw I, never felt, a calm so deep!
The river glideth at his own sweet will:
Dear God! the very houses seem asleep;
And all that mighty heart is lying still!

LINES WRITTEN A FEW MILES ABOVE TINTERN ABBEY

Five years have passed; five summers, with the length
Of five long winters! and again I hear
These waters, rolling from their mountain-springs
With a sweet inland murmur.—Once again
Do I behold these steep and lofty cliffs,   5
Which on a wild secluded scene impress
Thoughts of more deep seclusion; and connect
The landscape with the quiet of the sky.
The day is come when I again repose
Here, under this dark sycamore, and view   10
These plots of cottage-ground, these orchard-tufts,
Which, at this season, with their unripe fruits,
Among the woods and copses lose themselves,
Nor, with their green and simple hue, disturb
The wild green landscape. Once again I see   15
These hedge-rows, hardly hedge-rows, little lines
Of sportive wood run wild; these pastoral farms
Green to the very door; and wreaths of smoke
Sent up, in silence, from among the trees,
With some uncertain notice, as might seem,   20
Of vagrant dwellers in the houseless woods,
Or of some hermit's cave, where by his fire
The hermit sits alone.
                        Though absent long,
These forms of beauty have not been to me,   25
As is a landscape to a blind man's eye:
But oft, in lonely rooms, and mid the din
Of towns and cities, I have owed to them,
In hours of weariness, sensations sweet,
Felt in the blood, and felt along the heart,   30
And passing even into my purer mind,
With tranquil restoration:—feelings too
Of unremembered pleasure: such, perhaps,
As may have had no trivial influence
On that best portion of a good man's life;   35
His little, nameless, unremembered acts
Of kindness and of love. Nor less, I trust,
To them I may have owed another gift,
Of aspect more sublime; that blessed mood,
In which the burthen of the mystery,   40

In which the heavy and the weary weight
Of all this unintelligible world
Is lightened:—that serene and blessed mood,
In which the affections gently lead us on,
Until, the breath of this corporeal frame,   45
And even the motion of our human blood
Almost suspended, we are laid asleep
In body, and become a living soul:
While with an eye made quiet by the power
Of harmony, and the deep power of joy,   50
We see into the life of things.
                              If this
Be but a vain belief, yet, oh! how oft,
In darkness, and amid the many shapes
Of joyless daylight; when the fretful stir   55
Unprofitable, and the fever of the world,
Have hung upon the beatings of my heart,
How oft, in spirit, have I turned to thee,
O sylvan Wye! Thou wanderer through the woods,
How often has my spirit turned to thee!   60
   And now, with gleams of half-extinguished thought,
With many recognitions dim and faint,
And somewhat of a sad perplexity,
The picture of the mind revives again:
While here I stand, not only with the sense   65
Of present pleasure, but with pleasing thoughts
That in this moment there is life and food
For future years. And so I dare to hope,
Though changed, no doubt, from what I was, when first
I came among these hills; when like a roe   70
I bounded o'er the mountains, by the sides
Of the deep rivers, and the lonely streams,
Wherever nature led: more like a man
Flying from something that he dreads, than one
Who sought the thing he loved. For nature then   75
(The coarser pleasures of my boyish days,
And their glad animal movements all gone by)
To me was all in all.—I cannot paint
What then I was. The sounding cataract
Haunted me like a passion: the tall rock,   80
The mountain, and the deep and gloomy wood,
Their colors and their forms, were then to me

An appetite: a feeling and a love,
That had no need of a remoter charm,
By thought supplied, or any interest   85
Unborrowed from the eye.—that time is past,
And all its aching joys are now no more,
And all its dizzy raptures. Not for this
Faint I, nor mourn nor murmur: other gifts
Have followed, for such loss, I would believe,   90
Abundant recompense. For I have learned
To look on nature, not as in the hour
Of thoughtless youth, but hearing oftentimes
The still, sad music of humanity,
Nor harsh nor grating, though of ample power   95
To chasten and subdue. And I have felt
A presence that disturbs me with the joy
Of elevated thoughts; a sense sublime
Of something far more deeply interfused,
Whose dwelling is the light of setting suns,   100
And the round ocean, and the living air,
And the blue sky, and in the mind of man,
A motion and a spirit, that impels
All thinking things, all objects of all thought,
And rolls through all things. Therefore am I still   105
A lover of the meadows and the woods,
And mountains; and of all that we behold
From this green earth; of all the mighty world
Of eye and ear, both what they half create,
And what perceive; well pleased to recognize   110
In nature and the language of the sense,
The anchor of my purest thoughts, the nurse,
The guide, the guardian of my heart, and soul
Of all my moral being.
                            Nor, perchance,   115
If I were not thus taught, should I the more
Suffer my genial spirits to decay:
For thou art with me, here, upon the banks
Of this fair river; thou, my dearest friend,
My dear, dear friend, and in thy voice I catch   120
The language of my former heart, and read
My former pleasures in the shooting lights
Of thy wild eyes. Oh! yet a little while
May I behold in thee what I was once,

My dear, dear sister! And this prayer I make, 125
Knowing that Nature never did betray
The heart that loved her; 'tis her privilege,
Through all the years of this our life, to lead
From joy to joy: for she can so inform
The mind that is within us, so impress 130
With quietness and beauty, and so feed
With lofty thoughts, that neither evil tongues,
Rash judgments, nor the sneers of selfish men,
Nor greetings where no kindness is, nor all
The dreary intercourse of daily life, 135
Shall e'er prevail against us, or disturb
Our cheerful faith that all which we behold
Is full of blessings. Therefore let the moon
Shine on thee in thy solitary walk;
And let the misty mountain winds be free 140
To blow against thee: and in after years,
When these wild ecstasies shall be matured
Into a sober pleasure, when thy mind
Shall be a mansion for all lovely forms,
Thy memory be as a dwelling-place 145
For all sweet sounds and harmonies; Oh! then,
If solitude, or fear, or pain, or grief,
Should be thy portion, with what healing thoughts
Of tender joy wilt thou remember me,
And these my exhortations! Nor perchance, 150
If I should be where I no more can hear
Thy voice, nor catch from thy wild eyes these gleams
Of past existence, wilt thou then forget
That on the banks of this delightful stream
We stood together; and that I, so long 155
A worshiper of Nature, hither came,
Unwearied in that service: rather say
With warmer love, oh! with far deeper zeal
Of holier love. Nor wilt thou then forget,
That after many wanderings, many years 160
Of absence, these steep woods and lofty cliffs,
And this green pastoral landscape, were to me
More dear, both for themselves, and for thy sake.

THE SOLITARY REAPER

Behold her, single in the field,
Yon solitary Highland lass!
Reaping and singing by herself;
Stop here, or gently pass!
Alone she cuts, and binds the grain,   5
And sings a melancholy strain;
O listen! for the vale profound
Is overflowing with the sound.

No nightingale did ever chant
So sweetly to reposing bands   10
Of travelers in some shady haunt,
Among Arabian sands:
No sweeter voice was ever heard
In springtime from the cuckoo-bird,
Breaking the silence of the seas   15
Among the farthest Hebrides.

Will no one tell me what she sings?
Perhaps the plaintive numbers flow
For old, unhappy, far-off things,
And battles long ago: 20
Or is it some more humble lay,
Familiar matter of today?
Some natural sorrow, loss, or pain,
That has been, and may be again!

Whate'er the theme, the maiden sung   25
As if her song could have no ending;
I saw her singing at her work,
And o'er the sickle bending;
I listened till I had my fill:
And, as I mounted up the hill,   30
The music in my heart I bore,
Long after it was heard no more.

JOHN KEATS
(1795–1821)

ON FIRST LOOKING INTO CHAPMAN'S HOMER

Much have I traveled in the realms of gold,
   And many goodly states and kingdoms seen;
   Round many western islands have I been
Which bards in fealty to Apollo hold.
Oft of one wide expanse had I been told   5
   That deep-browed Homer ruled as his demesne;
   Yet did I never breathe its pure serene
Till I heard Chapman speak out loud and bold:
Then felt I like some watcher of the skies
   When a new planet swims into his ken;   10
Or like stout Cortez when with eagle eyes
   He stared at the Pacific—and all his men
Looked at each other with a wild surmise—
   Silent, upon a peak in Darien.

Chapman's Homer: George Chapman, an Elizabethan poet, translated both the *Iliad* and the *Odyssey.* **14.** *Darien:* Panama.

THE EVE OF ST. AGNES

I

St. Agnes' Eve—Ah, bitter chill it was!
The owl, for all his feathers, was a-cold;
The hare limped trembling through the frozen grass,
And silent was the flock in woolly fold:
Numb were the beadsman's fingers, while he told   5
His rosary, and while his frosted breath,
Like pious incense from a censer old,
Seemed taking flight for heaven, without a death,
Past the sweet Virgin's picture, while his prayer he saith.

II

His prayer he saith, this patient, holy man;   10
Then takes his lamp, and riseth from his knees,
And back returneth, meager, barefoot, wan,
Along the chapel aisle by slow degrees:
The sculptured dead, on each side, seem to freeze,
Emprisoned in black, purgatorial rails: 15
Knights, ladies, praying in dumb orat'ries,
He passeth by; and his weak spirit fails
To think how they may ache in icy hoods and mails.

III

Northward he turneth through a little door,
And scarce three steps, ere Music's golden tongue   20
Flattered to tears this aged man and poor;
But no—already had his deathbell rung:
The joys of all his life were said and sung:
His was harsh penance on St. Agnes' Eve:
Another way he went, and soon among   25
Rough ashes sat he for his soul's reprieve,
And all night kept awake, for sinners' sake to grieve.

IV

That ancient beadsman heard the prelude soft;
And so it chanced, for many a door was wide,
From hurry to and fro. Soon, up aloft,   30
The silver, snarling trumpets 'gan to chide:
The level chambers, ready with their pride,
Were glowing to receive a thousand guests:

The carved angels, ever eager-eyed,
Stared, where upon their heads the cornice rests,   35
With hair blown back, and wings put cross-wise on their breasts.

V

At length burst in the argent revelry,
With plume, tiara, and all rich array,
Numerous as shadows haunting faerily
The brain, new stuffed, in youth, with triumphs gay   40
Of old romance. These let us wish away,
And turn, sole-thoughted, to one lady there,
Whose heart had brooded, all that wintry day,
On love, and winged St. Agnes' saintly care,
As she had heard old dames full many times declare.   45

VI

They told her how, upon St. Agnes' Eve,
Young virgins might have visions of delight,
And soft adorings from their loves receive
Upon the honeyed middle of the night,
If ceremonies due they did aright;   50
As, supperless to bed they must retire,
And couch supine their beauties, lily white;
Nor look behind, nor sideways, but require
Of Heaven with upward eyes for all that they desire.

VII

Full of this whim was thoughtful Madeline: 55
The music, yearning like a god in pain,
She scarcely heard: her maiden eyes divine,
Fixed on the floor, saw many a sweeping train
Pass by—she heeded not at all: in vain
Came many a tiptoe, amorous cavalier,   60
And back retired; not cooled by high disdain,
But she saw not: her heart was otherwhere:
She sighed for Agnes' dreams, the sweetest of the year.

VIII

She danced along with vague, regardless eyes,
Anxious her lips, her breathing quick and short: 65
The hallowed hour was near at hand: she sighs
Amid the timbrels, and the thronged resort

Of whisperers in anger, or in sport;
    'Mid looks of love, defiance, hate, and scorn,
    Hoodwinked with faery fancy; all amort,   70
    Save to St. Agnes and her lambs unshorn,
And all the bliss to be before tomorrow morn.

IX

So, purposing each moment to retire,
    She lingered still. Meantime, across the moors,
    Had come young Porphyro, with heart on fire   75
    For Madeline. Beside the portal doors,
    Buttressed from moonlight, stands he, and implores
    All saints to give him sight of Madeline,
    But for one moment in the tedious hours,
    That he might gaze and worship all unseen;   80
Perchance speak, kneel, touch, kiss—in sooth such things have
        been.

X

He ventures in: let no buzzed whisper tell:
    All eyes be muffled, or a hundred swords
    Will storm his heart, love's fev'rous citadel:
    For him, those chambers held barbarian hordes,   85
    Hyena foemen, and hot-blooded lords,
    Whose very dogs would execrations howl
    Against his lineage: not one breast affords
    Him any mercy, in that mansion foul,
Save one old beldame, weak in body and in soul.   90

XI

Ah, happy chance! the aged creature came,
    Shuffling along with ivory-headed wand,
    To where he stood, hid from the torch's flame,
    Behind a broad hall-pillar, far beyond
    The sound of merriment and chorus bland: 95
    He startled her; but soon she knew his face,
    And grasped his fingers in her palsied hand,
    Saying, "Mercy, Porphyro! hie thee from this place:
They are all here tonight, the whole bloodthirsty race!

70. *amort:* lifeless.

XII

"Get hence! get hence! there's dwarfish Hildebrand;   100
He had a fever late, and in the fit
He cursed thee and thine, both house and land:
Then there's that old Lord Maurice, not a whit
More tame for his gray hairs—Alas me! flit!
Flit like a ghost away."—"Ah, Gossip dear,   105
We're safe enough; here in this armchair sit,
And tell me how"—"Good Saints! not here, not here;
Follow me, child, or else these stones will be thy bier."

XIII

He followed through a lowly arched way,
Brushing the cobwebs with his lofty plume,   110
And as she muttered, "Well-a—well-a-day!"
He found him in a little moonlight room,
Pale, latticed, chill, and silent as a tomb.
"Now tell me where is Madeline," said he,
"O tell me, Angela, by the holy loom   115
Which none but secret sisterhood may see,
When they St. Agnes' wool are weaving piously."

XIV

"St. Agnes! Ah! it is St. Agnes' Eve—
Yet men will murder upon holy days:
Thou must hold water in a witch's sieve   120
And be liege-lord of all the elves and fays,
To venture so: it fills me with amaze
To see thee, Porphyro!—St. Agnes' Eve!
God's help! my lady fair the conjuror plays
This very night: good angels her deceive!   125
But let me laugh awhile, I've mickle time to grieve."

XV

Feebly she laugheth in the languid moon,
While Porphyro upon her face doth look,
Like puzzled urchin on an aged crone
Who keepeth closed a wond'rous riddle-book,   130
As spectacled she sits in chimney nook.
But soon his eyes grew brilliant, when she told
His lady's purpose; and he scarce could brook
Tears, at the thought of those enchantments cold,
And Madeline asleep in lap of legends old.   135

XVI

Sudden a thought came like a full-blown rose,
 Flushing his brow, and in his pained heart
Made purple riot: then doth he propose
 A stratagem, that makes the beldame start:
"A cruel man and impious thou art: 140
Sweet lady, let her pray, and sleep, and dream
 Alone with her good angels, far apart
From wicked men like thee. Go, go!—I deem
Thou canst not surely be the same that thou didst seem."

XVII

"I will not harm her, by all saints I swear,"   145
 Quoth Porphyro: "O may I ne'er find grace
When my weak voice shall whisper its last prayer,
 If one of her soft ringlets I displace,
Or look with ruffian passion in her face:
Good Angela, believe me by these tears;   150
 Or I will, even in a moment's space,
Awake, with horrid shout, my foemen's ears,
And beard them, though they be more fanged than
   wolves and bears."

XVIII

"Ah! why wilt thou affright a feeble soul?
 A poor, weak, palsy-stricken, churchyard thing,
Whose passing-bell may ere the midnight toll;   155
 Whose prayers for thee, each morn and evening,
Were never missed."—Thus plaining, doth she bring
 A gentler speech from burning Porphyro;
So woeful, and of such deep sorrowing,
 That Angela gives promise she will do   160
Whatever he shall wish, betide her weal or woe.

XIX

Which was, to lead him, in close secrecy,
 Even to Madeline's chamber, and there hide
Him in a closet, of such privacy
 That he might see her beauty unespied,   165
And win perhaps that night a peerless bride,
 While legioned faeries paced the coverlet,

And pale enchantment held her sleepy-eyed.
Never on such a night have lovers met,   170
Since Merlin paid his Demon all the monstrous debt.

XX

"It shall be as thou wishest," said the dame:
All cates and dainties shall be stored there
Quickly on this feast-night: by the tambour frame
Her own lute thou wilt see: no time to spare,   175
For I am slow and feeble, and scarce dare
On such a catering trust my dizzy head.
Wait here, my child, with patience; kneel in prayer
The while: Ah! thou must needs the lady wed,
Or may I never leave my grave among the dead."   180

XXI

So saying, she hobbled off with busy fear.
The lover's endless minutes slowly passed;
The dame returned, and whispered in his ear
To follow her; with aged eyes aghast
From fright of dim espial. Safe at last,   185
Through many a dusky gallery, they gain
The maiden's chamber, silken, hushed, and chaste;
Where Porphyro took covert, pleased amain.
His poor guide hurried back with agues in her brain.

XXII

Her falt'ring hand upon the balustrade,   190
Old Angela was feeling for the stair,
When Madeline, St. Agnes' charmed maid,
Rose, like a missioned spirit, unaware:
With silver taper's light, and pious care,
She turned, and down the aged gossip led   195
To a safe level matting. Now prepare,
Young Porphyro, for gazing on that bed;
She comes, she comes again, like ring-dove frayed and fled.

---

171. *Merlin . . . debt:* Merlin was engendered by a demon; he paid the debt of his monstrous origin when he was enchanted by Vivian. The evening after his enchantment there was a great storm.   **198.** *frayed:* frightened.

XXIII

    Out went the taper as she hurried in;
    Its little smoke, in pallid moonshine, died: 200
    She closed the door, she panted, all akin
    To spirits of the air, and visions wide:
    No uttered syllable, or, woe betide!
    But to her heart, her heart was voluble,
    Paining with eloquence her balmy side;   205
    As though a tongueless nightingale should swell
Her throat in vain, and die, heart-stifled, in her dell.

XXIV

    A casement high and triple-arched there was,
    All garlanded with carven imag'ries
    Of fruits, and flowers, and bunches of knot-grass,   210
    And diamonded with panes of quaint device,
    Innumerable of stains and splendid dyes,
    As are the tiger-moth's deep-damasked wings;
    And in the midst, 'mong thousand heraldries,
    And twilight saints, and dim emblazonings,   215
A shielded scutcheon blushed with blood of queens and kings.

XXV

    Full on this casement shone the wintry moon,
    And threw warm gules on Madeline's fair breast,
    As down she knelt for heaven's grace and boon;
    Rose-bloom fell on her hands, together pressed,   220
    And on her silver cross soft amethyst,
    And on her hair a glory, like a saint:
    She seemed a splendid angel, newly dressed,
    Save wings, for heaven:—Porphyro grew faint:
She knelt, so pure a thing, so free from mortal taint.   225

XXVI

    Anon his heart revives: her vespers done,
    Of all its wreathed pearls her hair she frees;
    Unclasps her warmed jewels one by one;
    Loosens her fragrant bodice; by degrees
    Her rich attire creeps rustling to her knees: 230
    Half-hidden, like a mermaid in seaweed,
    Pensive awhile she dreams awake, and sees,
    In fancy, fair St. Agnes in her bed,
But dares not look behind, or all the charm is fled.

XXVII

Soon, trembling in her soft and chilly nest,   235
In sort of wakeful swoon, perplexed she lay,
Until the poppied warmth of sleep oppressed
Her soothed limbs, and soul fatigued away;
Flown, like a thought, until the morrow-day;
Blissfully havened both from joy and pain;   240
Clasped like a missal where swart Paynims pray;
Blinded alike from sunshine and from rain,
As though a rose should shut, and be a bud again.

XXVIII

Stolen to this paradise, and so entranced,
Porphyro gazed upon her empty dress,   245
And listened to her breathing, if it chanced
To wake into a slumberous tenderness;
Which when he heard, that minute did he bless,
And breathed himself: then from the closet crept,
Noiseless as fear in a wide wilderness,   250
And over the hushed carpet, silent, stepped,
And 'tween the curtains peeped, where, lo!—how fast she slept.

XXIX

Then by the bedside, where the faded moon
Made a dim, silver twilight, soft he set
A table, and, half anguished, threw thereon   255
A cloth of woven crimson, gold, and jet:—
O for some drowsy Morphean amulet!
The boisterous, midnight, festive clarion,
The kettle-drum, and far-heard clarinet,
Affray his ears, though but in dying tone:—   260
The hall door shuts again, and all the noise is gone.

XXX

And still she slept an azure-lidded sleep,
In blanched linen, smooth, and lavendered,
While he from forth the closet brought a heap
Of candied apple, quince, and plum, and gourd;   265
With jellies soother than the creamy curd,

---

241. *Paynims:* pagans, usually Moslems.   **257.** *Morphean:* sleep-giving, like the god Morpheus.

And lucent syrups, tinct with cinnamon;
Manna and dates, in argosy transferred
From Fez; and spiced dainties, every one,
From silken Samarcand to cedared Lebanon.   270

XXXI

These delicates he heaped with glowing hand
On golden dishes and in baskets bright
Of wreathed silver: sumptuous they stand
In the retired quiet of the night,
Filling the chilly room with perfume light.—   275
"And now, my love, my seraph fair, awake!
Thou art my heaven, and I thine eremite:
Open thine eyes, for meek St. Agnes' sake,
Or I shall drowse beside thee, so my soul doth ache."

XXXII

Thus whispering, his warm, unnerved arm
Sank in her pillow. Shaded was her dream   280
By the dusk curtains:—'twas a midnight charm
Impossible to melt as iced stream:
The lustrous salvers in the moonlight gleam;
Broad golden fringe upon the carpet lies: 285
It seemed he never, never could redeem
From such a steadfast spell his lady's eyes;
So mused awhile, entoiled in woofed fantasies.

XXXIII

Awakening up, he took her hollow lute,—
Tumultuous,—and, in chords that tenderest be,   290
He played an ancient ditty, long since mute,
In Provence called, "La belle dame sans mercy:"
Close to her ear touching the melody;—
Wherewith disturbed, she uttered a soft moan:
He ceased—she panted quick—and suddenly   295
Her blue affrayed eyes wide open shone:
Upon his knees he sank, pale as smooth-sculptured stone.

XXXIV

Her eyes were open, but she still beheld,
Now wide awake, the vision of her sleep:

277. *eremite:* worshiper.

There was a painful change, that nigh expelled   300
The blisses of her dream so pure and deep;
At which fair Madeline began to weep,
And moan forth witless words with many a sigh;
While still her gaze on Porphyro would keep;
Who knelt, with joined hands and piteous eye,   305
Fearing to move or speak, she looked so dreamingly.

XXXV

"Ah, Porphyro!" said she, "but even now
Thy voice was at sweet tremble in mine ear,
Made tuneable with every sweetest vow;
And those sad eyes were spiritual and clear: 310
How changed thou art! how pallid, chill, and drear!
Give me that voice again, my Porphyro,
Those looks immortal, those complainings dear!
Oh leave me not in this eternal woe,
For if thou diest, my love, I know not where to go."   315

XXXVI

Beyond a mortal man impassioned far
At these voluptuous accents, he arose,
Ethereal, flushed, and like a throbbing star
Seen mid the sapphire heaven's deep repose;
Into her dream he melted, as the rose   320
Blendeth its odor with the violet,—
Solution sweet: meantime the frost-wind blows
Like love's alarum pattering the sharp sleet
Against the windowpanes; St. Agnes' moon hath set.

XXXVII

'Tis dark: quick pattereth the flaw-blown sleet: 325
"This is no dream, my bride, my Madeline!"
'Tis dark: the iced gusts still rave and beat:
"No dream, alas! alas! and woe is mine!
Porphyro will leave me here to fade and pine.—
Cruel! what traitor could thee hither bring?   330
I curse not, for my heart is lost in thine,
Though thou forsakest a deceived thing;—
A dove forlorn and lost with sick unpruned wing."

XXXVIII

"My Madeline! sweet dreamer! lovely bride!
Say, may I be for aye thy vassal blest?   335
Thy beauty's shield, heart-shaped and vermeil dyed?
Ah, silver shrine, here will I take my rest
After so many hours of toil and quest,
A famished pilgrim,—saved by miracle.
Though I have found, I will not rob thy nest   340
Saving of thy sweet self; if thou think'st well
To trust, fair Madeline, to no rude infidel.

XXXIX

"Hark! 'tis an elfin-storm from faery land,
Of haggard seeming, but a boon indeed:
Arise—arise! the morning is at hand;—   345
The bloated wassailers will never heed:—
Let us away, my love, with happy speed;
There are no ears to hear, or eyes to see,—
Drowned all in Rhenish and the sleepy mead:
Awake! arise! my love, and fearless be,   350
For o'er the southern moors I have a home for thee."

XL

She hurried at his words, beset with fears,
For there were sleeping dragons all around,
At glaring watch, perhaps, with ready spears—
Down the wide stairs a darkling way they found.—   355
In all the house was heard no human sound.
A chain-drooped lamp was flickering by each door;
The arras, rich with horseman, hawk, and hound,
Fluttered in the besieging wind's uproar;
And the long carpets rose along the gusty floor.   360

XLI

They glide, like phantoms, into the wide hall;
Like phantoms, to the iron porch, they glide;
Where lay the porter, in uneasy sprawl,
With a huge empty flagon by his side:
The wakeful bloodhound rose, and shook his hide,   365
But his sagacious eye an inmate owns:

---

336. *vermeil:* vermilion.   **349.** *Rhenish:* Rhine wine.

By one, and one, the bolts full easy slide:—
The chains lie silent on the footworn stones;—
The key turns, and the door upon its hinges groans.

XLII
And they are gone: aye, ages long ago   370
These lovers fled away into the storm.
That night the baron dreamt of many a woe,
And all his warrior-guests, with shade and form
Of witch, and demon, and large coffin-worm,
Were long be-nightmared. Angela the old   375
Died palsy-twitched, with meager face deform;
The beadsman, after thousand aves told,
For aye unsought for slept among his ashes cold.

LA BELLE DAME SANS MERCI

I

"O, what can ail thee, knight-at-arms,
    Alone and palely loitering?
The sedge has withered from the lake,
    And no birds sing.

II

"O, what can ail thee, knight-at-arms,   5
    So haggard and so woe-begone?
The squirrel's granary is full,
    And the harvest's done.

III

"I see a lily on thy brow,
    With anguish moist and fever dew;   10
And on thy cheeks a fading rose
    Fast withereth too."

IV

"I met a lady in the meads,
    Full beautiful—a faery's child,
Her hair was long, her foot was light,   15
    And her eyes were wild.

V

"I made a garland for her head,
    And bracelets too, and fragrant zone;
She looked at me as she did love,
    And made sweet moan.   20

VI

"I set her on my pacing steed,
    And nothing else saw all day long;
For sidelong would she bend, and sing
    A faery's song.

VII

"She found me roots of relish sweet,   25
    And honey wild, and manna dew,
And sure in language strange she said—
    'I love thee true.'

VIII

"She took me to her elfin grot,
 And there she wept and sighed full sore,   30
And there I shut her wild wild eyes
 With kisses four.

IX

"And there she lulled me asleep
 And there I dreamed—Ah! woe betide!
The latest dream I ever dreamed   35
 On the cold hillside.

X

"I saw pale kings and princes too,
 Pale warriors, death-pale were they all;
They cried—'La Belle Dame sans Merci
 Hath thee in thrall!'   40

XI

"I saw their starved lips in the gloam,
 With horrid warning gaped wide,
And I awoke and found me here,
 On the cold hill's side.

XII

"And this is why I sojourn here
 Alone and palely loitering,   45
Though the sedge has withered from the lake,
 And no birds sing."

ODE TO A NIGHTINGALE

I

My heart aches, and a drowsy numbness pains
  My sense, as though of hemlock I had drunk,
Or emptied some dull opiate to the drains
  One minute past, and Lethe-wards had sunk:
'Tis not through envy of thy happy lot,   5
  But being too happy in thine happiness,—
    That thou, light-winged dryad of the trees,
      In some melodious plot
  Of beechen green, and shadows numberless,
    Singest of summer in full-throated ease.   10

II

O, for a draught of vintage! that hath been
  Cooled a long age in the deep-delved earth,
Tasting of Flora and the country green,
  Dance, and Provençal song, and sunburnt mirth!
O for a beaker full of the warm South,   15
  Full of the true, the blushful Hippocrene,
    With beaded bubbles winking at the brim,
      And purple-stained mouth;
  That I might drink, and leave the world unseen,
    And with thee fade away into the forest dim: 20

III

Fade far away, dissolve, and quite forget
  What thou among the leaves hast never known,
The weariness, the fever, and the fret
  Here, where men sit and hear each other groan;
Where palsy shakes a few, sad, last gray hairs,   25
  Where youth grows pale, and specter-thin, and dies;
    Where but to think is to be full of sorrow
      And leaden-eyed despairs,
  Where Beauty cannot keep her lustrous eyes,
    Or new Love pine at them beyond tomorrow.   30

---

4. *Lethe-wards:* toward Lethe, the river of oblivion in Hades.   **7.** *dryad:* wood nymph.   **16.** *Hippocrene:* a fountain on Mt. Helicon, the source of poetic inspiration.

IV

Away! away! for I will fly to thee,
  Not charioted by Bacchus and his pards,
But on the viewless wings of Poesy,
  Though the dull brain perplexes and retards:
Already with thee! tender is the night,   35
    And haply the Queen-Moon is on her throne,
      Clustered around by all her starry fays;
          But here there is no light,
    Save what from heaven is with the breezes blown
      Through verdurous glooms and winding mossy ways.   40

V

I cannot see what flowers are at my feet,
  Nor what soft incense hangs upon the boughs,
But, in embalmed darkness, guess each sweet
  Wherewith the seasonable month endows
The grass, the thicket, and the fruit-tree wild;   45
    White hawthorn, and the pastoral eglantine;
      Fast fading violets covered up in leaves;
          And mid-May's eldest child,
    The coming musk-rose, full of dewy wine,
      The murmurous haunt of flies on summer eves.   50

VI

Darkling I listen; and, for many a time
  I have been half in love with easeful Death,
Called him soft names in many a mused rhyme,
  To take into the air my quiet breath;
Now more than ever seems it rich to die,   55
    To cease upon the midnight with no pain,
      While thou art pouring forth thy soul abroad
          In such an ecstasy!
    Still wouldst thou sing, and I have ears in vain—
      To thy high requiem become a sod.   60

VII

Thou wast not born for death, immortal bird!
  No hungry generations tread thee down;

---

32. *pards:* the leopards that draw Bacchus's chariot.

The voice I hear this passing night was heard
  In ancient days by emperor and clown:
Perhaps the self-same song that found a path   65
    Through the sad heart of Ruth, when, sick for home,
      She stood in tears amid the alien corn;
          The same that oft-times hath
    Charmed magic casements, opening on the foam
      Of perilous seas, in faery lands forlorn.   70

VIII

Forlorn! the very word is like a bell
  To toll me back from thee to my sole self!
Adieu! the fancy cannot cheat so well
  As she is famed to do, deceiving elf.
Adieu! adieu! thy plaintive anthem fades   75
    Past the near meadows, over the still stream,
      Up the hillside; and now 'tis buried deep
          In the next valley-glades:
    Was it a vision, or a waking dream?
      Fled is that music:—Do I wake or sleep?   80

66. *Ruth:* The Old Testament Book of Ruth relates Ruth's journey into a foreign land out of love for her husband's mother.

ODE ON A GRECIAN URN

I

Thou still unravished bride of quietness,
   Thou foster-child of silence and slow time,
Sylvan historian, who canst thus express
   A flowery tale more sweetly than our rhyme:
What leaf-fringed legend haunts about thy shape   5
    Of deities or mortals, or of both,
      In Tempe or the dales of Arcady?
    What men or gods are these? What maidens loth?
What mad pursuit? What struggle to escape?
      What pipes and timbrels? What wild ecstasy?   10

II

Heard melodies are sweet, but those unheard
   Are sweeter; therefore, ye soft pipes, play on;
Not to the sensual ear, but, more endeared,
   Pipe to the spirit ditties of no tone:
Fair youth, beneath the trees, thou canst not leave   15
    Thy song, nor ever can those trees be bare;
      Bold lover, never, never canst thou kiss,
Though winning near the goal—yet, do not grieve;
    She cannot fade, though thou hast not thy bliss,
      For ever wilt thou love, and she be fair!   20

III

Ah, happy, happy boughs! that cannot shed
   Your leaves, nor ever bid the Spring adieu;
And, happy melodist, unwearied,
   For ever piping songs for ever new;
More happy love! more happy, happy love!   25
    For ever warm and still to be enjoyed,
      For ever panting, and for ever young;
All breathing human passion far above,
    That leaves a heart high-sorrowful and cloyed,
      A burning forehead, and a parching tongue.   30

IV

Who are these coming to the sacrifice?
   To what green altar, O mysterious priest,
Lead'st thou that heifer lowing at the skies,
    And all her silken flanks with garlands drest?

What little town by river or seashore,   35
  Or mountain-built with peaceful citadel,
    Is emptied of this folk, this pious morn?
And, little town, thy streets for evermore
  Will silent be; and not a soul to tell
    Why thou art desolate, can e'er return.   40

V

O Attic shape! Fair attitude! with brede
  Of marble men and maidens overwrought,
With forest branches and the trodden weed;
  Thou, silent form, dost tease us out of thought
As doth eternity: Cold Pastoral!   45
  When old age shall this generation waste,
    Thou shalt remain, in midst of other woe
Than ours, a friend to man, to whom thou say'st,
  "Beauty is truth, truth beauty,"—that is all
    Ye know on earth, and all ye need to know.   50

41. *Attic:* Belonging to the region around Athens, Greece; *brede:* embroidery.

TO AUTUMN

I

Season of mists and mellow fruitfulness,
   Close bosom-friend of the maturing sun;
Conspiring with him how to load and bless
   With fruit the vines that round the thatch-eaves run;
To bend with apples the mossed cottage-trees,   5
   And fill all fruit with ripeness to the core;
     To swell the gourd, and plump the hazel shells
   With a sweet kernel; to set budding more,
And still more, later flowers for the bees,
Until they think warm days will never cease,   10
     For Summer has o'er-brimmed their clammy cells.

II

Who hath not seen thee oft amid thy store?
   Sometimes whoever seeks abroad may find
Thee sitting careless on a granary floor,
   Thy hair soft-lifted by the winnowing wind;   15
Or on a half-reaped furrow sound asleep,
   Drowsed with the fume of poppies, while thy hook
     Spares the next swath and all its twined flowers:
And sometimes like a gleaner thou dost keep
   Steady thy laden head across a brook;   20
   Or by a cider-press, with patient look,
     Thou watchest the last oozings hours by hours.

III

Where are the songs of Spring? Ay, where are they?
   Think not of them, thou hast thy music too,—
While barred clouds bloom the soft-dying day,   25
   And touch the stubble-plains with rosy hue;
Then in a wailful choir the small gnats mourn
   Among the river sallows, borne aloft
     Or sinking as the light wind lives or dies;
And full-grown lambs loud bleat from hilly bourn;   30
   Hedge-crickets sing; and now with treble soft
   The red-breast whistles from a garden-croft;
     And gathering swallows twitter in the skies.

BRIGHT STAR

Bright star, would I were steadfast as thou art—
  Not in lone splendor hung aloft the night
And watching, with eternal lids apart,
  Like nature's patient, sleepless eremite,
The moving waters at their priestlike task   5
  Of pure ablution round earth's human shores,
Or gazing on the new soft-fallen mask
  Of snow upon the mountains and the moors—
No—yet still steadfast, still unchangeable,
  Pillowed upon my fair love's ripening breast,   10
To feel for ever its soft fall and swell,
  Awake for ever in a sweet unrest,
Still, still to hear her tender-taken breath,
And so live ever—or else swoon to death.

4. *eremite:* hermit, worshiper.

ALFRED, LORD TENNYSON
(1809–1892)

ULYSSES

It little profits that an idle king,
By this still hearth, among these barren crags,
Matched with an agèd wife, I mete and dole
Unequal laws unto a savage race,
That hoard, and sleep, and feed, and know not me. 5
I cannot rest from travel: I will drink
Life to the lees: all times I have enjoyed
Greatly, have suffered greatly, both with those
That loved me, and alone; on shore, and when
Through scudding drifts the rainy Hyades 10
Vexed the dim sea: I am become a name;
For always roaming with a hungry heart
Much have I seen and known; cities of men
And manners, climates, councils, governments,
Myself not least, but honored of them all; 15
And drunk delight of battle with my peers,
Far on the ringing plains of windy Troy.
I am a part of all that I have met;
Yet all experience is an arch wherethrough
Gleams that untraveled world, whose margin fades 20
Forever and forever when I move.
How dull it is to pause, to make an end,
To rust unburnished, not to shine in use!
As though to breathe were life. Life piled on life
Were all too little, and of one to me 25
Little remains: but every hour is saved
From that eternal silence, something more,
A bringer of new things; and vile it were
For some three suns to store and hoard myself,
And this gray spirit yearning in desire 30
To follow knowledge like a sinking star,
Beyond the utmost bound of human thought.

This is my son, mine own Telemachus,
To whom I leave the scepter and the isle—
Well-loved of me, discerning to fulfill 35
This labor, by slow prudence to make mild
A rugged people, and through soft degrees
Subdue them to the useful and the good.
Most blameless is he, centered in the sphere
Of common duties, decent not to fail 40
In offices of tenderness, and pay
Meet adoration to my household gods,
When I am gone. He works his work, I mine.

There lies the port; the vessel puffs her sail:
There gloom the dark broad seas. My mariners, 45
Souls that have toiled, and wrought, and thought with me—
That ever with a frolic welcome took
The thunder and the sunshine, and opposed
Free hearts, free foreheads—you and I are old;
Old age hath yet his honor and his toil; 50
Death closes all: but something ere the end,
Some work of noble note, may yet be done,
Not unbecoming men that strove with gods.
The lights begin to twinkle from the rocks:
The long day wanes: the slow moon climbs: the deep 55
Moans round with many voices. Come, my friends,
'Tis not too late to seek a newer world.
Push off, and sitting well in order smite
The sounding furrows; for my purpose holds
To sail beyond the sunset, and the baths 60
Of all the western stars, until I die.
It may be that the gulfs will wash us down:
It may be we shall touch the Happy Isles,
And see the great Achilles, whom we knew.
Though much is taken, much abides; and though 65
We are not now that strength which in old days
Moved earth and heaven; that which we are, we are;
One equal temper of heroic hearts,
Made weak by time and fate, but strong in will
To strive, to seek, to find, and not to yield. 70

MATTHEW ARNOLD
(1822–1888)

DOVER BEACH

The sea is calm tonight.
The tide is full, the moon lies fair
Upon the straits;—on the French coast the light
Gleams and is gone; the cliffs of England stand,
Glimmering and vast, out in the tranquil bay.   5
Come to the window, sweet is the night air!
Only, from the long line of spray
Where the sea meets the moon-blanched land,
Listen! you hear the grating roar
Of pebbles which the waves draw back, and fling,   10
At their return, up the high strand,
Begin, and cease, and then again begin,
With tremulous cadence slow, and bring
The eternal note of sadness in.

Sophocles long ago   15
Heard it on the Ægæan, and it brought
Into his mind the turbid ebb and flow
Of human misery; we
Find also in the sound a thought,
Hearing it by this distant northern sea.   20

The Sea of Faith
Was once, too, at the full, and round earth's shore
Lay like the folds of a bright girdle furled.
But now I only hear
Its melancholy, long, withdrawing roar,   25
Retreating, to the breath
Of the night wind, down the vast edges drear
And naked shingles of the world.

28. *shingles:* gravel beaches.

Ah, love, let us be true
To one another! for the world, which seems   30
To lie before us like a land of dreams,
So various, so beautiful, so new,
Hath really neither joy, nor love, nor light,
Nor certitude, nor peace, nor help for pain;
And we are here as on a darkling plain   35
Swept with confused alarms of struggle and flight,
Where ignorant armies clash by night.

ROBERT BROWNING
(1812–1889)

PORPHYRIA'S LOVER

The rain set early in tonight,
   The sullen wind was soon awake,
It tore the elm-tops down for spite,
   And did its worst to vex the lake:
   I listened with heart fit to break. 5
When glided in Porphyria; straight
   She shut the cold out and the storm,
And kneeled and made the cheerless grate
   Blaze up, and all the cottage warm;
   Which done, she rose, and from her form 10
Withdrew the dripping cloak and shawl,
   And laid her soiled gloves by, untied
Her hat and let the damp hair fall,
   And, last, she sat down by my side
   And called me. When no voice replied, 15
She put my arm about her waist,
   And made her smooth white shoulder bare,
And all her yellow hair displaced,
   And, stooping, made my cheek lie there,
   And spread, o'er all, her yellow hair, 20
Murmuring how she loved me—she
   Too weak, for all her heart's endeavor,
To set its struggling passion free
   From pride, and vainer ties dissever,
   And give herself to me for ever. 25
But passion sometimes would prevail,
   Nor could tonight's gay feast restrain
A sudden thought of one so pale
   For love of her, and all in vain:
   So, she was come through wind and rain. 30
Be sure I looked up at her eyes
   Happy and proud; at last I knew
Porphyria worshiped me; surprise
   Made my heart swell, and still it grew
   While I debated what to do. 35

That moment she was mine, mine, fair,
    Perfectly pure and good: I found
A thing to do, and all her hair
    In one long yellow string I wound
    Three times her little throat around,   40
And strangled her. No pain felt she;
    I am quite sure she felt no pain.
As a shut bud that holds a bee,
    I warily oped her lids: again
    Laughed the blue eyes without a stain.   45
And I untightened next the tress
    About her neck; her cheek once more
Blushed bright beneath my burning kiss:
    I propped her head up as before,
    Only, this time my shoulder bore   50
Her head, which droops upon it still:
    The smiling rosy little head,
So glad it has its utmost will,
    That all it scorned at once is fled,
    And I, its love, am gained instead!   55
Porphyria's love: she guessed not how
    Her darling one wish would be heard.
And thus we sit together now,
    And all night long we have not stirred,
    And yet God has not said a word!   60

SOLILOQUY OF THE SPANISH CLOISTER

I

Gr-r-r—there go, my heart's abhorrence!
   Water your damned flowerpots, do!
If hate killed men, Brother Lawrence,
   God's blood, would not mine kill you!
What? your myrtle-bush wants trimming?   5
   Oh, that rose has prior claims—
Needs its leaden vase filled brimming?
   Hell dry you up with its flames!

II

At the meal we sit together:
   Salve tibi! I must hear   10
Wise talk of the kind of weather,
   Sort of season, time of year:
Not a plenteous cork-crop: scarcely
   Dare we hope oak-galls, I doubt:
What's the Latin name for "parsley"?   15
   What's the Greek name for Swine's Snout?

III

Whew! We'll have our platter burnished,
   Laid with care on our own shelf!
With a fire-new spoon we're furnished,
   And a goblet for ourself,   20
Rinsed like something sacrificial
   Ere 'tis fit to touch our chaps—
Marked with L. for our initial!
   (He-he! There his lily snaps!)

IV

Saint, forsooth! While brown Dolores   25
   Squats outside the Convent bank
With Sanchicha, telling stories,
   Steeping tresses in the tank,
Blue-black, lustrous, thick like horsehairs,
   —Can't I see his dead eye glow,   30
Bright as 'twere a Barbary corsair's?
   (That is, if he'd let it show!)

10. *Salve tibi:* bless you.

V

When he finishes refection,
 Knife and fork he never lays
Cross-wise, to my recollection,   35
 As do I, in Jesu's praise.
I the Trinity illustrate,
 Drinking watered orange-pulp—
In three sips the Arian frustrate;
 While he drains his at one gulp.   40

VI

Oh, those melons? If he's able
 We're to have a feast! so nice!
One goes to the Abbot's table,
 All of us get each a slice.
How go on your flowers? None double? 45
 Not one fruit-sort can you spy?
Strange!—And I, too, at such trouble,
 Keep them close-nipped on the sly!

VII

There's a great text in Galatians,
 Once you trip on it, entails   50
Twenty-nine distinct damnations,
 One sure, if another fails:
If I trip him just a-dying,
 Sure of heaven as sure as can be,
Spin him round and send him flying 55
 Off to hell, a Manichee?

VIII

Or, my scrofulous French novel
 On gray paper with blunt type!
Simply glance at it, you grovel
 Hand and foot in Belial's gripe: 60

39. *Arian:* The Arian heresy denies the Trinity, which conceives of God as three persons in one being. 56. *Manichee:* The Manichean heresy viewed the world as the battlefield of equally balanced forces of good and evil, thus denying God's role as controlling Providence. 60. *Belial:* a sensual Miltonic devil.

If I double down its pages
   At the woeful sixteenth print,
When he gathers his greengages,
   Ope a sieve and slip it in't?

IX

Or, there's Satan!—one might venture   65
   Pledge one's soul to him, yet leave
Such a flaw in the indenture
   As he'd miss till, past retrieve,
Blasted lay that rose-acacia
   We're so proud of! *Hy, Zy, Hine* . . .   70
'St, there's Vespers! *Plena gratiâ*
   Ave, Virgo! Gr-r-r—you swine!

71–72. *Plena* . . . *Virgo:* "Hail Mary, full of grace."

THE BISHOP ORDERS HIS TOMB
AT SAINT PRAXED'S CHURCH

rome, 15—

Vanity, saith the preacher, vanity!
Draw round my bed: is Anselm keeping back?
Nephews—sons mine . . . ah God, I know not! Well—
She, men would have to be your mother once,
Old Gandolf envied me, so fair she was!   5
What's done is done, and she is dead beside,
Dead long ago, and I am Bishop since,
And as she died so must we die ourselves,
And thence ye may perceive the world's a dream.
Life, how and what is it? As here I lie   10
In this state-chamber, dying by degrees,
Hours and long hours in the dead night, I ask
"Do I live, am I dead?" Peace, peace seems all.
Saint Praxed's ever was the church for peace;
And so, about this tomb of mine. I fought   15
With tooth and nail to save my niche, ye know:
—Old Gandolf cozened me, despite my care;
Shrewd was that snatch from out the corner South
He graced his carrion with, God curse the same!
Yet still my niche is not so cramped but thence   20
One sees the pulpit o' the epistle-side,
And somewhat of the choir, those silent seats,
And up into the airy dome where live
The angels, and a sunbeam's sure to lurk:
And I shall fill my slab of basalt there,   25
And 'neath my tabernacle take my rest,
With those nine columns round me, two and two,
The odd one at my feet where Anselm stands:
Peach-blossom marble all, the rare, the ripe
As fresh-poured red wine of a mighty pulse.   30
—Old Gandolf with his paltry onion-stone,
Put me where I may look at him! True peach,
Rosy and flawless: how I earned the prize!

21. *epistle-side:* the right side of the altar, as you face it, where the epistle is read. **26.** *tabernacle:* literally the tent, or canopy, over his tomb.

Draw close: that conflagration of my church
—What then? So much was saved if aught were missed!   35
My sons, ye would not be my death? Go dig
The white-grape vineyard where the oil-press stood,
Drop water gently till the surface sink,
And if ye find . . . Ah God, I know not, I! . . .
Bedded in store of rotten fig-leaves soft,   40
And corded up in a tight olive-frail,
Some lump, ah God, of lapis lazuli,
Big as a Jew's head cut off at the nape,
Blue as a vein o'er the Madonna's breast. . . .
Sons, all have I bequeathed you, villas, all,   45
That brave Frascati villa with its bath,
So, let the blue lump poise between my knees,
Like God the Father's globe on both his hands
Ye worship in the Jesu Church so gay,
For Gandolf shall not choose but see and burst!   50
Swift as a weaver's shuttle fleet our years:
Man goeth to the grave, and where is he?
Did I say basalt for my slab, sons? Black—
'Twas ever antique-black I meant! How else
Shall ye contrast my frieze to come beneath?   55
The bas-relief in bronze ye promised me,
Those Pans and Nymphs ye wot of, and perchance
Some tripod, thyrsus, with a vase or so,
The Saviour at his sermon on the mount,
Saint Praxed in a glory, and one Pan   60
Ready to twitch the Nymph's last garment off,
And Moses with the tables . . . but I know
Ye mark me not! What do they whisper thee,
Child of my bowels, Anselm? Ah, ye hope
To revel down my villas while I gasp   65
Bricked o'er with beggar's moldy travertine
Which Gandolf from his tomb-top chuckles at!
Nay, boys, ye love me—all of jasper, then!
'Tis jasper ye stand pledged to, lest I grieve
My bath must needs be left behind, alas!   70
One block, pure green as a pistachio-nut,
There's plenty jasper somewhere in the world—

41. *olive-frail:* a basket of rushes.

And have I not Saint Praxed's ear to pray
Horses for ye, and brown Greek manuscripts,
And mistresses with great smooth marbly limbs? 75
—That's if ye carve my epitaph aright,
Choice Latin, picked phrase, Tully's every word,
No gaudy ware like Gandolf's second line—
Tully, my masters? Ulpian serves his need!
And then how I shall lie through centuries, 80
And hear the blessed mutter of the mass,
And see God made and eaten all day long,
And feel the steady candle-flame, and taste
Good strong thick stupefying incense-smoke!
For as I lie here, hours of the dead night, 85
Dying in state and by such slow degrees,
I fold my arms as if they clasped a crook,
And stretch my feet forth straight as stone can point,
And let the bedclothes, for a mortcloth, drop
Into great laps and folds of sculptor's-work: 90
And as yon tapers dwindle, and strange thoughts
Grow, with a certain humming in my ears,
About the life before I lived this life,
And this life too, popes, cardinals and priests,
Saint Praxed at his sermon on the mount, 95
Your tall pale mother with her talking eyes,
And new-found agate urns as fresh as day,
And marble's language, Latin pure, discreet,
—Aha, ELUCESCEBAT quoth our friend!
No Tully, said I, Ulpian at the best! 100
Evil and brief hath been my pilgrimage.
All lapis, all, sons! Else I give the Pope
My villas! Will ye ever eat my heart?
Ever your eyes were as a lizard's quick,
They glitter like your mother's for my soul, 105
Or ye would heighten my impoverished frieze,
Piece out its starved design, and fill my vase
With grapes, and add a visor and a term,
And to the tripod ye would tie a lynx
That in his struggle throws the thyrsus down, 110

77. *Tully:* Cicero, the model for Latin prose. **79.** *Ulpian:* Domitius Ulpianus, an inferior Latin writer. **89.** *mortcloth:* a funeral pall. **99.** *ELUCESCEBAT:* "he was famous." **108.** *term:* a memorial sculpture.

To comfort me on my entablature
Whereon I am to lie till I must ask
"Do I live, am I dead?" There, leave me, there!
For ye have stabbed me with ingratitude
To death—ye wish it—God, ye wish it! Stone—   115
Gritstone, a-crumble! Clammy squares which sweat
As if the corpse they keep were oozing through—
And no more lapis to delight the world!
Well, go! I bless ye. Fewer tapers there,
But in a row: and, going, turn your backs   120
—Ay, like departing altar-ministrants,
And leave me in my church, the church for peace,
That I may watch at leisure if he leers—
Old Gandolf, at me, from his onion-stone,
As still he envied me, so fair she was!   125

CHARLES DODGSON (LEWIS CARROLL)
(1832–1898)

JABBERWOCKY

'Twas brillig, and the slithy toves
　　Did gyre and gimble in the wabe;
All mimsy were the borogoves,
　　　And the mome raths outgrabe.

"Beware the Jabberwock, my son !　　　　　　　　　5
　　The jaws that bite, the claws that catch !
Beware the Jubjub bird, and shun
　　　The frumious Bandersnatch !"

He took his vorpal sword in hand:
　　Long time the manxome foe he sought—　　　　10
So rested he by the Tumtum tree,
　　　And stood awhile in thought.

And as in uffish thought he stood,
　　The Jabberwock, with eyes of flame,
Came whiffling through the tulgey wood,　　　　　15
　　　And burbled as it came !

One, two ! One, two ! And through and through
　　The vorpal blade went snicker-snack !
He left it dead, and with its head
　　　He went galumphing back.　　　　　　　　　20

"And hast thou slain the Jabberwock?
　　Come to my arms, my beamish boy !
O frabjous day ! Callooh ! Callay !"
　　　He chortled in his joy.

'Twas brillig, and the slithy toves　　　　　　　　25
　　Did gyre and gimble in the wabe;
All mimsy were the borogoves,
　　　And the mome raths outgrabe.

WALT WHITMAN
(1819–1892)

From SONG OF MYSELF

I
I celebrate myself, and sing myself,
And what I assume you shall assume,
For every atom belonging to me as good belongs to you.

I loaf and invite my soul,
I lean and loaf at my ease observing a spear of summer grass.   5

My tongue, every atom of my blood, formed from this soil,
    this air,
Born here of parents born here from parents the same, and their
    parents the same,
I, now thirty-seven years old in perfect health begin,
Hoping to cease not till death.

Creeds and schools in abeyance,   10
Retiring back a while sufficed at what they are, but never
    forgotten,
I harbor for good or bad, I permit to speak at every hazard,
Nature without check with original energy.

XXIV
Walt Whitman, a kosmos, of Manhattan the son,
Turbulent, fleshy, sensual, eating, drinking and breeding,
No sentimentalist, no stander above men and women or apart
    from them,
No more modest than immodest.

Unscrew the locks from the doors!   5
Unscrew the doors themselves from their jambs!

Whoever degrades another degrades me,
And whatever is done or said returns at last to me.

Through me the afflatus surging and surging, through me the
    current and index.

I speak the pass-word primeval, I give the sign of democracy, 10
By God! I will accept nothing which all cannot have their
  counterpart of on the same terms.

Through me many long dumb voices,
Voices of the interminable generations of prisoners and slaves,
Voices of the diseased and despairing and of thieves and dwarfs,
Voices of cycles of preparation and accretion, 15
And of the threads that connect the stars, and of wombs and
  of the father-stuff,
And of the rights of them the others are down upon,
Of the deformed, trivial, flat, foolish, despised,
Fog in the air, beetles rolling balls of dung.

Through me forbidden voices, 20
Voices of sexes and lusts, voices veiled and I remove the veil,
Voices indecent by me clarified and transfigured.

I do not press my fingers across my mouth,
I keep as delicate around the bowels as around the head and
  heart,
Copulation is no more rank to me than death is. 25

I believe in the flesh and the appetites,
Seeing, hearing, feeling, are miracles, and each part and tag of
  me is a miracle.

Divine am I inside and out, and I make holy whatever I touch
  or am touched from,
The scent of these arm-pits aroma finer than prayer,
This head more than churches, bibles, and all the creeds. 30

If I worship one thing more than another it shall be the spread
  of my own body, or any part of it,
Translucent mold of me it shall be you!
Shaded ledges and rests it shall be you!
Firm masculine colter it shall be you!
Whatever goes to the tilth of me it shall be you! 35
You my rich blood! your milky stream pale strippings of my life!
Breast that presses against other breasts it shall be you!
My brain it shall be your occult convolutions!

Root of washed sweet-flag! timorous pond-snipe! nest of
    guarded duplicate eggs! it shall be you!
Mixed tussled hay of head, beard, brawn, it shall be you!   40
Trickling sap of maple, fiber of manly wheat, it shall be you!
Sun so generous it shall be you!
Vapors lighting and shading my face it shall be you!
You sweaty brooks and dews it shall be you!
Winds whose soft-tickling genitals rub against me it shall be
    you!   45
Broad muscular fields, branches of live oak, loving lounger in
    my winding paths, it shall be you!
Hands I have taken, face I have kissed, mortal I have ever
    touched, it shall be you.

I dote on myself, there is that lot of me and all so luscious,
Each moment and whatever happens thrills me with joy,
I cannot tell how my ankles bend, nor whence the cause of my
    faintest wish,   50
Nor the cause of the friendship I emit, nor the cause of the
    friendship I take again.

That I walk up my stoop, I pause to consider if it really be,
A morning-glory at my window satisfies me more than the
    metaphysics of books.

To behold the day-break!
The little light fades the immense and diaphanous shadows,   55
The air tastes good to my palate.

Hefts of the moving world at innocent gambols silently rising
    freshly exuding,
Scooting obliquely high and low.

Something I cannot see puts upward libidinous prongs,
Seas of bright juice suffuse heaven.   60

The earth by the sky stayed with, the daily close of their junc-
    tion,
The heaved challenge from the east that moment over my head,
The mocking taunt, "See then whether you shall be master!"

XLVII

I am the teacher of athletes,
He that by me spreads a wider breast than my own proves the
  width of my own,
He most honors my style who learns under it to destroy the
  teacher.

The boy I love, the same becomes a man not through derived
  power, but in his own right,
Wicked rather than virtuous out of conformity or fear,   5
Fond of his sweetheart, relishing well his steak,
Unrequited love or a slight cutting him worse than sharp steel
  cuts,
First-rate to ride, to fight, to hit the bull's eye, to sail a skiff, to
  sing a song or play on the banjo,
Preferring scars and the beard and faces pitted with small-pox
  over all latherers,
And those well-tanned to those that keep out of the sun.   10

I teach straying from me, yet who can stray from me?
I follow you whoever you are from the present hour,
My words itch at your ears till you understand them.

I do not say these things for a dollar or to fill up the time while
  I wait for a boat,
(It is you talking just as much as myself, I act as the tongue of
  you,
                                                                          15
Tied in your mouth, in mine it begins to be loosened.)

I swear I will never again mention love or death inside a house,
And I swear I will never translate myself at all, only to him or
  her who privately stays with me in the open air.

If you would understand me go to the heights or water-shore,
The nearest gnat is an explanation, and a drop or motion of
  waves a key,
                                                                          20
The maul, the oar, the hand-saw, second my words.

No shuttered room or school can commune with me,
But roughs and little children better than they.

The young mechanic is closest to me, he knows me well,
The woodman that takes his axe and jug with him shall take me
  with him all day,   25
The farm-boy plowing in the field feels good at the sound of
  my voice,
In vessels that sail my words sail, I go with fishermen and sea-
  men and love them.

The soldier camped or upon the march is mine,
On the night ere the pending battle many seek me, and I do
  not fail them,
On that solemn night (it may be their last) those that know me
  seek me.   30

My face rubs to the hunter's face when he lies down alone in
  his blanket,
The driver thinking of me does not mind the jolt of his wagon,
The young mother and old mother comprehend me,
The girl and the wife rest the needle a moment and forget
  where they are,
They and all would resume what I have told them.   35

LI
The past and present wilt—I have filled them, emptied them,
And proceed to fill my next fold of the future.

Listener up there! what have you to confide to me?
Look in my face while I snuff the sidle of evening,
(Talk honestly, no one else hears you, and I stay only a minute
  longer.)   5

Do I contradict myself?
Very well then I contradict myself,
(I am large, I contain multitudes.)

I concentrate toward them that are nigh, I wait on the door-
  slab.

Who has done his day's work? who will soonest be through
  with his supper?   10
Who wishes to walk with me?

Will you speak before I am gone? will you prove already too
  late?

LII

The spotted hawk swoops by and accuses me, he complains of
    my gab and my loitering.

I too am not a bit tamed, I too am untranslatable,
I sound my barbaric yawp over the roofs of the world.

The last scud of day holds back for me,
It flings my likeness after the rest and true as any on the
    shadowed wilds,
It coaxes me to the vapor and the dusk.   5

I depart as air, I shake my white locks at the runaway sun,
I effuse my flesh in eddies, and drift it in lacy jags.

I bequeath myself to the dirt to grow from the grass I love,
If you want me again look for me under your boot-soles.   10

You will hardly know who I am or what I mean,
But I shall be good health to you nevertheless,
And filter and fiber your blood.

Failing to fetch me at first keep encouraged,
Missing me one place search another,   15
I stop somewhere waiting for you.

WHILE THE SCHOOLS AND
THE TEACHERS ARE TEACHING

While the schools and the teachers are teaching after their kind,
Some, obedience to look to the protection of the laws,
Some, to assert a sovereign and God, over all, to rely on,
Some, enjoining to build outside forts and embankments;
Solitary, I here, I to enjoin for you whoever you are you to
    build inside, invisible forts,   5
Counseling every man and woman to become the fortress, the
    lord and sovereign, of himself or herself,
To grow through infinite time finally to be a supreme God
    himself or herself,
Acknowledging none greater, now or after death, than himself
    or herself.

GERARD MANLEY HOPKINS
(1844–1889)

GOD'S GRANDEUR

The world is charged with the grandeur of God.
It will flame out, like shining from shook foil;
It gathers to a greatness, like the ooze of oil
Crushed. Why do men then now not reck his rod?
Generations have trod, have trod, have trod;   5
And all is seared with trade; bleared, smeared with toil;
And wears man's smudge and shares man's smell: the soil
Is bare now, nor can foot feel, being shod.

And for all this, nature is never spent;
There lives the dearest freshness deep down things;   10
And though the last lights off the black West went
Oh, morning, at the brown brink eastward, springs—
Because the Holy Ghost over the bent
World broods with warm breast and with ah! bright wings.

THE LANTERN OUT OF DOORS

Sometimes a lantern moves along the night,
   That interests our eyes. And who goes there?
   I think; where from and bound, I wonder, where,
With, all down darkness wide, his wading light?

Men go by me whom either beauty bright   5
   In mold or mind or what not else makes rare:
   They rain against our much-thick and marsh air
Rich beams, till death or distance buys them quite.

Death or distance soon consumes them: wind
   What most I may eye after, be in at the end   10
I cannot, and out of sight is out of mind.

Christ minds; Christ's interest, what to avow or amend
   There, éyes them, heart wánts, care haúnts, foot fóllows
     kínd,
Their ránsom, théir rescue, ánd first, fást, last friénd.

THE WINDHOVER:

to christ our lord

I caught this morning morning's minion, king-
    dom of daylight's dauphin, dapple-dawn-drawn Falcon, in
      his riding
Of the rolling level underneath him steady air, and striding
High there, how he rung upon the rein of a wimpling wing
In his ecstasy! then off, off forth on swing,   5
    As a skate's heel sweeps smooth on a bow-bend: the hurl
      and gliding
    Rebuffed the big wind. My heart in hiding
Stirred for a bird,—the achieve of, the mastery of the thing!

Brute beauty and valor and act, oh, air, pride, plume, here
    Buckle! AND the fire that breaks from thee then, a billion   10
Times told lovelier, more dangerous, O my chevalier!

    No wonder of it: shéer plód makes plough down sillion
Shine, and blue-bleak embers, ah my dear,
    Fall, gall themselves, and gash gold-vermilion.

PIED BEAUTY

Glory be to God for dappled things—
    For skies of couple-color as a brinded cow;
      For rose-moles all in stipple upon trout that swim;
Fresh-firecoal chestnut-falls; finches' wings;
    Landscape plotted and pieced—fold, fallow, and plough;   5
    And áll trádes, their gear and tackle and trim.

All things counter, original, spare, strange;
    Whatever is fickle, freckled (who knows how?)
    With swift, slow; sweet, sour; adazzle, dim;
He fathers-forth whose beauty is past change: 10
           Praise him.

Windhover: a small undistinguished hawk. **1.** *minion:* the favorite of a king.
2. *dauphin:* prince, heir-apparent. **4.** *rung:* flew in a circle; or, made a
ringing sound; perhaps with the suggestion of "wrung"; *wimpling:* rippling.
12. *sillion:* furrow.

HURRAHING IN HARVEST

Summer ends now; now, barbarous in beauty, the stooks arise
 Around; up above, what wind-walks! what lovely behavior
 Of silk-sack clouds! has wilder, willful-wavier
Meal-drift molded ever and melted across skies?

I walk, I lift up, I lift up heart, eyes,   5
 Down all that glory in the heavens to glean our Saviour;
 And, éyes, heárt, what looks, what lips yet gave you a
Rapturous love's greeting of realer, of rounder replies?

And the azurous hung hills are his world-wielding shoulder
 Majestic—as a stallion stalwart, very-violet-sweet!—   10
These things, these things were here and but the beholder
 Wanting; which two when they once meet,
The heart rears wings bold and bolder
 And hurls for him, O half hurls earth for him off under his
  feet.

THE CAGED SKYLARK

As a dare-gale skylark scanted in a dull cage
 Man's mounting spirit in his bone-house, mean house, dwells—
 That bird beyond the remembering his free fells;
This in drudgery, day-laboring-out life's age.

Though aloft on turf or perch or poor low stage,   5
 Both sing sometímes the sweetest, sweetest spells,
 Yet both droop deadly sómetimes in their cells
Or wring their barriers in bursts of fear or rage.

Not that the sweet-fowl, song-fowl, needs no rest—
Why, hear him, hear him babble and drop down to his nest,   10
 But his own nest, wild nest, no prison.

Man's spirit will be flesh-bound when found at best,
But uncumbered: meadow-down is not distressed
 For a rainbow footing it nor he for his bónes rísen.

SPRING AND FALL:

to a young child

Márgarét, are you gríeving
Over Goldengrove unleaving?
Leáves, líke the things of man, you
With your fresh thoughts care for, can you?
Áh! ás the heart grows older   5
It will come to such sights colder
By and by, nor spare a sigh
Though worlds of wanwood leafmeal lie;
And yet you wíll weep and know why.
Now no matter, child, the name: 10
Sórrow's spríngs áre the same.
Nor mouth had, no nor mind, expressed
What heart heard of, ghost guessed:
It ís the blight man was born for,
It is Margaret you mourn for.   15

[CARRION COMFORT]

Not, I'll not, carrion comfort, Despair, not feast on thee;
Not untwist—slack they may be—these last strands of man
In me ór, most weary, cry *I can no more*. I can;
Can something, hope, wish day come, not choose not to be.
But ah, but O thou terrible, why wouldst thou rude on me   5
Thy wring-world right foot rock? lay a lionlimb against me? scan
With darksome devouring eyes my bruisèd bones? and fan,
O in turns of tempest, me heaped there; me frantic to avoid thee
     and flee?

   Why? That my chaff might fly; my grain lie, sheer and clear.
Nay in all that toil, that coil, since (seems) I kissed the rod,   10
Hand rather, my heart lo! lapped strength, stole joy, would
     laugh, chéer.
Cheer whom though? the hero whose heaven-handling flung
     me, fóot tród
Me? or me that fought him? O which one? is it each one? That
     night, that year
Of now done darkness I wretch lay wrestling with (my God!)
     my God.

THAT NATURE IS A HERACLITEAN FIRE
AND OF THE COMFORT OF THE RESURRECTION

Cloud-puffball, torn tufts, tossed pillows | flaunt forth, then
    chevy on an air-
built thoroughfare: heaven-roysterers, in gay-gangs | they
    throng; they glitter in marches.
Down roughcast, down dazzling whitewash, | wherever an elm
    arches,
Shivelights and shadowtackle in long | lashes lace, lance, and
    pair.
Delightfully the bright wind boisterous | ropes, wrestles, beats
    earth bare   5
Of yestertempest's creases; | in pool and rut peel parches
Squandering ooze to squeezed | dough, crust, dust; stanches,
    starches
Squadroned masks and manmarks | treadmire toil there
Footfretted in it. Million-fuelèd, | nature's bonfire burns on.
But quench her bonniest, dearest | to her, her clearest-selvèd
    spark   10
Man, how fast his firedint, | his mark on mind, is gone!
Both are in an unfathomable, all is in an enormous dark
Drowned. O pity and indig | nation! Manshape, that shone
Sheer off, disseveral, a star, | death blots black out; nor mark
                Is any of him at all so stark   15
But vastness blurs and time | beats level. Enough! the Resurrec-
    tion,
A heart's-clarion! Away grief's gasping, | joyless days, dejec-
    tion.
                Across my foundering deck shone
A beacon, an eternal beam. | Flesh fade, and mortal trash
Fall to the residuary worm; | world's wildfire, leave but ash: 20
                In a flash, at a trumpet crash,
I am all at once what Christ is, | since he was what I am, and
This Jack, joke, poor potsherd, | patch, matchwood, immortal
    diamond,
                Is immortal diamond.

Heraclitean Fire: Heraclitus, a fifth-century B.C. Greek philosopher, held that
the basic substance of all the elements was an eternal fire, which was con-
tinually being extinguished and renewed.

EMILY DICKINSON
(1830–1886)

SUCCESS IS COUNTED SWEETEST

Success is counted sweetest
By those who ne'er succeed.
To comprehend a nectar
Requires sorest need.

Not one of all the purple Host   5
Who took the Flag today
Can tell the definition
So clear of Victory

As he defeated—dying—
On whose forbidden ear   10
The distant strains of triumph
Burst agonized and clear!

I DIED FOR BEAUTY

I died for Beauty—but was scarce
Adjusted in the Tomb
When One who died for Truth, was lain
In an adjoining Room—

He questioned softly "Why I failed"?   5
"For Beauty", I replied—
"And I—for Truth—Themself are One—
We Bretheren, are", He said—

And so, as Kinsmen, met a Night—
We talked between the Rooms—   10
Until the Moss had reached our lips—
And covered up—our names—

I HEARD A FLY BUZZ—WHEN I DIED

I heard a Fly buzz—when I died—
The Stillness in the Room
Was like the Stillness in the Air—
Between the Heaves of Storm—

The Eyes around—had wrung them dry—   5
And Breaths were gathering firm
For that last Onset—when the King
Be witnessed—in the Room—

I willed my Keepsakes—Signed away
What portion of me be   10
Assignable—and then it was
There interposed a Fly—

With Blue—uncertain stumbling Buzz—
Between the light—and me—
And then the Windows failed—and then   15
I could not see to see

BECAUSE I COULD NOT STOP FOR DEATH

Because I could not stop for Death—
He kindly stopped for me—
The Carriage held but just Ourselves—
And Immortality.

We slowly drove—He knew no haste   5
And I had put away
My labor and my leisure too,
For His Civility—

We passed the School, where Children strove
At Recess—in the Ring—   10
We passed the Fields of Gazing Grain—
We passed the Setting Sun—

Or rather—He passed Us—
The Dews drew quivering and chill—
For only Gossamer, my Gown—   15
My Tippet—only Tulle—

We paused before a House that seemed
A Swelling of the Ground—
The Roof was scarcely visible—
The Cornice—in the Ground—   20

Since then—'tis Centuries—and yet
Feels shorter than the Day
I first surmised the Horses Heads
Were toward Eternity—

16. *Tippet:* a scarf or hood; *Tulle:* thin silk.

I TASTE A LIQUOR NEVER BREWED

I taste a liquor never brewed—
From Tankards scooped in Pearl—
Not all the Frankfort Berries
Yield such an Alcohol!

Inebriate of Air—am I—   5
And Debauchee of Dew—
Reeling—thro endless summer days—
From inns of Molten Blue—

When "Landlords" turn the drunken Bee
Out of the Foxglove's door—   10
When Butterflies—renounce their "drams"—
I shall but drink the more!

Till Seraphs swing their snowy Hats—
And Saints—to windows run—
To see the little Tippler   15
From Manzanilla come!

16. *Manzanilla:* probably Manzanillo, a Cuban city here associated with the export of rum.

A NARROW FELLOW IN THE GRASS

A narrow Fellow in the Grass
Occasionally rides—
You may have met Him—did you not
His notice sudden is—

The Grass divides as with a Comb—   5
A spotted shaft is seen—
And then it closes at your feet
And opens further on—

He likes a Boggy Acre
A Floor too cool for Corn—   10
Yet when a Boy, and Barefoot—
I more than once at Noon

Have passed, I thought, a Whip lash
Unbraiding in the Sun
When stooping to secure it   15
It wrinkled, and was gone—

Several of Nature's People
I know, and they know me—
I feel for them a transport
Of cordiality—   20

But never met this Fellow
Attended, or alone
Without a tighter breathing
And Zero at the Bone—

I DREADED THAT FIRST ROBIN, SO

I dreaded that first Robin, so,
But He is mastered, now,
I'm some accustomed to Him grown,
He hurts a little, though—

I thought if I could only live   5
Till that first Shout got by—
Not all Pianos in the Woods
Had power to mangle me—

I dared not meet the Daffodils—
For fear their Yellow Gown   10
Would pierce me with a fashion
So foreign to my own—

I wished the Grass would hurry—
So—when 'twas time to see—
He'd be too tall, the tallest one   15
Could stretch—to look at me—

I could not bear the Bees should come,
I wished they'd stay away
In those dim countries where they go,
What word had they, for me?   20

They're here, though; not a creature failed—
No Blossom stayed away
In gentle deference to me—
The Queen of Calvary—

Each one salutes me, as he goes,   25
And I, my childish Plumes,
Lift, in bereaved acknowledgement
Of their unthinking Drums—

DEATH IS THE SUPPLE SUITOR

Death is the supple Suitor
That wins at last—
It is a stealthy Wooing
Conducted first
By pallid innuendoes   5
And dim approach
But brave at last with Bugles
And a bisected Coach
It bears away in triumph
To Troth unknown   10
And Kinsmen as divulgeless
As throngs of Down—

FOREVER—IS COMPOSED OF NOWS

Forever—is composed of Nows—
'Tis not a different time—
Except for Infiniteness—
And Latitude of Home—

From this—experienced Here—   5
Remove the Dates—to These—
Let Months dissolve in further Months—
And Years—exhale in Years—

Without Debate—or Pause—
Or Celebrated Days—   10
No different Our Years would be
From Anno Dominies—

WILLIAM BUTLER YEATS
(1865–1939)

LEDA AND THE SWAN

A sudden blow: the great wings beating still
Above the staggering girl, her thighs caressed
By the dark webs, her nape caught in his bill,
He holds her helpless breast upon his breast.

How can those terrified vague fingers push   5
The feathered glory from her loosening thighs?
And how can body, laid in that white rush,
But feel the strange heart beating where it lies?

A shudder in the loins engenders there
The broken wall, the burning roof and tower   10
And Agamemnon dead.
                        Being so caught up,
So mastered by the brute blood of the air,
Did she put on his knowledge with his power
Before the indifferent beak could let her drop?

Leda: the mother of Helen of Troy and Clytemnestra (who murdered her
husband Agamemnon upon his return from Troy). Zeus assumed the form
of a swan to make love to Leda.

THE WILD SWANS AT COOLE

The trees are in their autumn beauty,
The woodland paths are dry,
Under the October twilight the water
Mirrors a still sky;
Upon the brimming water among the stones   5
Are nine-and-fifty swans.

The nineteenth autumn has come upon me
Since I first made my count;
I saw, before I had well finished,
All suddenly mount   10
And scatter wheeling in great broken rings
Upon their clamorous wings.

I have looked upon those brilliant creatures,
And now my heart is sore.
All's changed since I, hearing at twilight,   15
The first time on this shore,
The bell-beat of their wings above my head,
Trod with a lighter tread.

Unwearied still, lover by lover,
They paddle in the cold   20
Companionable streams or climb the air;
Their hearts have not grown old;
Passion or conquest, wander where they will,
Attend upon them still.

But now they drift on the still water,   25
Mysterious, beautiful;
Among what rushes will they build,
By what lake's edge or pool
Delight men's eyes when I awake some day
To find they have flown away?   30

THE SECOND COMING

Turning and turning in the widening gyre
The falcon cannot hear the falconer;
Things fall apart; the centre cannot hold;
Mere anarchy is loosed upon the world,
The blood-dimmed tide is loosed, and everywhere   5
The ceremony of innocence is drowned;
The best lack all conviction, while the worst
Are full of passionate intensity.

Surely some revelation is at hand;
Surely the Second Coming is at hand.   10
The Second Coming! Hardly are those words out
When a vast image out of *Spiritus Mundi*
Troubles my sight: somewhere in sands of the desert
A shape with lion body and the head of a man,
A gaze blank and pitiless as the sun,   15
Is moving its slow thighs, while all about it
Reel shadows of the indignant desert birds.
The darkness drops again; but now I know
That twenty centuries of stony sleep
Were vexed to nightmare by a rocking cradle,   20
And what rough beast, its hour come round at last,
Slouches towards Bethlehem to be born?

12. *Spiritus Mundi:* for Yeats this means the world's collective spirit or memory.

A STICK OF INCENSE

Whence did all that fury come?
From empty tomb or Virgin womb?
Saint Joseph thought the world would melt
But liked the way his finger smelt.

AMONG SCHOOL CHILDREN

I

I walk through the long schoolroom questioning;
A kind old nun in a white hood replies;
The children learn to cipher and to sing,
To study reading-books and history,
To cut and sew, be neat in everything   5
In the best modern way—the children's eyes
In momentary wonder stare upon
A sixty-year-old smiling public man.

II

I dream of a Ledaean body, bent
Above a sinking fire, a tale that she   10
Told of a harsh reproof, or trivial event
That changed some childish day to tragedy—
Told, and it seemed that our two natures blent
Into a sphere from youthful sympathy,
Or else, to alter Plato's parable,   15
Into the yolk and white of the one shell.

III

And thinking of that fit of grief or rage
I look upon one child or t'other there
And wonder if she stood so at that age—
For even daughters of the swan can share   20
Something of every paddler's heritage—
And had that colour upon cheek or hair,
And thereupon my heart is driven wild:
She stands before me as a living child.

IV

Her present image floats into the mind—   25
Did Quattrocento finger fashion it
Hollow of cheek as though it drank the wind

---

9. *Ledaean:* like Leda (see note, p. 213). **15.** *Plato's parable:* In Plato's *Symposium,* Aristophanes relates a fable in which men and women, originally joined in one body, were separated into two sexes by a jealous Zeus; and ever since they have been trying to become reunited as the parts of an egg might be rejoined. **26.** *Quattrocento:* the fifteenth century in Italy, used especially to refer to the art of painting in that century.

And took a mess of shadows for its meat?
And I though never of Ledaean kind
Had pretty plumage once—enough of that, 30
Better to smile on all that smile, and show
There is a comfortable kind of old scarecrow.

V
What youthful mother, a shape upon her lap
Honey of generation had betrayed,
And that must sleep, shriek, struggle to escape 35
As recollection or the drug decide,
Would think her son, did she but see that shape
With sixty or more winters on its head,
A compensation for the pang of his birth,
Or the uncertainty of his setting forth? 40

VI
Plato thought nature but a spume that plays
Upon a ghostly paradigm of things;
Solider Aristotle played the taws
Upon the bottom of a king of kings;
World-famous golden-thighed Pythagoras 45
Fingered upon a fiddle-stick or strings
What a star sang and careless Muses heard:
Old clothes upon old sticks to scare a bird.

VII
Both nuns and mothers worship images,
But those the candles light are not as those 50
That animate a mother's reveries,
But keep a marble or a bronze repose.
And yet they too break hearts—O Presences
That passion, piety or affection knows,
And that all heavenly glory symbolise— 55
O self-born mockers of man's enterprise;

34. *honey of generation:* according to Plotinus, the drug that makes each
soul at birth oblivious of its previous life. 41–42. Plato assumes that the
visible world is the reflection ("spume") of a set of abstract forms ("ghostly
paradigm"). 43–44. Aristotle, who assumed an empirical ("Solider")
epistemology, or concept of reality, was tutor to Alexander the Great ("king
of kings"). 45–47. Pythagoras, who was reputed to have a golden thigh,
is associated with the mathematics of musical harmony.

VIII
Labour is blossoming or dancing where
The body is not bruised to pleasure soul,
Nor beauty born out of its own despair,
Nor blear-eyed wisdom out of midnight oil.   60
O chestnut-tree, great-rooted blossomer,
Are you the leaf, the blossom or the bole?
O body swayed to music, O brightening glance,
How can we know the dancer from the dance?

58. *pleasure:* used here as a verb.

THE LOVER'S SONG

Bird sighs for the air,
Thought for I know not where,
For the womb the seed sighs.
Now sinks the same rest
On mind, on nest,   5
On straining thighs.

THE CHAMBERMAID'S FIRST SONG

How came this ranger
Now sunk in rest,
Stranger with stranger,
On my cold breast?
What's left to sigh for?   5
Strange night has come;
God's love has hidden him
Out of all harm,
Pleasure has made him
Weak as a worm.   10

THE CHAMBERMAID'S SECOND SONG

From pleasure of the bed,
Dull as a worm,
His rod and its butting head
Limp as a worm,
His spirit that has fled   5
Blind as a worm.

SAILING TO BYZANTIUM

I

That is no country for old men. The young
In one another's arms, birds in the trees
—Those dying generations—at their song,
The salmon-falls, the mackerel-crowded seas,
Fish, flesh, or fowl, commend all summer long   5
Whatever is begotten, born, and dies.
Caught in that sensual music all neglect
Monuments of unageing intellect.

II

An aged man is but a paltry thing,
A tattered coat upon a stick, unless   10
Soul clap its hands and sing, and louder sing
For every tatter in its mortal dress,
Nor is there singing school but studying
Monuments of its own magnificence;
And therefore I have sailed the seas and come   15
To the holy city of Byzantium.

III

O sages standing in God's holy fire
As in the gold mosaic of a wall,
Come from the holy fire, perne in a gyre,
And be the singing-masters of my soul.   20
Consume my heart away; sick with desire
And fastened to a dying animal
It knows not what it is; and gather me
Into the artifice of eternity.

IV

Once out of nature I shall never take   25
My bodily form from any natural thing,
But such a form as Grecian goldsmiths make
Of hammered gold and gold enamelling
To keep a drowsy Emperor awake;
Or set upon a golden bough to sing   30
To lords and ladies of Byzantium
Of what is past, or passing, or to come.

19. *perne:* a spool of thread; here apparently a verb expressing a movement
like the winding of the thread about the spool.

LONG-LEGGED FLY

That civilisation may not sink,
Its great battle lost,
Quiet the dog, tether the pony
To a distant post;
Our master Caesar is in the tent   5
Where the maps are spread,
His eyes fixed upon nothing,
A hand under his head.
Like a long-legged fly upon the stream
His mind moves upon silence.   10

That the topless towers be burnt
And men recall that face,
Move most gently if move you must
In this lonely place.
She thinks, part woman, three parts a child,   15
That nobody looks; her feet
Practise a tinker shuffle
Picked up on a street.
Like a long-legged fly upon the stream
Her mind moves upon silence.   20

That girls at puberty may find
The first Adam in their thought,
Shut the door of the Pope's chapel,
Keep those children out.
There on that scaffolding reclines   25
Michael Angelo.
With no more sound than the mice make
His hand moves to and fro.
Like a long-legged fly upon the stream
His mind moves upon silence.   30

11. *topless towers:* the city of Troy.   **12.** *that face:* Helen of Troy, "the face that launched a thousand ships," the cause of the Trojan War.

CRAZY JANE AND THE BISHOP

Bring me to the blasted oak
That I, midnight upon the stroke,
(*All find safety in the tomb.*)
May call down curses on his head
Because of my dear Jack that's dead.   5
Coxcomb was the least he said:
The solid man and the coxcomb.

Nor was he Bishop when his ban
Banished Jack the Journeyman,
(*All find safety in the tomb.*)   10
Nor so much as parish priest,
Yet he, an old book in his fist,
Cried that we lived like beast and beast:
The solid man and the coxcomb.

The Bishop has a skin, God knows,   15
Wrinkled like the foot of a goose,
(*All find safety in the tomb.*)
Nor can he hide in holy black
The heron's hunch upon his back,
But a birch-tree stood my Jack: 20
The solid man and the coxcomb.

Jack had my virginity,
And bids me to the oak, for he
(*All find safety in the tomb.*)
Wanders out into the night   25
And there is shelter under it,
But should that other come, I spit:
The solid man and the coxcomb.

CRAZY JANE TALKS WITH THE BISHOP

I met the Bishop on the road
And much said he and I.
"Those breasts are flat and fallen now,
Those veins must soon be dry;
Live in a heavenly mansion,   5
Not in some foul sty."

"Fair and foul are near of kin,
And fair needs foul," I cried.
"My friends are gone, but that's a truth
Nor grave nor bed denied,   10
Learned in bodily lowliness
And in the heart's pride.

"A woman can be proud and stiff
When on love intent;
But Love has pitched his mansion in   15
The place of excrement;
For nothing can be sole or whole
That has not been rent."

SWEET DANCER

The girl goes dancing there
On the leaf-sown, new-mown, smooth
Grass plot of the garden;
Escaped from bitter youth,
Escaped out of her crowd,   5
Or out of her black cloud.
Ah, dancer, ah, sweet dancer!

If strange men come from the house
To lead her away, do not say
That she is happy being crazy;
Lead them gently astray;   10
Let her finish her dance,
Let her finish her dance.
Ah, dancer, ah, sweet dancer!

LAPIS LAZULI

(for harry clifton)

I have heard that hysterical women say
They are sick of the palette and fiddle-bow,
Of poets that are always gay,
For everybody knows or else should know
That if nothing drastic is done   5
Aeroplane and Zeppelin will come out,
Pitch like King Billy bomb-balls in
Until the town lie beaten flat.

All perform their tragic play,
There struts Hamlet, there is Lear,   10
That's Ophelia, that Cordelia;
Yet they, should the last scene be there,
The great stage curtain about to drop,
If worthy their prominent part in the play,
Do not break up their lines to weep.   15
They know that Hamlet and Lear are gay;
Gaiety transfiguring all that dread.
All men have aimed at, found and lost;
Black out; Heaven blazing into the head:
Tragedy wrought to its uttermost.   20
Though Hamlet rambles and Lear rages,
And all the drop-scenes drop at once
Upon a hundred thousand stages,
It cannot grow by an inch or an ounce.

On their own feet they came, or on shipboard,   25
Camel-back, horse-back, ass-back, mule-back,
Old civilisations put to the sword.
Then they and their wisdom went to rack:
No handiwork of Callimachus,
Who handled marble as if it were bronze,   30
Made draperies that seemed to rise
When sea-wind swept the corner, stands;
His long lamp-chimney shaped like the stem

7. *King Billy:* Kaiser Wilhelm II.

Of a slender palm, stood but a day;
All things fall and are built again,   35
And those that build them again are gay.

Two Chinamen, behind them a third,
Are carved in lapis lazuli,
Over them flies a long-legged bird,
A symbol of longevity;   40
The third, doubtless a serving-man,
Carries a musical instrument.

Every discoloration of the stone,
Every accidental crack or dent,
Seems a water-course or an avalanche,   45
Or lofty slope where it still snows
Though doubtless plum or cherry-branch
Sweetens the little half-way house
Those Chinamen climb towards, and I
Delight to imagine them seated there;   50
There, on the mountain and the sky,
On all the tragic scene they stare.
One asks for mournful melodies;
Accomplished fingers begin to play.
Their eyes mid many wrinkles, their eyes,   55
Their ancient, glittering eyes, are gay.

ROBERT FROST
(1874–1963)

NOTHING GOLD CAN STAY

Nature's first green is gold,
Her hardest hue to hold.
Her early leaf's a flower;
But only so an hour.
Then leaf subsides to leaf.
So Eden sank to grief,
So dawn goes down to day.
Nothing gold can stay.

5

"OUT, OUT—"

The buzz saw snarled and rattled in the yard
And made dust and dropped stove-length sticks of wood,
Sweet-scented stuff when the breeze drew across it.
And from there those that lifted eyes could count
Five mountain ranges one behind the other   5
Under the sunset far into Vermont.
And the saw snarled and rattled, snarled and rattled,
As it ran light, or had to bear a load.
And nothing happened: day was all but done.
Call it a day, I wish they might have said   10
To please the boy by giving him the half hour
That a boy counts so much when saved from work.
His sister stood beside them in her apron
To tell them "Supper." At the word, the saw,
As if to prove saws knew what supper meant,   15
Leaped out at the boy's hand, or seemed to leap—
He must have given the hand. However it was,
Neither refused the meeting. But the hand!
The boy's first outcry was a rueful laugh,
As he swung toward them holding up the hand,   20
Half in appeal, but half as if to keep
The life from spilling. Then the boy saw all—
Since he was old enough to know, big boy
Doing a man's work, though a child at heart—
He saw all spoiled. "Don't let him cut my hand off—   25
The doctor, when he comes. Don't let him, sister!"
So. But the hand was gone already.
The doctor put him in the dark of ether.
He lay and puffed his lips out with his breath.
And then—the watcher at his pulse took fright.   30
No one believed. They listened at his heart.
Little—less—nothing!—and that ended it.
No more to build on there. And they, since they
Were not the one dead, turned to their affairs.

THE WOOD-PILE

Out walking in the frozen swamp one gray day,
I paused and said, "I will turn back from here.
No, I will go on farther—and we shall see."
The hard snow held me, save where now and then
One foot went through. The view was all in lines   5
Straight up and down of tall slim trees
Too much alike to mark or name a place by
So as to say for certain I was here
Or somewhere else: I was just far from home.
A small bird flew before me. He was careful   10
To put a tree between us when he lighted,
And say no word to tell me who he was
Who was so foolish as to think what *he* thought.
He thought that I was after him for a feather—
The white one in his tail; like one who takes   15
Everything said as personal to himself.
One flight out sideways would have undeceived him.
And then there was a pile of wood for which
I forgot him and let his little fear
Carry him off the way I might have gone,   20
Without so much as wishing him good-night.
He went behind it to make his last stand.
It was a cord of maple, cut and split
And piled—and measured, four by four by eight.
And not another like it could I see.   25
No runner tracks in this year's snow looped near it.
And it was older sure than this year's cutting,
Or even last year's or the year's before.
The wood was gray and the bark warping off it
And the pile somewhat sunken. Clematis   30
Had wound strings round and round it like a bundle.
What held it, though, on one side was a tree
Still growing, and on one a stake and prop,
These latter about to fall. I thought that only
Someone who lived in turning to fresh tasks   35
Could so forget his handiwork on which
He spent himself, the labor of his ax,
And leave it there far from a useful fireplace
To warm the frozen swamp as best it could
With the slow smokeless burning of decay.   40

FIRE AND ICE

Some say the world will end in fire,
Some say in ice.
From what I've tasted of desire
I hold with those who favor fire.
But if it had to perish twice,   5
I think I know enough of hate
To say that for destruction ice
Is also great
And would suffice.

AN OLD MAN'S WINTER NIGHT

All out-of-doors looked darkly in at him
Through the thin frost, almost in separate stars,
That gathers on the pane in empty rooms.
What kept his eyes from giving back the gaze
Was the lamp tilted near them in his hand.   5
What kept him from remembering what it was
That brought him to that creaking room was age.
He stood with barrels round him—at a loss.
And having scared the cellar under him
In clomping here, he scared it once again   10
In clomping off—and scared the outer night,
Which has its sounds, familiar, like the roar
Of trees and crack of branches, common things,
But nothing so like beating on a box.
A light he was to no one but himself   15
Where now he sat, concerned with he knew what,
A quiet light, and then not even that.
He consigned to the moon—such as she was,
So late-arising—to the broken moon,
As better than the sun in any case   20
For such a charge, his snow upon the roof,
His icicles along the wall to keep;
And slept. The log that shifted with a jolt
Once in the stove, disturbed him and he shifted,
And eased his heavy breathing, but still slept.   25
One aged man—one man—can't keep a house,
A farm, a countryside, or if he can,
It's thus he does it of a winter night.

THE STRONG ARE SAYING NOTHING

The soil now gets a rumpling soft and damp,
And small regard to the future of any weed.
The final flat of the hoe's approval stamp
Is reserved for the bed of a few selected seed.

There is seldom more than a man to a harrowed piece.   5
Men work alone, their lots plowed far apart,
One stringing a chain of seed in an open crease,
And another stumbling after a halting cart.

To the fresh and black of the squares of early mould
The leafless bloom of a plum is fresh and white;   10
Though there's more than a doubt if the weather is not too cold
For the bees to come and serve its beauty aright.

Wind goes from farm to farm in wave on wave,
But carries no cry of what is hoped to be.
There may be little or much beyond the grave,   15
But the strong are saying nothing until they see.

DESIGN

I found a dimpled spider, fat and white,
On a white heal-all, holding up a moth
Like a white piece of rigid satin cloth—
Assorted characters of death and blight
Mixed ready to begin the morning right,   5
Like the ingredients of a witches' broth—
A snow-drop spider, a flower like froth,
And dead wings carried like a paper kite.

What had that flower to do with being white,
The wayside blue and innocent heal-all?   10
What brought the kindred spider to that height,
Then steered the white moth thither in the night?
What but design of darkness to appall?—
If design govern in a thing so small.

FORGIVE, O LORD

Forgive, O Lord, my little jokes on Thee
And I'll forgive Thy great big one on me.

T. S. ELIOT
(1888–1965)

THE NAMING OF CATS

The Naming of Cats is a difficult matter,
    It isn't just one of your holiday games;
You may think at first I'm as mad as a hatter
When I tell you, a cat must have THREE DIFFERENT NAMES.
First of all, there's the name that the family use daily,   5
    Such as Peter, Augustus, Alonzo or James,
Such as Victor or Jonathan, George or Bill Bailey—
    All of them sensible everyday names.
There are fancier names if you think they sound sweeter,
    Some for the gentlemen, some for the dames: 10
Such as Plato, Admetus, Electra, Demeter—
    But all of them sensible everyday names.
But I tell you, a cat needs a name that's particular,
    A name that's peculiar, and more dignified,
Else how can he keep up his tail perpendicular,   15
    Or spread out his whiskers, or cherish his pride?
Of names of this kind, I can give you a quorum,
    Such as Munkustrap, Quaxo, or Coricopat,
Such as Bombalurina, or else Jellylorum—
    Names that never belong to more than one cat.   20
But above and beyond there's still one name left over,
    And that is the name that you never will guess;
The name that no human research can discover—
    But THE CAT HIMSELF KNOWS, and will never confess.
When you notice a cat in profound meditation,   25
    The reason, I tell you, is always the same:
His mind is engaged in a rapt contemplation
    Of the thought, of the thought, of the thought of his name:
        His ineffable effable
        Effanineffable
Deep and inscrutable singular Name.   30

THE HIPPOPOTAMUS

*Similiter et omnes revereantur Diaconos, ut mandatum Jesu
Christi; et Episcopum, ut Jesum Christum, existentem filium Patris;
Presbyteros autem, ut concilium Dei et conjunctionem Apostolorum.
Sine his Ecclesia non vocatur; de quibus suadeo vos sic habeo.*

—S. Ignatii Ad Trallianos

*And when the epistle is read among you, cause that it be read
also in the church of the Laodiceans.*

The broad-backed hippopotamus
Rests on his belly in the mud;
Although he seems so firm to us
He is merely flesh and blood.

Flesh and blood is weak and frail,   5
Susceptible to nervous shock;
While the True Church can never fail
For it is based upon a rock.

The hippo's feeble steps may err
In compassing material ends,   10
While the True Church need never stir
To gather in its dividends.

The 'potamus can never reach
The mango on the mango-tree;
But fruits of pomegranate and peach   15
Refresh the Church from over sea.

At mating time the hippo's voice
Betrays inflexions hoarse and odd,
But every week we hear rejoice
The Church, at being one with God.   20

Similiter . . . habeo: "Likewise let all reverence both the deacons as rep-
resentative of Jesus Christ; and the bishops as types of Jesus Christ the
Son who manifests the Father; and likewise the presbyters as God's high
council and the society of the Apostles. Apart from these, the Church does not
deserve the name; concerning these things I am persuaded that such is
your attitude." Saint Ignatius, to whom this Epistle to the Trallians is ascribed,
was the third bishop of Antioch; he was martyred c. 110 A.D. *And . . .
Laodiceans:* Colossians 4:16; see also Revelation 3:14–18.

The hippopotamus's day
Is passed in sleep; at night he hunts;
God works in a mysterious way—
The Church can sleep and feed at once.

I saw the 'potamus take wing   25
Ascending from the damp savannas,
And quiring angels round him sing
The praise of God, in loud hosannas.

Blood of the Lamb shall wash him clean
And him shall heavenly arms enfold,   30
Among the saints he shall be seen
Performing on a harp of gold.

He shall be washed as white as snow,
By all the martyr'd virgins kist,
While the True Church remains below   35
Wrapt in the old miasmal mist.

THE HOLLOW MEN

Mistah Kurtz—he dead.

A penny for the Old Guy

I

We are the hollow men
We are the stuffed men
Leaning together
Headpiece filled with straw. Alas!
Our dried voices, when   5
We whisper together
Are quiet and meaningless
As wind in dry grass
Or rats' feet over broken glass
In our dry cellar   10

   Shape without form, shade without colour,
Paralysed force, gesture without motion;

   Those who have crossed
With direct eyes, to death's other Kingdom
Remember us—if at all—not as lost   15
Violent souls, but only
As the hollow men
The stuffed men.

II

Eyes I dare not meet in dreams
In death's dream kingdom   20
These do not appear:
There, the eyes are
Sunlight on a broken column
There, is a tree swinging
And voices are   25

Mistah . . . dead: In Conrad's *Heart of Darkness,* Kurtz is an idealistic
European ivory-trader who is converted to primitive savagery. *the Old Guy:*
Guy Fawkes, one of the conspirators who attempted to blow up the Houses
of Parliament in 1605. On Guy Fawkes Day, November 5, straw effigies are
traditionally carried through the streets and pennies begged for them.

In the wind's singing
More distant and more solemn
Than a fading star.

   Let me be no nearer
In death's dream kingdom   30
Let me also wear
Such deliberate disguises
Rat's coat, crowskin, crossed staves
In a field
Behaving as the wind behaves   35
No nearer—

   Not that final meeting
In the twilight kingdom

III

This is the dead land
This is cactus land
Here the stone images   40
Are raised, here they receive
The supplication of a dead man's hand
Under the twinkle of a fading star.

   Is it like this   45
In death's other kingdom
Waking alone
At the hour when we are
Trembling with tenderness
Lips that would kiss   50
Form prayers to broken stone.

IV

The eyes are not here
There are no eyes here
In this valley of dying stars
In this hollow valley
This broken jaw of our lost kingdoms   55

   In this last of meeting places
We grope together
And avoid speech
Gathered on this beach of the tumid river   60

    Sightless, unless
The eyes reappear
As the perpetual star
Multifoliate rose
Of death's twilight kingdom   65
The hope only
Of empty men.

V

Here we go round the prickly pear
Prickly pear prickly pear
Here we go round the prickly pear   70
At five o'clock in the morning.

    Between the idea
And the reality
Between the motion
And the act   75
Falls the Shadow
             For Thine is the Kingdom

    Between the conception
And the creation
Between the emotion   80
And the response
Falls the Shadow
            Life is very long

    Between the desire
And the spasm   85
Between the potency
And the existence
Between the essence
And the descent
Falls the Shadow   90
            For Thine is the Kingdom

    For Thine is
Life is
For Thine is the

    This is the way the world ends   95
This is the way the world ends
This is the way the world ends
Not with a bang but a whimper.

LA FIGLIA CHE PIANGE

O quam te memorem virgo . . .

Stand on the highest pavement of the stair—
Lean on a garden urn—
Weave, weave the sunlight in your hair—
Clasp your flowers to you with a pained surprise—
Fling them to the ground and turn   5
With a fugitive resentment in your eyes:
But weave, weave the sunlight in your hair.

  So I would have had him leave,
So I would have had her stand and grieve,
So he would have left   10
As the soul leaves the body torn and bruised,
As the mind deserts the body it has used.
I should find
Some way incomparably light and deft,
Some way we both should understand,   15
Simple and faithless as a smile and shake of the hand.

  She turned away, but with the autumn weather
Compelled my imagination many days,
Many days and many hours:
Her hair over her arms and her arms full of flowers.   20
And I wonder how they should have been together!
I should have lost a gesture and a pose.
Sometimes these cogitations still amaze
The troubled midnight and the noon's repose.

La . . . Piange: the girl who weeps. *O . . . virgo:* "Oh what shall I call
you, virgin?" Aeneas' words to his mother, Venus, who appears to him
disguised as a huntress in Book II of the *Aeneid.*

THE LOVE SONG OF J. ALFRED PRUFROCK

*S'io credesse che mia risposta fosse
A persona che mai tornasse al mondo,
Questa fiamma staria senza piu scosse.
Ma perciocche giammai di questo fondo
Non torno vivo alcun, s'i'odo il vero,
Senza tema d'infamia ti rispondo.*

Let us go then, you and I,
When the evening is spread out against the sky
Like a patient etherised upon a table;
Let us go, through certain half-deserted streets,
The muttering retreats   5
Of restless nights in one-night cheap hotels
And sawdust restaurants with oyster-shells:
Streets that follow like a tedious argument
Of insidious intent
To lead you to an overwhelming question . . .   10
Oh, do not ask, "What is it?"
Let us go and make our visit.

In the room the women come and go
Talking of Michelangelo.

The yellow fog that rubs its back upon the window-panes,   15
The yellow smoke that rubs its muzzle on the window-panes
Licked its tongue into the corners of the evening,
Lingered upon the pools that stand in drains,
Let fall upon its back the soot that falls from chimneys,
Slipped by the terrace, made a sudden leap,   20
And seeing that it was a soft October night,
Curled once about the house, and fell asleep.

And indeed there will be time
For the yellow smoke that slides along the street,
Rubbing its back upon the window-panes;   25
There will be time, there will be time

To prepare a face to meet the faces that you meet;
There will be time to murder and create,
And time for all the works and days of hands
That lift and drop a question on your plate;   30
Time for you and time for me,
And time yet for a hundred indecisions,
And for a hundred visions and revisions,
Before the taking of a toast and tea.

    In the room the women come and go   35
Talking of Michelangelo.

    And indeed there will be time
To wonder, "Do I dare?" and, "Do I dare?"
Time to turn back and descend the stair,
With a bald spot in the middle of my hair—   40
[They will say: "How his hair is growing thin!"]
My morning coat, my collar mounting firmly to the chin,
My necktie rich and modest, but asserted by a simple pin—
[They will say: "But how his arms and legs are thin!"]
Do I dare   45
Disturb the universe?
In a minute there is time
For decisions and revisions which a minute will reverse.

    For I have known them all already, known them all:—
Have known the evenings, mornings, afternoons,   50
I have measured out my life with coffee spoons;
I know the voices dying with a dying fall
Beneath the music from a farther room.
    So how should I presume?

    And I have known the eyes already, known them all—   55
The eyes that fix you in a formulated phrase,
And when I am formulated, sprawling on a pin,
When I am pinned and wriggling on the wall,
Then how should I begin
To spit out all the butt-ends of my days and ways?   60
    And how should I presume?

    And I have known the arms already, known them all—
Arms that are braceleted and white and bare
[But in the lamplight, downed with light brown hair!]

Is it perfume from a dress   65
That makes me so digress?
Arms that lie along a table, or wrap about a shawl.
    And should I then presume?
    And how should I begin?

       .   .   .   .

Shall I say, I have gone at dusk through narrow streets   70
And watched the smoke that rises from the pipes
Of lonely men in shirt-sleeves, leaning out of windows? . . .

    I should have been a pair of ragged claws
Scuttling across the floors of silent seas.

       .   .   .   .   .

And the afternoon, the evening, sleeps so peacefully!   75
Smoothed by long fingers,
Asleep . . . tired . . . or it malingers,
Stretched on the floor, here beside you and me.
Should I, after tea and cakes and ices,
Have the strength to force the moment to its crisis?   80
But though I have wept and fasted, wept and prayed,
Though I have seen my head [grown slightly bald] brought in
      upon a platter,
I am no prophet—and here's no great matter;
I have seen the moment of my greatness flicker,
And I have seen the eternal Footman hold my coat, and snicker,   85
And in short, I was afraid.

    And would it have been worth it, after all,
After the cups, the marmalade, the tea,
Among the porcelain, among some talk of you and me,
Would it have been worth while,   90
To have bitten off the matter with a smile,
To have squeezed the universe into a ball
To roll it toward some overwhelming question,
To say: "I am Lazarus, come from the dead,
Come back to tell you all, I shall tell you all"—   95
If one, settling a pillow by her head,
    Should say: "That is not what I meant at all.
    That is not it, at all."

And would it have been worth it, after all,
Would it have been worth while,   100
After the sunsets and the dooryards and the sprinkled streets,
After the novels, after the teacups, after the skirts that trail along
    the floor—
And this, and so much more?—
It is impossible to say just what I mean!
But as if a magic lantern threw the nerves in patterns on a screen: 105
Would it have been worth while
If one, settling a pillow or throwing off a shawl,
And turning toward the window, should say:
    "That is not it at all,
    That is not what I meant, at all."   110

.   .   .   .   .

No! I am not Prince Hamlet, nor was meant to be;
Am an attendant lord, one that will do
To swell a progress, start a scene or two,
Advise the prince; no doubt, an easy tool,
Deferential, glad to be of use,   115
Politic, cautious, and meticulous;
Full of high sentence, but a bit obtuse;
At times, indeed, almost ridiculous—
Almost, at times, the Fool.

    I grow old . . . I grow old . . .   120
I shall wear the bottoms of my trousers rolled.

    Shall I part my hair behind? Do I dare to eat a peach?
I shall wear white flannel trousers, and walk upon the beach.
I have heard the mermaids singing, each to each.

    I do not think that they will sing to me.   125

    I have seen them riding seaward on the waves
Combing the white hair of the waves blown back
When the wind blows the water white and black.

    We have lingered in the chambers of the sea
By sea-girls wreathed with seaweed red and brown   130
Till human voices wake us, and we drown.

SWEENEY ERECT

> *And the trees about me,*
> *Let them be dry and leafless; let the rocks*
> *Groan with continual surges; and behind me*
> *Make all a desolation. Look, look, wenches!*

Paint me a cavernous waste shore
    Cast in the unstilled Cyclades,
Paint me the bold anfractuous rocks
    Faced by the snarled and yelping seas.

Display me Aeolus above   5
    Reviewing the insurgent gales
Which tangle Ariadne's hair
    And swell with haste the perjured sails.

Morning stirs the feet and hands
    (Nausicaa and Polypheme).   10
Gesture of orang-outang
    Rises from the sheets in steam.

This withered root of knots of hair
    Slitted below and gashed with eyes,
This oval O cropped out with teeth: 15
    The sickle motion from the thighs

Jackknifes upward at the knees
    Then straightens out from heel to hip
Pushing the framework of the bed
    And clawing at the pillow slip.   20

Sweeney addressed full length to shave
    Broadbottomed, pink from nape to base,
Knows the female temperament
    And wipes the suds around his face.

And . . . wenches! From Beaumont and Fletcher, *The Maid's Tragedy,*
II.ii. **2.** *Cyclades:* the Aegean islands where Theseus abandoned Ariadne
after she had helped him escape the labyrinth and the Minotaur of Crete.
10. *Nausicaa:* the young Phaeacian princess with whom Odysseus fell in
love; *Polypheme:* Polyphemus, the one-eyed giant that devoured men and
women and was killed by Odysseus.

(The lengthened shadow of a man 25
   Is history, said Emerson
Who had not seen the silhouette
   Of Sweeney straddled in the sun.)

Tests the razor on his leg
   Waiting until the shriek subsides. 30
The epileptic on the bed
   Curves backward, clutching at her sides.

The ladies of the corridor
   Find themselves involved, disgraced,
Call witness to their principles 35
   And deprecate the lack of taste

Observing that hysteria
   Might easily be misunderstood;
Mrs. Turner intimates
   It does the house no sort of good. 40

But Doris, towelled from the bath,
   Enters padding on broad feet,
Bringing sal volatile
   And a glass of brandy neat.

GERONTION

> *Thou hast nor youth nor age*
> *But as it were an after dinner sleep*
> *Dreaming of both.*

Here I am, an old man in a dry month,
Being read to by a boy, waiting for rain.
I was neither at the hot gates
Nor fought in the warm rain
Nor knee deep in the salt marsh, heaving a cutlass,   5
Bitten by flies, fought.
My house is a decayed house,
And the jew squats on the window sill, the owner,
Spawned in some estaminet of Antwerp,
Blistered in Brussels, patched and peeled in London.   10
The goat coughs at night in the field overhead;
Rocks, moss, stonecrop, iron, merds.
The woman keeps the kitchen, makes tea,
Sneezes at evening, poking the peevish gutter.
       I an old man,   15
A dull head among windy spaces.

Signs are taken for wonders. "We would see a sign!"
The word within a word, unable to speak a word,
Swaddled with darkness. In the juvescence of the year
Came Christ the tiger   20

In depraved May, dogwood and chestnut, flowering judas,
To be eaten, to be divided, to be drunk
Among whispers; by Mr. Silvero
With caressing hands, at Limoges
Who walked all night in the next room;   25

By Hakagawa, bowing among the Titians;
By Madame de Tornquist, in the dark room
Shifting the candles; Fräulein von Kulp
Who turned in the hall, one hand on the door.

Thou . . . both: From *Shakespeare, Measure for Measure* III.i.32–34, where
the Duke attempts to persuade Claudio to be courageous in the face of death.
9. *estaminet:* a cheap cabaret. **12.** *merds:* dung.

Vacant shuttles   30
Weave the wind. I have no ghosts,
An old man in a draughty house
Under a windy knob.

After such knowledge, what forgiveness? Think now
History has many cunning passages, contrived corridors   35
And issues, deceives with whispering ambitions,
She gives when our attention is distracted
And what she gives, gives with such supple confusions
That the giving famishes the craving. Gives too late   40
What's not believed in, or if still believed,
In memory only, reconsidered passion. Gives too soon
Into weak hands, what's thought can be dispensed with
Till the refusal propagates a fear. Think
Neither fear nor courage saves us. Unnatural vices   45
Are fathered by our heroism. Virtues
Are forced upon us by our impudent crimes.
These tears are shaken from the wrath-bearing tree.

The tiger springs in the new year. Us he devours. Think at last
We have not reached conclusion, when I   50
Stiffen in a rented house. Think at last
I have not made this show purposelessly
And it is not by any concitation
Of the backward devils.
I would meet you upon this honestly.   55
I that was near your heart was removed therefrom
To lose beauty in terror, terror in inquisition.
I have lost my passion: why should I need to keep it
Since what is kept must be adulterated?
I have lost my sight, smell, hearing, taste and touch: 60
How should I use them for your closer contact?

These with a thousand small deliberations
Protract the profit of their chilled delirium,
Excite the membrane, when the sense has cooled,
With pungent sauces, multiply variety   65
In a wilderness of mirrors. What will the spider do,
Suspend its operations, will the weevil
Delay? De Bailhache, Fresca, Mrs. Cammel, whirled

Beyond the circuit of the shuddering Bear
In fractured atoms. Gull against the wind, in the windy straits   70
Of Belle Isle, or running on the Horn,
White feathers in the snow, the Gulf claims,
And an old man driven by the Trades
To a sleepy corner.

                    Tenants of the house,   75
Thoughts of a dry brain in a dry season.

WALLACE STEVENS
(1879–1955)

THE EMPEROR OF ICE-CREAM

Call the roller of big cigars,
The muscular one, and bid him whip
In kitchen cups concupiscent curds.
Let the wenches dawdle in such dress
As they are used to wear, and let the boys   5
Bring flowers in last month's newspapers.
Let be be finale of seem.
The only emperor is the emperor of ice-cream.

Take from the dresser of deal,
Lacking the three glass knobs, that sheet   10
On which she embroidered fantails once
And spread it so as to cover her face.
If her horny feet protrude, they come
To show how cold she is, and dumb.
Let the lamp affix its beam.   15
The only emperor is the emperor of ice-cream.

PETER QUINCE AT THE CLAVIER

I

Just as my fingers on these keys
Make music, so the selfsame sounds
On my spirit make a music, too.

Music is feeling, then, not sound;
And thus it is that what I feel,
Here in this room, desiring you,   5

Thinking of your blue-shadowed silk,
Is music. It is like the strain
Waked in the elders by Susanna.

Of a green evening, clear and warm,   10
She bathed in her still garden, while
The red-eyed elders watching, felt
The basses of their beings throb
In witching chords, and their thin blood
Pulse pizzicati of Hosanna.   15

II

In the green water, clear and warm,
Susanna lay.
She searched
The touch of springs,
And found
Concealed imaginings.   20
She sighed,
For so much melody.

Upon the bank, she stood
In the cool
Of spent emotions.   25
She felt, among the leaves,
The dew
Of old devotions.

9ff. *Susanna:* In the apocryphal Book of Daniel, Susanna is spied upon by
a group of lecherous old men while she is bathing. When she rejects one
of them, he accuses her of adultery, but she is vindicated by Daniel.

She walked upon the grass, 30
Still quavering.
The winds were like her maids,
On timid feet,
Fetching her woven scarves,
Yet wavering. 35

A breath upon her hand
Muted the night.
She turned—
A cymbal crashed,
And roaring horns. 40

III
Soon, with a noise like tambourines,
Came her attendant Byzantines.

They wondered why Susanna cried
Against the elders by her side;

And as they whispered, the refrain 45
Was like a willow swept by rain.

Anon, their lamps' uplifted flame
Revealed Susanna and her shame.

And then, the simpering Byzantines
Fled, with a noise like tambourines. 50

IV
Beauty is momentary in the mind—
The fitful tracing of a portal;
But in the flesh it is immortal.

The body dies; the body's beauty lives.
So evenings die, in their green going, 55
A wave, interminably flowing.
So gardens die, their meek breath scenting
The cowl of winter, done repenting.
So maidens die, to the auroral
Celebration of a maiden's choral. 60

Susanna's music touched the bawdy strings
Of those white elders; but, escaping,
Left only Death's ironic scraping.
Now, in its immortality, it plays
On the clear viol of her memory,
And makes a constant sacrament of praise.

65

THE IDEA OF ORDER AT KEY WEST

She sang beyond the genius of the sea.
The water never formed to mind or voice,
Like a body wholly body, fluttering
Its empty sleeves; and yet its mimic motion
Made constant cry, caused constantly a cry,   5
That was not ours although we understood,
Inhuman, of the veritable ocean.

The sea was not a mask. No more was she.
The song and water were not medleyed sound
Even if what she sang was what she heard,   10
Since what she sang was uttered word by word.
It may be that in all her phrases stirred
The grinding water and the gasping wind;
But it was she and not the sea we heard.

For she was the maker of the song she sang.   15
The ever-hooded, tragic-gestured sea
Was merely a place by which she walked to sing.
Whose spirit is this? we said, because we knew
It was the spirit that we sought and knew
That we should ask this often as she sang.   20

If it was only the dark voice of the sea
That rose, or even colored by many waves;
If it was only the outer voice of sky
And cloud, of the sunken coral water-walled,
However clear, it would have been deep air,   25
The heaving speech of air, a summer sound
Repeated in a summer without end
And sound alone. But it was more than that,
More even than her voice, and ours, among
The meaningless plungings of water and the wind,   30
Theatrical distances, bronze shadows heaped
On high horizons, mountainous atmospheres
Of sky and sea.
                It was her voice that made
The sky acutest at its vanishing.
She measured to the hour its solitude.   35
She was the single artificer of the world

In which she sang. And when she sang, the sea,
Whatever self it had, became the self
That was her song, for she was the maker. Then we,
As we beheld her striding there alone,   40
Knew that there never was a world for her
Except the one she sang and, singing, made.

Ramon Fernandez, tell me, if you know,
Why, when the singing ended and we turned
Toward the town, tell why the glassy lights,   45
The lights in the fishing boats at anchor there,
As the night descended, tilting in the air,
Fixing emblazoned zones and fiery poles,
Arranging, deepening, enchanting night.   50

Oh! Blessed rage for order, pale Ramon,
The maker's rage to order words of the sea,
Words of the fragrant portals, dimly-starred,
And of ourselves and of our origins,
In ghostlier demarcations, keener sounds.   55

43. *Ramon Fernandez:* a French critic (1894–1944). His *Messages* (1926) asserts that the business of the artist is to create a personality and a world that imposes a sense of order upon the disorder of experience.

JOHN CROWE RANSOM
(1888–   )

BELLS FOR JOHN WHITESIDE'S DAUGHTER

There was such speed in her little body,
And such lightness in her footfall,
It is no wonder her brown study
Astonishes us all.

Her wars were bruited in our high window.   5
We looked among orchard trees and beyond,
Where she took arms against her shadow,
Or harried unto the pond

The lazy geese, like a snow cloud
Dripping their snow on the green grass,   10
Tricking and stopping, sleepy and proud,
Who cried in goose, Alas,

For the tireless heart within the little
Lady with rod that made them rise
From their noon apple-dreams and scuttle   15
Goose-fashion under the skies!

But now go the bells, and we are ready,
In one house we are sternly stopped
To say we are vexed at her brown study,
Lying so primly propped.   20

e. e. cummings
(1894–1962)

plato told him

plato told

him:he couldn't
believe it(jesus

told him;he
wouldn't believe
it)lao   5

tsze
certainly told
him, and general
(yes   10

mam)
sherman;
and even
(believe it
or   15

not) you
told him:i told
him;we told him
(he didn't believe it, no

sir)it took   20
a nipponized bit of
the old sixth

avenue
el;in the top of his head:to tell

him   25

here is little Effie's head

here is little Effie's head
whose brains are made of gingerbread
when the judgment day comes
God will find six crumbs

stooping by the coffinlid   5
waiting for something to rise
as the other somethings did—
you imagine His surprise

bellowing through the general noise
Where is Effie who was dead?   10
—to God in a tiny voice,
i am may the first crumb said

whereupon its fellow five
crumbs chuckled as if they were alive
and number two took up the song,   15
might i'm called and did no wrong

cried the third crumb, i am should
and this is my little sister could
with our big brother who is would
don't punish us for we were good;   20

and the last crumb with some shame
whispered unto God, my name
is must and with the others i've
been Effie who isn't alive

just imagine it I say   25
God amid a monstrous din
watch your step and follow me
stooping by Effie's little, in

(want a match or can you see?)
which the six subjunctive crumbs   30
twitch like mutilated thumbs:
picture His peering biggest whey

coloured face on which a frown
puzzles, but I know the way—
(nervously Whose eyes approve   35
the blessed while His ears are crammed

with the strenuous music of
the innumerable capering damned)
—staring wildly up and down
the here we are now judgment day   40

cross the threshold have no dread
lift the sheet back in this way.
here is little Effie's head
whose brains are made of gingerbread

love is more thicker than forget

love is more thicker than forget
more thinner than recall
more seldom than a wave is wet
more frequent than to fail

it is most mad and moonly   5
and less it shall unbe
than all the sea which only
is deeper than the sea

love is less always than to win
less never than alive   10
less bigger than the least begin
less littler than forgive

it is most sane and sunly
and more it cannot die
than all the sky which only   15
is higher than the sky

anyone lived in a pretty how town

anyone lived in a pretty how town
(with up so floating many bells down)
spring summer autumn winter
he sang his didn't he danced his did.

Women and men(both little and small)   5
cared for anyone not at all
they sowed their isn't they reaped their same
sun moon stars rain

children guessed(but only a few
and down they forgot as up they grew   10
autumn winter spring summer)
that noone loved him more by more

when by now and tree by leaf
she laughed his joy she cried his grief
bird by snow and stir by still   15
anyone's any was all to her

someones married their everyones
laughed their cryings and did their dance
(sleep wake hope and then)they
said their nevers they slept their dream   20

stars rain sun moon
(and only the snow can begin to explain
how children are apt to forget to remember
with up so floating many bells down)

one day anyone died i guess   25
(and noone stooped to kiss his face)
busy folk buried them side by side
little by little and was by was

all by all and deep by deep
and more by more they dream their sleep   30
noone and anyone earth by april
wish by spirit and if by yes.

Women and men(both dong and ding)
summer autumn winter spring
reaped their sowing and went their came   35
sun moon stars rain

my father moved through dooms of love

my father moved through dooms of love
through sames of am through haves of give,
singing each morning out of each night
my father moved through depths of height

this motionless forgetful where   5
turned at his glance to shining here;
that if(so timid air is firm)
under his eyes would stir and squirm

newly as from unburied which
floats the first who, his april touch   10
drove sleeping selves to swarm their fates
woke dreamers to their ghostly roots

and should some why completely weep
my father's fingers brought her sleep:
vainly no smallest voice might cry   15
for he could feel the mountains grow.

Lifting the valleys of the sea
my father moved through griefs of joy;
praising a forehead called the moon
singing desire into begin   20

joy was his song and joy so pure
a heart of star by him could steer
and pure so now and now so yes
the wrists of twilight would rejoice

keen as midsummer's keen beyond   25
conceiving mind of sun will stand,
so strictly(over utmost him
so hugely)stood my father's dream

his flesh was flesh his blood was blood:
no hungry man but wished him food;   30
no cripple wouldn't creep one mile
uphill to only see him smile.

Scorning the pomp of must and shall
my father moved through dooms of feel;
his anger was as right as rain
his pity was as green as grain

septembering arms of year extend
less humbly wealth to foe and friend
than he to foolish and to wise
offered immeasurable is

proudly and(by octobering flame
beckoned)as earth will downward climb,
so naked for immortal work
his shoulders marched against the dark

his sorrow was as true as bread:
no liar looked him in the head;
if every friend became his foe
he'd laugh and build a world with snow.

My father moved through theys of we,
singing each new leaf out of each tree
(and every child was sure that spring
danced when she heard my father sing)

then let men kill which cannot share,
let blood and flesh be mud and mire,
scheming imagine,passion willed,
freedom a drug that's bought and sold

giving to steal and cruel kind,
a heart to fear,to doubt a mind,
to differ a disease of same,
conform the pinnacle of am

though dull were all we taste as bright,
bitter all utterly things sweet,
maggoty minus and dumb death
all we inherit,all bequeath

and nothing quite so least as truth
—i say though hate were why men breathe—
because my father lived his soul
love is the whole and more than all

35

40

45

50

55

60

65

my sweet old etcetera

my sweet old etcetera
aunt lucy during the recent

war could and what
is more did tell you just
what everybody was fighting   5

for,
my sister

isabel created hundreds
(and
hundreds)of socks not to   10
mention shirts fleaproof earwarmers

etcetera wristers etcetera, my
mother hoped that

i would die etcetera
bravely of course my father used   15
to become hoarse talking about how it was
a privilege and if only he
could meanwhile my

self etcetera lay quietly
in the deep mud et   20

cetera
(dreaming,
et
    cetera, of
Your smile   25
eyes knees and of your Etcetera)

i like my body when it is with your body

i like my body when it is with your
body. It is so quite new a thing.
Muscles better and nerves more.
i like your body. i like what it does,
i like its hows. i like to feel the spine   5
of your body and its bones, and the trembling
-firm-smooth ness and which i will
again and again and again
kiss, i like kissing this and that of you,
i like, slowly stroking the, shocking fuzz   10
of your electric fur, and what-is-it comes
over parting flesh . . . . And eyes big love-crumbs,

and possibly i like the thrill

of under me you so quite new

MARIANNE MOORE
(1887–   )

POETRY

I, too, dislike it: there are things that are important beyond all
  this fiddle.
  Reading it, however, with a perfect contempt for it, one
    discovers in
  it after all, a place for the genuine.
      Hands that can grasp, eyes
      that can dilate, hair that can rise   5
        if it must, these things are important not because a

high-sounding interpretation can be put upon them but because
  they are
  useful. When they become so derivative as to become unin-
    telligible,
  the same thing may be said for all of us, that we
      do not admire what   10
      we cannot understand: the bat
        holding on upside down or in quest of something to

eat, elephants pushing, a wild horse taking a roll, a tireless wolf
  under
  a tree, the immovable critic twitching his skin like a horse
    that feels a flea, the base-
  ball fan, the statistician—   15
      nor is it valid
        to discriminate against "business documents and

school-books"; all these phenomena are important. One must
  make a distinction
  however: when dragged into prominence by half poets, the
    result is not poetry,
  nor till the poets among us can be   20
      "literalists of
      the imagination"—above
        insolence and triviality and can present

for inspection, "imaginary gardens with real toads in them,"
    shall we have
  it. In the meantime, if you demand on the one hand,   25
  the raw material of poetry in
    all its rawness and
    that which is on the other hand
      genuine, you are interested in poetry.

W. H. AUDEN
(1907–   )

MUSÉE DES BEAUX ARTS

About suffering they were never wrong,
The Old Masters: how well they understood
Its human position; how it takes place
While someone else is eating or opening a window or just
    walking dully along;
How, when the aged are reverently, passionately waiting   5
For the miraculous birth, there always must be
Children who did not specially want it to happen, skating
On a pond at the edge of the wood:
They never forgot
That even the dreadful martyrdom must run its course   10
Anyhow in a corner, some untidy spot
Where the dogs go on with their doggy life and the torturer's
    horse
Scratches its innocent behind on a tree.

In Brueghel's *Icarus*, for instance: how everything turns away
Quite leisurely from the disaster; the ploughman may   15
Have heard the splash, the forsaken cry,
But for him it was not an important failure; the sun shone
As it had to on the white legs disappearing into the green
Water; and the expensive delicate ship that must have seen
Something amazing, a boy falling out of the sky,   20
Had somewhere to get to and sailed calmly on.

14. *Brueghel's Icarus:* Icarus was the son of Daedalus, the master artist; he
flew too near the sun with his wax-covered wings and fell into the sea. In
the painting by Pieter Brueghel (1525?–1569), his fall is made insignificant
in relation to the landscape in the foreground.

THE VOICE OF CAESAR: from "FOR THE TIME BEING"

Narrator
Now let the wife look up from her stove, the husband
Interrupt his work, the child put down its toy,
That His voice may be heard in our Just Society
   Who under the sunlight
Of His calm, possessing the good earth, do well. Pray   5
Silence for Caesar: stand motionless and hear
In a concourse of body and concord of soul
   His proclamation.

Recitative
CITIZENS OF THE EMPIRE, GREETING. ALL MALE PERSONS WHO
SHALL HAVE ATTAINED THE AGE OF TWENTY-ONE YEARS OR OVER 10
MUST PROCEED IMMEDIATELY TO THE VILLAGE, TOWNSHIP, CITY,
PRECINCT OR OTHER LOCAL ADMINISTRATIVE AREA IN WHICH THEY
WERE BORN AND THERE REGISTER THEMSELVES AND THEIR DE-
PENDENTS IF ANY WITH THE POLICE. WILFUL FAILURE TO COM-
PLY WITH THIS ORDER IS PUNISHABLE BY CONFISCATION OF GOODS 15
AND LOSS OF CIVIL RIGHTS.

Narrator
You have been listening to the voice of Caesar
Who overcame implacable Necessity
By His endurance and by His skill has subdued the
   Welter of Fortune.   20
It is meet, therefore, that, before dispersing
In pious equanimity to obey His orders,
With well-tuned instruments and grateful voices
   We should praise Caesar.

Fugal-Chorus
Great is Caesar: He has conquered Seven Kingdoms.   25
The First was the Kingdom of Abstract Idea:
Last night it was Tom, Dick and Harry; tonight it is S's with P's;
Instead of inflexions and accents
There are prepositions and word-order;

For the Time Being: A Christmas oratorio, or dramatic reading of the
Christmas narrative with individual and choral meditations.

Instead of aboriginal objects excluding each other 30
There are specimens reiterating a type;
Instead of wood-nymphs and river-demons,
There is one unconditioned ground of Being.
Great is Caesar: God must be with Him.

Great is Caesar: He has conquered Seven Kingdoms. 35
The Second was the Kingdom of Natural Cause:
Last night it was Sixes and Sevens; tonight it is One and Two;
Instead of saying, "Strange are the whims of the Strong,"
We say, "Harsh is the Law but it is certain";
Instead of building temples, we build laboratories; 40
Instead of offering sacrifices, we perform experiments;
Instead of reciting prayers, we note pointer-readings;
Our lives are no longer erratic but efficient.
Great is Caesar: God must be with Him.

Great is Caesar; He has conquered Seven Kingdoms. 45
The Third was the Kingdom of Infinite Number:
Last night it was Rule-of-Thumb, tonight it is To-a-T;
Instead of Quite-a-lot, there is Exactly-so-many;
Instead of Only-a-few, there is Just-these;
Instead of saying, "You must wait until I have counted," 50
We say, "Here you are. You will find this answer correct";
Instead of a nodding acquaintance with a few integers
The Transcendentals are our personal friends.
Great is Caesar: God must be with Him.

Great is Caesar: He has conquered Seven Kingdoms. 55
The Fourth was the Kingdom of Credit Exchange:
Last night it was Tit-for-Tat, tonight it is C.O.D.;
When we have a surplus, we need not meet someone with a
    deficit;
When we have a deficit, we need not meet someone with a
    surplus;
Instead of heavy treasures, there are paper symbols of value; 60
Instead of Pay at Once, there is Pay when you can;
Instead of My Neighbour, there is Our Customers;
Instead of Country Fair, there is World Market.
Great is Caesar: God must be with Him.

Great is Caesar; He has conquered Seven Kingdoms. 65
The Fifth was the Kingdom of Inorganic Giants:
Last night it was Heave-Ho, tonight it is Whee-Spree;
When we want anything, They make it;
When we dislike anything, They change it;
When we want to go anywhere, They carry us; 70
When the Barbarian invades us, They raise immovable shields;
When we invade the Barbarian, They brandish irresistible
    swords;
Fate is no longer a fiat of Matter, but a freedom of Mind.
Great is Caesar: God must be with Him.

Great is Caesar: He has conquered Seven Kingdoms. 75
The Sixth was the Kingdom of Organic Dwarfs:
Last night it was Ouch-Ouch, tonight it is Yum-Yum;
When diseases waylay us, They strike them dead;
When worries intrude on us, They throw them out;
When pain accosts us, They save us from embarrassment; 80
When we feel like sheep, They make us lions;
When we feel like geldings, They make us stallions;
Spirit is no longer under Flesh, but on top.
Great is Caesar: God must be with Him.

Great is Caesar: He has conquered Seven Kingdoms. 85
The Seventh was the Kingdom of Popular Soul:
Last night it was Order-Order, tonight it is Hear-Hear;
When he says, You are happy, we laugh;
When he says, You are wretched, we cry;
When he says, It is true, everyone believes it; 90
When he says, It is false, no one believes it;
When he says, This is good, this is loved;
When he says, That is bad, that is hated.
Great is Caesar: God must be with Him.

THE FALL OF ROME

[for cyril connolly]

The piers are pummelled by the waves;
In a lonely field the rain
Lashes an abandoned train;
Outlaws fill the mountain caves.

Fantastic grow the evening gowns;   5
Agents of the Fisc pursue
Absconding tax-defaulters through
The sewers of provincial towns.

Private rites of magic send
The temple prostitutes to sleep;   10
All the literati keep
An imaginary friend.

Cerebrotonic Cato may
Extoll the Ancient Disciplines,
But the muscle-bound Marines   15
Mutiny for food and pay.

Caesar's double-bed is warm
As an unimportant clerk
Writes *I DO NOT LIKE MY WORK*
On a pink official form.   20

Unendowed with wealth or pity,
Little birds with scarlet legs,
Sitting on their speckled eggs,
Eye each flu-infected city.

Altogether elsewhere, vast   25
Herds of reindeer move across
Miles and miles of golden moss,
Silently and very fast.

---

14. *cerebrotonic:* from cerebrotonia, a personality type characterized by introversion, sensitivity, and dominant intellectuality.

THE SHIELD OF ACHILLES

        She looked over his shoulder
            For vines and olive trees,
        Marble well-governed cities
            And ships upon untamed seas,
        But there on the shining metal   5
            His hands had put instead
        An artificial wilderness
            And a sky like lead.

A plain without a feature, bare and brown,
    No blade of grass, no sign of neighbourhood,   10
Nothing to eat and nowhere to sit down,
    Yet, congregated on its blankness, stood
        An unintelligible multitude,
A million eyes, a million boots in line,
Without expression, waiting for a sign.   15

Out of the air a voice without a face
    Proved by statistics that some cause was just
In tones as dry and level as the place:
    No one was cheered and nothing was discussed;
        Column by column in a cloud of dust   20
They marched away enduring a belief
Whose logic brought them, somewhere else, to grief.

        She looked over his shoulder
            For ritual pieties,
        White flower-garlanded heifers,
            Libation and sacrifice,   25
        But there on the shining metal
            Where the altar should have been,
        She saw by his flickering forge-light
            Quite another scene.   30

The Shield of Achilles: Auden recalls Book XVIII of the *Iliad,* in which, at the request of Achilles' mother Thetis, Hephaestos, the god of fire, forges a shield whose engravings depict the totality of human existence.

Barbed wire enclosed an arbitrary spot
   Where bored officials lounged (one cracked a joke)
And sentries sweated for the day was hot:
   A crowd of ordinary decent folk
   Watched from without and neither moved nor spoke   35
As three pale figures were led forth and bound
To three posts driven upright in the ground.

The mass and majesty of this world, all
   That carries weight and always weighs the same
Lay in the hands of others; they were small   40
   And could not hope for help and no help came:
   What their foes liked to do was done, their shame
Was all the worst could wish; they lost their pride
And died as men before their bodies died.

        She looked over his shoulder   45
           For athletes at their games,
        Men and women in a dance
           Moving their sweet limbs
        Quick, quick, to music,
           But there on the shining shield   50
        His hands had set no dancing-floor
           But a weed-choked field.

A ragged urchin, aimless and alone,
   Loitered about that vacancy, a bird
Flew up to safety from his well-aimed stone: 55
   That girls are raped, that two boys knife a third,
   Were axioms to him, who'd never heard
Of any world where promises were kept,
Or one could weep because another wept.

        The thin-lipped armourer,   60
           Hephaestos hobbled away,
        Thetis of the shining breasts
           Cried out in dismay
        At what the god had wrought
           To please her son, the strong   65
        Iron-hearted man-slaying Achilles
           Who would not live long.

DYLAN THOMAS
(1914–1953)

THE FORCE THAT THROUGH
THE GREEN FUSE DRIVES THE FLOWER

The force that through the green fuse drives the flower
Drives my green age; that blasts the roots of trees
Is my destroyer.
And I am dumb to tell the crooked rose
My youth is bent by the same wintry fever.   5

The force that drives the water through the rocks
Drives my red blood; that dries the mouthing streams
Turns mine to wax.
And I am dumb to mouth unto my veins
How at the mountain spring the same mouth sucks.   10

The hand that whirls the water in the pool
Stirs the quicksand; that ropes the blowing wind
Hauls my shroud sail.
And I am dumb to tell the hanging man
How of my clay is made the hangman's lime.   15

The lips of time leech to the fountain head;
Love drips and gathers, but the fallen blood
Shall calm her sores.
And I am dumb to tell a weather's wind
How time has ticked a heaven round the stars.   20

And I am dumb to tell the lover's tomb
How at my sheet goes the same crooked worm.

A REFUSAL TO MOURN THE DEATH,
BY FIRE, OF A CHILD
IN LONDON

Never until the mankind making
Bird beast and flower
Fathering and all humbling darkness
Tells with silence the last light breaking
And the still hour   5
Is come of the sea tumbling in harness

And I must enter again the round
Zion of the water bead
And the synagogue of the ear of corn
Shall I let pray the shadow of a sound   10
Or sow my salt seed
In the least valley of sackcloth to mourn

The majesty and burning of the child's death.
I shall not murder
The mankind of her going with a grave truth   15
Nor blaspheme down the stations of the breath
With any further
Elegy of innocence and youth.

Deep with the first dead lies London's daughter,
Robed in the long friends,
The grains beyond age, the dark veins of her mother,   20
Secret by the unmourning water
Of the riding Thames.
After the first death, there is no other.

THEODORE ROETHKE
(1908–1963)

OPEN HOUSE

My secrets cry aloud.
I have no need for tongue.
My heart keeps open house,
My doors are widely swung.
An epic of the eyes   5
My love, with no disguise.

My truths are all foreknown,
This anguish self-revealed.
I'm naked to the bone,
With nakedness my shield.   10
Myself is what I wear:
I keep the spirit spare.

The anger will endure,
The deed will speak the truth
In language strict and pure.
I stop the lying mouth: 15
Rage warps my clearest cry
To witless agony.

THE CHAIR

A funny thing about a Chair:
You hardly ever think it's *there*.
To know a Chair is really it,
You sometimes have to go and sit.

ORCHIDS

They lean over the path,
Adder-mouthed,
Swaying close to the face,
Coming out, soft and deceptive,
Limp and damp, delicate as a young bird's tongue;   5
Their fluttery fledgling lips
Move slowly,
Drawing in the warm air.

And at night,
The faint moon falling through whitewashed glass,   10
The heat going down
So their musky smell comes even stronger,
Drifting down from their mossy cradles:
So many devouring infants!
Soft luminescent fingers,   15
Lips neither dead nor alive,
Loose ghostly mouths
Breathing.

CUTTINGS

Sticks-in-a-drowse droop over sugary loam,
Their intricate stem-fur dries;
But still the delicate slips keep coaxing up water;
The small cells bulge;

One nub of growth   5
Nudges a sand-crumb loose,
Pokes through a musty sheath
Its pale tendrilous horn.

CUTTINGS (later)

This urge, wrestle, resurrection of dry sticks,
Cut stems struggling to put down feet,
What saint strained so much,
Rose on such lopped limbs to a new life?

I can hear, underground, that sucking and sobbing,   5
In my veins, in my bones I feel it,—
The small waters seeping upward,
The tight grains parting at last.
When sprouts break out,
Slippery as fish,   10
I quail, lean to beginnings, sheath-wet.

WEED PULLER

Under the concrete benches,
Hacking at black hairy roots,—
Those lewd monkey-tails hanging from drainholes,—
Digging into the soft rubble underneath,
Webs and weeds,   5
Grubs and snails and sharp sticks,
Or yanking tough fern-shapes,
Coiled green and thick, like dripping smilax,
Tugging all day at perverse life:
The indignity of it!—   10
With everything blooming above me,
Lilies, pale-pink cyclamen, roses,
Whole fields lovely and inviolate,—
Me down in that fetor of weeds,
Crawling on all fours,   15
Alive, in a slippery grave.

BIG WIND

Where were the greenhouses going,
Lunging into the lashing
Wind driving water
So far down the river
All the faucets stopped?—   5
So we drained the manure-machine
For the steam plant,
Pumping the stale mixture
Into the rusty boilers,
Watching the pressure gauge   10
Waver over to red,
As the seams hissed
And the live steam
Drove to the far
End of the rose-house,   15
Where the worst wind was,
Creaking the cypress window-frames,
Cracking so much thin glass
We stayed all night,
Stuffing the holes with burlap;   20
But she rode it out,
That old rose-house,
She hove into the teeth of it,
The core and pith of that ugly storm,
Ploughing with her stiff prow,   25
Bucking into the wind-waves
That broke over the whole of her,
Flailing her sides with spray,
Flinging long strings of wet across the roof-top,
Finally veering, wearing themselves out, merely   30
Whistling thinly under the wind-vents;
She sailed until the calm morning,
Carrying her full cargo of roses.

MY PAPA'S WALTZ

The whiskey on your breath
Could make a small boy dizzy;
But I hung on like death:
Such waltzing was not easy.

We romped until the pans
Slid from the kitchen shelf;
My mother's countenance
Could not unfrown itself.

The hand that held my wrist
Was battered on one knuckle;
At every step you missed
My right ear scraped a buckle.

You beat time on my head
With a palm caked hard by dirt,
Then waltzed me off to bed
Still clinging to your shirt.

PICKLE BELT

The fruit rolled by all day.
They prayed the cogs would creep;
They thought about Saturday pay,
And Sunday sleep.

Whatever he smelled was good:
The fruit and flesh smells mixed.
There beside him she stood,—
And he, perplexed;

He, in his shrunken britches,
Eyes rimmed with pickle dust,
Prickling with all the itches
Of sixteen-year-old lust.

DOLOR

I have known the inexorable sadness of pencils,
Neat in their boxes, dolor of pad and paper-weight,
All the misery of manilla folders and mucilage,
Desolation in immaculate public places,
Lonely reception room, lavatory, switchboard,   5
The unalterable pathos of basin and pitcher,
Ritual of multigraph, paper-clip, comma,
Endless duplication of lives and objects.
And I have seen dust from the walls of institutions,
Finer than flour, alive, more dangerous than silica,   10
Sift, almost invisible, through long afternoons of tedium,
Dropping a fine film on nails and delicate eyebrows,
Glazing the pale hair, the duplicate grey standard faces.

THE YOUNG GIRL

What can the spirit believe?—
It takes in the whole body;
I, on coming to love,
Make that my study.

We are one, and yet we are more,   5
I am told by those who know,—
At times content to be two.
Today I skipped on the shore,
My eyes neither here nor there,
My thin arms to and fro,   10
A bird my body,
My bird-blood ready.

HER RETICENCE

If I could send him only
One sleeve with my hand in it,
Disembodied, unbloody,
For him to kiss or caress
As he would or would not,—
But never the full look of my eyes,
Nor the whole heart of my thought,
Nor the soul haunting my body,
Nor my lips, my breasts, my thighs
That shiver in the wind
When the wind sighs.

5

10

LIGHT LISTENED

O what could be more nice
Than her ways with a man?
She kissed me more than twice
Once we were left alone.
Who'd look when he could feel?
She'd more sides than a seal.

The close air faintly stirred.
Light deepened to a bell,
The love-beat of a bird.
She kept her body still
And watched the weather flow.
We live by what we do.

All's known, all, all around:
The shape of things to be;
A green thing loves the green
And loves the living ground.
The deep shade gathers night;
She changed with changing light.

We met to leave again
The time we broke from time;
A cold air brought its rain,
The singing of a stem.
She sang a final song;
Light listened when she sang.

WISH FOR A YOUNG WIFE

My lizard, my lively writher,
May your limbs never wither,
May the eyes in your face
Survive the green ice
Of envy's mean gaze;   5
May you live out your life
Without hate, without grief,
And your hair ever blaze,
In the sun, in the sun,
When I am undone,   10
When I am no one.

I KNEW A WOMAN

I knew a woman, lovely in her bones,
When small birds sighed, she would sigh back at them;
Ah, when she moved, she moved more ways than one:
The shapes a bright container can contain!
Of her choice virtues only gods should speak,   5
Or English poets who grew up on Greek
(I'd have them sing in chorus, cheek to cheek).

How well her wishes went! She stroked my chin,
She taught me Turn, and Counter-turn, and Stand;
She taught me Touch, that undulant white skin;   10
I nibbled meekly from her proffered hand;
She was the sickle; I, poor I, the rake,
Coming behind her for her pretty sake
(But what prodigious mowing we did make).

Love likes a gander, and adores a goose: 15
Her full lips pursed, the errant note to seize;
She played it quick, she played it light and loose;
My eyes, they dazzled at her flowing knees;
Her several parts could keep a pure repose,
Or one hip quiver with a mobile nose   20
(She moved in circles, and those circles moved).

Let seed be grass, and grass turn into hay:
I'm martyr to a motion not my own;
What's freedom for? To know eternity.
I swear she cast a shadow white as stone.   25
But who would count eternity in days?
These old bones live to learn her wanton ways:
(I measure time by how a body sways).

ROBERT LOWELL
(1917–   )

THE FAT MAN IN THE MIRROR

What's filling up the mirror? O, it is not I;
Hair-belly like a beaver's house? An old dog's eye?
   The forenoon was blue
   In the mad King's zoo
Nurse was swinging me so high, so high!   5

The bullies wrestled on the royal bowling green;
Hammers and sickles on their hoods of black sateen. . . .
   Sulking on my swing
   The tobacco King
Sliced apples with a pen-knife for the Queen.   10

This *I*, who used to mouse about the paraffined preserves,
And jammed a finger in the coffee-grinder, serves
   Time before the mirror.
   But this pursey terror . . .
Nurse, it is a person. *It is nerves.*   15

Where's the Queen-Mother waltzing like a top to staunch
The blood of Lewis, King of Faerie? Hip and haunch
   Lard the royal grotto;
   Straddling Lewis' motto,
Time, the Turk, its sickle on its paunch.   20

Nurse, Nurse, it rises on me . . . O, it starts to roll,
My apples, O, are ashes in the meerschaum bowl. . . .
   If you'd only come,
   If you'd only come,
Darling, if . . . The apples that I stole,   25

While Nurse and I were swinging in the Old One's eye . . .
Only a fat man with his beaver on his eye
   Only a fat man,
   Only a fat man
Bursts the mirror. O, it is not I!   30

MR. EDWARDS AND THE SPIDER

I saw the spiders marching through the air,
Swimming from tree to tree that mildewed day
 In latter August when the hay
 Came creaking to the barn. But where
  The wind is westerly,   5
Where gnarled November makes the spiders fly
Into the apparitions of the sky,
They purpose nothing but their ease and die
Urgently beating east to sunrise and the sea;

What are we in the hands of the great God?   10
It was in vain you set up thorn and briar
 In battle array against the fire
 And treason crackling in your blood;
  For the wild thorns grow tame
And will do nothing to oppose the flame;   15
Your lacerations tell the losing game
You play against a sickness past your cure.
How will the hands be strong? How will the heart endure?

A very little thing, a little worm,
Or hourglass-blazoned spider, it is said,   20
 Can kill a tiger. Will the dead
 Hold up his mirror and affirm
  To the four winds the smell
And flash of his authority? It's well
If God who holds you to the pit of hell,   25
Much as one holds a spider, will destroy,
Baffle and dissipate your soul. As a small boy

On Windsor Marsh, I saw the spider die
When thrown into the bowels of fierce fire:
 There's no long struggle, no desire
 To get up on its feet and fly—   30
  It stretches out its feet
And dies. This is the sinner's last retreat;
Yes, and no strength exerted on the heat
Then sinews the abolished will, when sick   35
And full of burning, it will whistle on a brick.

But who can plumb the sinking of that soul?
Josiah Hawley, picture yourself cast
   Into a brick-kiln where the blast
   Fans your quick vitals to a coal—   40
     If measured by a glass,
How long would it seem burning! Let there pass
A minute, ten, ten trillion; but the blaze
Is infinite, eternal: this is death,
To die and know it. This is the Black Widow, death.   45

THE DRUNKEN FISHERMAN

Wallowing in this bloody sty,
I cast for fish that pleased my eye
(Truly Jehovah's bow suspends
No pots of gold to weight its ends);
Only the blood-mouthed rainbow trout   5
Rose to my bait. They flopped about
My canvas creel until the moth
Corrupted its unstable cloth.

A calendar to tell the day;
A handkerchief to wave away   10
The gnats; a couch unstuffed with storm
Pouching a bottle in one arm;
A whiskey bottle full of worms;
And bedroom slacks: are these fit terms
To mete the worm whose molten rage   15
Boils in the belly of old age?

Once fishing was a rabbit's foot—
O wind blow cold, O wind blow hot,
Let suns stay in or suns step out:
Life danced a jig on the sperm-whale's spout— 20
The fisher's fluent and obscene
Catches kept his conscience clean.
Children, the raging memory drools
Over the glory of past pools.

Now the hot river, ebbing, hauls   25
Its bloody waters into holes;
A grain of sand inside my shoe
Mimics the moon that might undo
Man and Creation too; remorse,
Stinking, has puddled up its source;   30
Here tantrums thrash to a whale's rage.
This is the pot-hole of old age.

Is there no way to cast my hook
Out of this dynamited brook?
The Fisher's sons must cast about   35

When shallow waters peter out.
I will catch Christ with a greased worm,
And when the Prince of Darkness stalks
My bloodstream to its Stygian term . . .
On water the Man-Fisher walks.   40

HOWARD NEMEROV
(1920–   )

A LIFE

Innocence?
In a sense.
In no sense!

Was that *it?*
Was *that* it?
Was that it?

That was it.

TWO GIRLS

I saw again in a dream the other night
Something I saw in daylight years ago,
A path in the rainy woods, a shaft of light,
And two girls walking together through shadow,
Through dazzle, till I lost them on their way
In gloom embowering beyond the glade.
The bright oblivion that belongs to day
Covered their steps, nothing of them remained,

Until the darkness brought them forth again
To the rainy glitter and the silver light,
The ancient leaves that had not fallen then.
Two girls, going forever out of sight,
Talking of lovers, maybe, and of love:
Not that blind life they'd be the mothers of.

THE FIRST DAY

Below the ten thousand billionth of a centimeter
Length ceases to exist. Beyond three billion light years
The nebulae would have to exceed the speed of light
In order to be, which is impossible: no universe.
The long and short of it seems to be that thought   5
Can make itself unthinkable, and that measurement
Of reach enough and scrupulosity will find its home
In the incommensurable. We shall not, nonetheless,
Admit to our discourse a Final Cause, but only
Groucho Marx, who said, "Closer? Any closer, lady,   10
And I'll be standing behind you." Now we're in the movies,
It may be said that within limits the Creation is
A going concern, imaginable because the film supplies
An image, a thin but absolute membrane whose surfaces
Divide the darkness from the light while at the same time   15
Uniting light and darkness, and whose linear motion,
Divided into frames, or moments, is at the same time
Continuous with itself and may be made to pace itself
Indistinguishably from the pace of time; being also
Able to be repeated, speeded up, slowed down, stopped,   20
And even run backwards, its model represents to us
Memory, concentration, causal sequence, analysis,
Time's irreversibility together with our doubt of this,
And a host of notions that from time long out of mind
Belong to the mind. That was the first day, and in that day   25
Of pure distinction, movies were without color, without sound.
Much later, words began to issue from the silence, and
The single light broke into spectral iridescence;
Meanwhile, in black and white and meddling into gray
Results, the Fall already is recorded on the film.   30
For "nothing in the universe can travel at the speed
Of light," they say, forgetful of the shadow's speed.

THE GREAT SOCIETY, MARK X

The engine and transmission and the wheels
Are made of greed, fear, and invidiousness
Fueled by super-pep high octane money
And lubricated with hypocrisy,
Interior upholstery is all handsewn   5
Of the skins of children of the very poor,
Justice and mercy, charity and peace,
Are optional items at slight extra cost,
The steering gear is newsprint powered by
Expediency but not connected with   10
The wheels, and finally there are no brakes.

However, the rear-view mirror and the horn
Are covered by our lifetime guarantee.

CREATION OF ANGUISH

Whatever sleeping in the world awakes,
We are the ones who to become ourselves
Awaken it, we are the ones who reach
Forever further, where the forest and the sky
And the incessantly restless sea invite   5
The voice that tells them fables of themselves
Till they shall make antiphonal response,
Confirming or else violently denying:
The hurricane's correction, or the fire
At night that scribbles out a city state.   10

Great pain was in the world before we came.
The shriek had learned to answer to the claw
Before we came; the gasp, the sigh, the groan,
Did not need our invention. But all these
Immediacies refused to signify   15
Till in the morning of the mental sun
One moment shuddered under stress and broke
Irreparably into before and after,
Inventing patience, panic, doubt, despair,
And with a single thrust producing thought   20
Beyond the possible, building the vaults
Of debt and the high citadels of guilt,
The segregating walls of obligation,
All that imposing masonry of time
Secretly rooted at the earth's cracked hearth,   25
In the Vishnu schist and the Bright Angel shale,
But up aspiring past the visible sky.
So was the material of pain
First metamorphosed, by the human touch,
Into significance, whence every man   30
And every woman, every child, becomes
Communicant: Shall I get better, or die?
Will they bring the electrodes soon again?
No, tell me what you really think of me.
Hence from nose-picking to the Crucifixion   35
One terrible continuum extends
Binding disaster to discovery.

And so the dog first entered in the door,
Whining and cringing, till we learned from him
Something of sympathy. Before we could,   40
We'd learned to wait as the condemned man waits
For the first light, his darkness, in the east,
And as the hunter waits before his trap,
The theorist before his question, or
The boy before his first time with a girl.   45
We learned, the soldier says, to sweat it out.

GRACE TO BE SAID AT THE SUPERMARKET

That God of ours, the Great Geometer,
Does something for us here, where He hath put
(if you want to put it that way) things in shape,
Compressing the little lambs in orderly cubes,
Making the roast a decent cylinder, 5
Fairing the tin ellipsoid of a ham,
Getting the luncheon meat anonymous
In squares and oblongs with the edges beveled
Or rounded (streamlined, maybe, for greater speed).

Praise Him, He hath conferred aesthetic distance 10
Upon our appetites, and on the bloody
Mess of our birthright, our unseemly need,
Imposed significant form. Through Him the brutes
Enter the pure Euclidean kingdom of number,
Free of their bulging and blood-swollen lives 15
They come to us holy, in cellophane
Transparencies, in the mystical body,

That we may look unflinchingly on death
As the greatest good, like a philosopher should.

LOBSTERS

Here at the Super Duper, in a glass tank
Supplied by a rill of cold fresh water
Running down a glass washboard at one end
And siphoned off at the other, and so
Perpetually renewed, a herd of lobster   5
Is made available to the customer
Who may choose whichever one he wants
To carry home and drop into boiling water
And serve with a sauce of melted butter.

Meanwhile, the beauty of strangeness marks   10
These creatures, who move (when they do)
With a slow, vague wavering of claws,
The somnambulist's effortless clambering
As he crawls over the shell of a dream
Resembling himself. Their velvet colors,   15
Mud red, bruise purple, cadaver green
Speckled with black, their camouflage at home,
Make them conspicuous here in the strong
Day-imitating light, the incommensurable
Philosophers and at the same time victims   20
Herded together in the marketplace, asleep
Except for certain tentative gestures
Of their antennae, or their imperial claws
Pegged shut with a whittled stick at the wrist.
We inlanders, buying our needful food,   25
Pause over these slow, gigantic spiders
That spin not. We pause and are bemused,
And sometimes it happens that a mind sinks down
To the blind abyss in a swirl of sand, goes cold
And archaic in a carapace of horn,   30
Thinking: There's something underneath the world. . . .

The flame beneath the pot that boils the water.

THE FLAME OF A CANDLE

Old fabulous rendering up,
Light on a shoestring, fire out of fat
Consuming oil and cup
Together, what

Miracle! the soul's splatter and flap   5
Aloft, enlightened lamb
That spurting through the beastly trap
Is able to say *I am*
That I am—

Our fathers lived on these   10
Desperate certainties;
Ate manna in the desert, it is said,
And are dead.

THIS, THAT & THE OTHER

a dialogue in disregard

This: I stand and watch for minutes by the pond
       The snowflakes falling on the open water.
       Though I get cold, and though it tells me nothing,
       Or maybe just because it tells me nothing,
       I have to stand and watch the infinite white   5
       Particulate chaos of the falling snow
       Abolished in the black and waiting water.
       An instantaneous thing, time and again
       It happens, quicker than the eye can count:
       The snowflake drifting down erratically,   10
       Reflected for a second, suddenly
       Annihilated; no disturbance to
       The silent mirror spread beneath the sky.

That: I hasten to attend, I take it in.
       I think I see something of what you mean: 15
       It's just as Hermes Trismegistus said
       (Or as the scholars say that Hermes said),
       The things below are as the things above.
       A parable of universal love,
       To see the water taking in the snow   20
       Like that, a something neither quick nor slow,
       Eternal in an instant, as the All
       Unchanged receives the individual.

This: If that's the way you want it, courtesy
       Must say it's yours to make of what you will.   25
       But I was speaking only of the snow
       (They say that no two snowflakes are alike,
       How can they know?) touching the water's face
       So gently that to meet and melt are one.
       There's no more reason in it than in dreams.   30

16. *Hermes Trismegistus:* the putative author of a body of mystical writings, in which the most frequent theme is the symbolic unity of all things.

That: Then I'll interpret you this dream of yours
      And make some sense of it; rather, of course,
      Some mind of it, for sense is what you make,
      And your provision is for me to take.
      First, I observe a pretty polarity   35
      Of black and white, and I ask, could this be
      A legend of the mingling of the races?
      The whites, with cold and isolated faces,
      Falling, a million Lucifers, out of
      Their self-made heaven into the primitive   40
      Beginnings that for centuries they hated,
      In fact into the undifferentiated?
      Political and metaphysical
      At once I read your little parable.

This: Water has many forms and still is water.   45
      The snow, the ice, the steam, the sailing cloud;
      Has many ways, between the raindrop and
      The great sea wave. One of the things it does
      Is mirror, and there's a model for all thought.

That: And more's to come, for mirroring reminds   50
      Me of Narcissus and his Echo, kinds
      One of the other, though unkind to him.
      Poor beauty pausing by the fountain's brim,
      Is he not imaged in the snowflake's last
      Moment of vanity, mirrored in the vast   55
      Abyss and yearning toward the steepdown gulf
      That seems to be, as it destroys, the self?

This: Echo, reflexion, radar of all sorts,
      The beauty of the mind is mediate,
      Its beauty and its sorrow. A poet said,   60
      Or had a political old fool say for him,
      "By indirections find directions out."
      A thought is thinking in my head: maybe
      The mind is not a spider, but a web.

---

51. Echo wasted away from unrequited love for Narcissus, until only the sound of her voice remained. In revenge, the gods made Narcissus fall in love with his reflection in a pool, and while admiring himself he drowned. **60–62.** *A poet . . . out:* Shakespeare gives this line to Polonius in *Hamlet* II.i.63.

That: The physicists are vexed between the wave   65
      And particle—would it not somehow save
      The appearances to think about the snow
      As particles becoming waves below,
      Exchanging not their natures but their shapes?
      And then, what's said of parity, perhaps   70
      That's pictured, and its overthrow as well,
      In this weakest of reactions: if, of all,
      One snowflake fell and somehow failed to drown
      But was deflected to the sky again . . .
      But there I'll stop, being compelled to see   75
      This isn't physics, but theology.

This: Sleeveless speculation, someone said,
      I disremember who, and never knew
      What it could mean. For even if a sleeve
      Could speculate, the arm of action still   80
      Would thrust a grasping hand out at the cuff,
      Bring morsels of this world up to the mouth
      To feed these dreams of immortality
      That end in death and defecation. See,
      The snow has stopped, the sun breaks out of cloud,   85
      A golden light is drifting through the glass.

That: A wind springs up that shatters images.

Both: The Other is deeply meddled in this world.
      We see no more than that the fallen light
      Is wrinkled in and with the wrinkling wave.   90

THE BLUE SWALLOWS

Across the millstream below the bridge
Seven blue swallows divide the air
In shapes invisible and evanescent,
Kaleidoscopic beyond the mind's
Or memory's power to keep them there.   5

"History is where tensions were,"
"Form is the diagram of forces."
Thus, helplessly, there on the bridge,
While gazing down upon those birds—
How strange, to be above the birds!—   10
Thus helplessly the mind in its brain
Weaves up relation's spindrift web,
Seeing the swallows' tails as nibs
Dipped in invisible ink, writing . . .

Poor mind, what would you have them write?
Some cabalistic history   15
Whose authorship you might ascribe
To God? to Nature? Ah, poor ghost,
You've capitalized your Self enough.
That villainous William of Occam   20
Cut out the feet from under that dream
Some seven centuries ago.
It's taken that long for the mind
To waken, yawn and stretch, to see
With opened eyes emptied of speech   25
The real world where the spelling mind
Imposes with its grammar book
Unreal relations on the blue
Swallows. Perhaps when you will have
Fully awakened, I shall show you   30
A new thing: even the water
Flowing away beneath those birds

20. *William of Occam* (or Ockham): a fourteenth-century English theologian.
His metaphysical principle that existence is always individual, that individuals
should not be expanded or subsumed in generalizations or subdivided in
arbitrary parts, is known as "Occam's razor." In effect, this means that we
must deal with each entity in terms of itself.

Will fail to reflect their flying forms,
And the eyes that see become as stones
Whence never tears shall fall again.   35

O swallows, swallows, poems are not
The point. Finding again the world,
That is the point, where loveliness
Adorns intelligible things
Because the mind's eye lit the sun.   40

SYLVIA PLATH
(1932–1963)

WORDS

Axes
After whose stroke the wood rings,
And the echoes!
Echoes travelling
Off from the centre like horses.   5

The sap
Wells like tears, like the
Water striving
To re-establish its mirror
Over the rock   10

That drops and turns,
A white skull,
Eaten by weedy greens.
Years later I
Encounter them on the road——   15

Words dry and riderless,
The indefatigable hoof-taps.
While
From the bottom of the pool, fixed stars
Govern a life.   20

TWO VIEWS OF A CADAVER ROOM

I

The day she visited the dissecting room
They had four men laid out, black as burnt turkey,
Already half unstrung. A vinegary fume
Of the death vats clung to them;
The white-smocked boys started working.   5
The head of his cadaver had caved in,
And she could scarcely make out anything
In that rubble of skull plates and old leather.
A sallow piece of string held it together.

In their jars the snail-nosed babies moon and glow.   10
He hands her the cut-out heart like a cracked heirloom.

II

In Brueghel's panorama of smoke and slaughter
Two people only are blind to the carrion army:
He, afloat in the sea of her blue satin
Skirts, sings in the direction   15
Of her bare shoulder, while she bends,
Fingering a leaflet of music, over him,
Both of them deaf to the fiddle in the hands
Of the death's-head shadowing their song.
These Flemish lovers flourish; not for long.   20

Yet desolation, stalled in paint, spares the little country
Foolish, delicate, in the lower right-hand corner.

---

12. *Brueghel:* Pieter Brueghel (1525?–1569), Flemish painter; the painting described is his *Triumph of Death,* now in the Prado, Madrid.

SOW

God knows how our neighbor managed to breed
His great sow:
Whatever his shrewd secret, he kept it hid

In the same way
He kept the sow—impounded from public stare,   5
Prize ribbon and pig show.

But one dusk our questions commended us to a tour
Through his lantern-lit
Maze of barns to the lintel of the sunk sty door

To gape at it: 10
This was no rose-and-larkspurred china suckling
With a penny slot

For thrifty children, nor dolt pig ripe for heckling,
About to be
Glorified for prime flesh and golden crackling   15

In a parsley halo;
Nor even one of the common barnyard sows,
Mire-smirched, blowzy,

Maunching thistle and knotweed on her snout-cruise—
Bloat tun of milk   20
On the move, hedged by a litter of feat-foot ninnies

Shrilling her hulk
To halt for a swig at the pink teats. No. This vast
Brobdingnag bulk

Of a sow lounged belly-bedded on that black compost,   25
Fat-rutted eyes
Dream-filmed. What a vision of ancient hoghood must

24. *Brobdingnag:* of monstrous size, like the creatures encountered in Book
II of *Gulliver's Travels.*

Thus wholly engross
The great grandam!—our marvel blazoned a knight,
Helmed, in cuirass,   30

Unhorsed and shredded in the grove of combat
By a grisly-bristled
Boar, fabulous enough to straddle that sow's heat.

But our farmer whistled,
Then, with a jocular fist thwacked the barrel nape,   35
And the green-copse-castled

Pig hove, letting legend like dried mud drop,
Slowly, grunt
On grunt, up in the flickering light to shape

A monument   40
Prodigious in gluttonies as that hog whose want
Made lean Lent

Of kitchen slops and, stomaching no constraint,
Proceeded to swill
The seven troughed seas and every earthquaking continent.   45

THE COLOSSUS

I shall never get you put together entirely,
Pieced, glued, and properly jointed.
Mule-bray, pig-grunt and bawdy cackles
Proceed from your great lips.
It's worse than a barnyard.   5

Perhaps you consider yourself an oracle,
Mouthpiece of the dead, or of some god or other.
Thirty years now I have labored
To dredge the silt from your throat.
I am none the wiser.   10

Scaling little ladders with gluepots and pails of lysol
I crawl like an ant in mourning
Over the weedy acres of your brow
To mend the immense skull plates and clear
The bald, white tumuli of your eyes.   15

A blue sky out of the Oresteia
Arches above us. O father, all by yourself
You are pithy and historical as the Roman Forum.
I open my lunch on a hill of black cypress.
Your fluted bones and acanthine hair are littered   20

In their old anarchy to the horizon-line.
It would take more than a lightning-stroke
To create such a ruin.
Nights, I squat in the cornucopia
Of your left ear, out of the wind,   25

Counting the red stars and those of plum-color.
The sun rises under the pillar of your tongue.
My hours are married to shadow.
No longer do I listen for the scrape of a keel
On the blank stones of the landing.   30

16. *Oresteia:* Aeschylus' dramatic trilogy that recounts the death of Agamemnon at the hands of his wife and her lover. His daughter Electra awaits the return of her brother Orestes from exile and joins him in avenging her father.

ALL THE DEAD DEARS

In the Archaeological Museum in Cambridge
is a stone coffin of the fourth century A.D.
containing the skeletons of a woman, a mouse and a
shrew. The ankle-bone of the woman has been slightly gnawn.

Rigged poker-stiff on her back
With a granite grin
This antique museum-cased lady
Lies, companioned by the gimcrack
Relics of a mouse and a shrew   5
That battened for a day on her ankle-bone.

These three, unmasked now, bear
Dry witness
To the gross eating game
We'd wink at if we didn't hear   10
Stars grinding, crumb by crumb,
Our own grist down to its bony face.

How they grip us through thin and thick,
These barnacle dead!
This lady here's no kin   15
Of mine, yet kin she is: she'll suck
Blood and whistle my marrow clean
To prove it. As I think now of her head,

From the mercury-backed glass
Mother, grandmother, greatgrandmother   20
Reach hag hands to haul me in,
And an image looms under the fishpond surface
Where the daft father went down
With orange duck-feet winnowing his hair—

All the long gone darlings: they   25
Get back, though, soon,
Soon: be it by wakes, weddings,
Childbirths or a family barbecue:
Any touch, taste, tang's
Fit for those outlaws to ride home on,   30

And to sanctuary: usurping the armchair
Between tick
And tack of the clock, until we go,
Each skulled-and-crossboned Gulliver
Riddled with ghosts, to lie   35
Deadlocked with them, taking root as cradles rock.

LADY LAZARUS

I have done it again.
One year in every ten
I manage it——

A sort of walking miracle, my skin
Bright as a Nazi lampshade,   5
My right foot

A paperweight,
My face a featureless, fine
Jew linen.

Peel off the napkin   10
O my enemy.
Do I terrify?——

The nose, the eye pits, the full set of teeth?
The sour breath
Will vanish in a day.   15

Soon, soon the flesh
The grave cave ate will be
At home on me

And I a smiling woman.
I am only thirty.   20
And like the cat I have nine times to die.

This is Number Three.
What a trash
To annihilate each decade.

What a million filaments.   25
The peanut-crunching crowd
Shoves in to see

Them unwrap me hand and foot——
The big strip tease.
Gentlemen, ladies   30

These are my hands
My knees.
I may be skin and bone,

Nevertheless, I am the same, identical woman.
The first time it happened I was ten.   35
It was an accident.

The second time I meant
To last it out and not come back at all.
I rocked shut

As a seashell.   40
They had to call and call
And pick the worms off me like sticky pearls.

Dying
Is an art, like everything else.
I do it exceptionally well.   45

I do it so it feels like hell.
I do it so it feels real.
I guess you could say I've a call.

It's easy enough to do it in a cell.
It's easy enough to do it and stay put.   50
It's the theatrical

Comeback in broad day
To the same place, the same face, the same brute
Amused shout:

'A miracle!'   55
That knocks me out.
There is a charge

For the eyeing of my scars, there is a charge
For the hearing of my heart——
It really goes.   60

And there is a charge, a very large charge
For a word or a touch
Or a bit of blood

Or a piece of my hair or my clothes.
So, so, Herr Doktor.
So, Herr Enemy.

I am your opus,
I am your valuable,
The pure gold baby

That melts to a shriek.
I turn and burn.
Do not think I underestimate your great concern.

Ash, ash—
You poke and stir.
Flesh, bone, there is nothing there——

A cake of soap,
A wedding ring,
A gold filling.

Herr God, Herr Lucifer
Beware
Beware.

Out of the ash
I rise with my red hair
And I eat men like air.

DADDY

You do not do, you do not do
Any more, black shoe
In which I have lived like a foot
For thirty years, poor and white,
Barely daring to breathe or Achoo.   5

Daddy, I have had to kill you.
You died before I had time——
Marble-heavy, a bag full of God,
Ghastly statue with one grey toe
Big as a Frisco seal   10

And a head in the freakish Atlantic
Where it pours bean green over blue
In the waters off beautiful Nauset.
I used to pray to recover you.
Ach, du.   15

In the German tongue, in the Polish town
Scraped flat by the roller
Of wars, wars, wars.
But the name of the town is common.
My Polack friend   20

Says there are a dozen or two.
So I never could tell where you
Put your foot, your root,
I never could talk to you.
The tongue stuck in my jaw.   25

It stuck in a barb wire snare.
Ich, ich, ich, ich,
I could hardly speak.
I thought every German was you.
And the language obscene   30

An engine, an engine
Chuffing me off like a Jew.
A Jew to Dachau, Auschwitz, Belsen.
I began to talk like a Jew.
I think I may well be a Jew.   35

The snows of the Tyrol, the clear beer of Vienna
Are not very pure or true.
With my gypsy ancestress and my weird luck
And my Taroc pack and my Taroc pack
I may be a bit of a Jew.   40

I have always been scared of *you*,
With your Luftwaffe, your gobbledygoo.
And your neat moustache
And your Aryan eye, bright blue.
Panzer-man, panzer-man, O You——   45

Not God but a swastika
So black no sky could squeak through.
Every woman adores a Fascist,
The boot in the face, the brute
Brute heart of a brute like you.   50

You stand at the blackboard, daddy,
In the picture I have of you,
A cleft in your chin instead of your foot
But no less a devil for that, no not
Any less the black man who   55

Bit my pretty red heart in two.
I was ten when they buried you.
At twenty I tried to die
And get back, back, back to you.
I thought even the bones would do.   60

But they pulled me out of the sack,
And they stuck me together with glue.
And then I knew what to do.
I made a model of you,
A man in black with a Meinkampf look   65

And a love of the rack and the screw.
And I said I do, I do.
So daddy, I'm finally through.
The black telephone's off at the root,
The voices just can't worm through.   70

If I've killed one man, I've killed two——
The vampire who said he was you
And drank my blood for a year,
Seven years, if you want to know.
Daddy, you can lie back now.   75

There's a stake in your fat black heart
And the villagers never liked you.
They are dancing and stamping on you.
They always *knew* it was you.
Daddy, daddy, you bastard, I'm through.   80

FEVER 103°

Pure? What does it mean?
The tongues of hell
Are dull, dull as the triple

Tongues of dull, fat Cerberus
Who wheezes at the gate. Incapable   5
Of licking clean

The aguey tendon, the sin, the sin.
The tinder cries.
The indelible smell

Of a snuffed candle!   10
Love, love, the low smokes roll
From me like Isadora's scarves, I'm in a fright

One scarf will catch and anchor in the wheel.
Such yellow sullen smokes
Make their own element. They will not rise,   15

But trundle round the globe
Choking the aged and the meek,
The weak

Hothouse baby in its crib,
The ghastly orchid   20
Hanging its hanging garden in the air,

Devilish leopard!
Radiation turned it white
And killed it in an hour.

Greasing the bodies of adulterers   25
Like Hiroshima ash and eating in.
The sin. The sin.

Darling, all night
I have been flickering, off, on, off, on.
The sheets grow heavy as a lecher's kiss.   30

Three days. Three nights.
Lemon water, chicken
Water, water make me retch.

I am too pure for you or anyone.
Your body   35
Hurts me as the world hurts God. I am a lantern——

My head a moon
Of Japanese paper, my gold beaten skin
Infinitely delicate and infinitely expensive.

Does not my heat astound you. And my light.   40
All by myself I am a huge camellia
Glowing and coming and going, flush on flush.

I think I am going up,
I think I may rise——
The beads of hot metal fly, and I, love, I   45

Am a pure acetylene
Virgin
Attended by roses,

By kisses, by cherubim,
By whatever these pink things mean.   50
Not you, nor him

Not him, nor him
(My selves dissolving, old whore petticoats)——
To Paradise.

ARIEL

Stasis in darkness.
Then the substanceless blue
Pour of tor and distances.

God's lioness,
How one we grow,
Pivot of heels and knees!—The furrow   5

Splits and passes, sister to
The brown arc
Of the neck I cannot catch,

Nigger-eye
Berries cast dark   10
Hooks——

Black sweet blood mouthfuls,
Shadows.
Something else   15

Hauls me through air——
Thighs, hair;
Flakes from my heels.

White
Godiva, I unpeel——   20
Dead hands, dead stringencies.

And now I
Foam to wheat, a glitter of seas.
The child's cry

Melts in the wall.   25
And I
Am the arrow,

The dew that flies
Suicidal, at one with the drive
Into the red   30

Eye, the cauldron of morning.

3. *tor:* the peak of a bare or rocky mountain.

WELDON KEES
(1914–   )

WHITE COLLAR BALLAD

There are lots of places to go:
Guaranteed headaches at every club,
Plush-and-golden cinemas that always show
How cunningly the heroine and hero rub.
Put on your hat, put on your gloves.   5
But there isn't any love, there isn't any love.

There are endless things we could do:
Walk around the block, watch the skaters whirl,
Promenade the park or see the newest zoo,
Plan for the future in a sensible world.   10
The water boils on the stove,
But there isn't any love, there isn't any love.

Our best friends lived in the house next door.
Went around to call on them the other day,
But they hadn't left an address or a word before   15
They packed their bags and moved away.
We could call on the people on the floor above,
But there wouldn't be any love, there wouldn't be any love.

It didn't use to be like this at all.
You wanted lots of money and I got it somehow.   20
Once it was Summer. Here it's almost Fall.
It isn't any season now.
There are seasons in the future to be thinking of,
But there won't be any love, there won't be any love.

THE PATIENT IS RALLYING

Difficult to recall an emotion that is dead,
Particularly so among these unbelieved fanfares
And admonitions from a camouflaged sky.

I should have remained burdened with destinations
Perhaps, or stayed quite drunk, or obeyed
The undertaker, who was fairly charming, after all.

Or was there a room like that one, worn
With our whispers, and a great tree blossoming
Outside blue windows, warm rain blowing in the night?

There seems to be some doubt. No doubt, however,
Of the chilled and empty tissues of the mind
—Cold, cold, a great gray winter entering—
Like spines of air, frozen in an ice cube.

CRIME CLUB

No butler, no second maid, no blood upon the stair.
No eccentric aunt, no gardener, no family friend
Smiling among the bric-a-brac and murder.
Only a suburban house with the front door open
And a dog barking at a squirrel, and the cars
Passing. The corpse quite dead. The wife in Florida.

Consider the clues: the potato masher in a vase,
The torn photograph of a Wesleyan basketball team,
Scattered with check stubs in the hall;
The unsent fan letter to Shirley Temple,
The Hoover button on the lapel of the deceased,
The note: "To be killed this way is quite all right with me."

Small wonder that the case remains unsolved,
Or that the sleuth, Le Roux, is now incurably insane,
And sits alone in a white room in a white gown,
Screaming that all the world is mad, that clues
Lead nowhere, or to walls so high their tops cannot be seen;
Screaming all day of war, screaming that nothing can be solved.

ASPECTS OF ROBINSON

Robinson at cards at the Algonquin; a thin
Blue light comes down once more outside the blinds.
Gray men in overcoats are ghosts blown past the door.
The taxis streak the avenues with yellow, orange, and red.
This is Grand Central, Mr. Robinson.   5

Robinson on a roof above the Heights; the boats
Mourn like the lost. Water is slate, far down.
Through sounds of ice cubes dropped in glass, an osteopath,
Dressed for the links, describes an old Intourist tour.
—Here's where old Gibbons jumped from, Robinson.   10

Robinson walking in the Park, admiring the elephant.
Robinson buying the *Tribune*, Robinson buying the *Times*.
    Robinson
Saying, "Hello. Yes, this is Robinson. Sunday
At five? I'd love to. Pretty well. And you?"
Robinson alone at Longchamps, staring at the wall.   15

Robinson afraid, drunk, sobbing Robinson
In bed with a Mrs. Morse. Robinson at home;
Decisions: Toynbee or luminol? Where the sun
Shines, Robinson in flowered trunks, eyes toward
The breakers. Where the night ends, Robinson in East Side bars.   20

Robinson in Glen plaid jacket, Scotch-grain shoes,
Black four-in-hand and oxford button-down,
The jeweled and silent watch that winds itself, the brief-
Case, covert topcoat, clothes for spring, all covering
His sad and usual heart, dry as a winter leaf.   25

ROBINSON

The dog stops barking after Robinson has gone.
His act is over. The world is a gray world,
Not without violence, and he kicks under the grand piano,
The nightmare chase well under way.

The mirror from Mexico, stuck to the wall, 5
Reflects nothing at all. The glass is black.
Robinson alone provides the image Robinsonian.

Which is all of the room—walls, curtains,
Shelves, bed, the tinted photograph of Robinson's first wife,
Rugs, vases, panatellas in a humidor. 10
They would fill the room if Robinson came in.

The pages in the books are blank
The books that Robinson has read. That is his favorite chair,
Or where the chair would be if Robinson were here.

All day the phone rings. It could be Robinson 15
Calling. It never rings when he is here.

Outside, white buildings yellow in the sun.
Outside, the birds circle continuously
Where trees are actual and take no holiday.

ROBINSON AT HOME

Curtains drawn back, the door ajar.
All winter long, it seemed, a darkening
Began. But now the moonlight and the odors of the street
Conspire and combine toward one community.

These are the rooms of Robinson.   5
Bleached, wan, and colorless this light, as though
All the blurred daybreaks of the spring
Found an asylum here, perhaps for Robinson alone,

Who sleeps. Were there more music sifted through the floors
And moonlight of a different kind,   10
He might awake to hear the news at ten,
Which will be shocking, moderately.

This sleep is from exhaustion, but his old desire
To die like this has known a lessening.
Now there is only this coldness that he has to wear.   15
But not in sleep.—Observant scholar, traveller,

Or uncouth bearded figure squatting in a cave,
A keen-eyed sniper on the barricades,
A heretic in catacombs, a famed roué,
A beggar on the streets, the confidant of Popes—   20

All these are Robinson in sleep, who mumbles as he turns,
"There is something in this madhouse that I symbolize—
This city—nightmare—black—"
                                            He wakes in sweat
To the terrible moonlight and what might be   25
Silence. It drones like wires far beyond the roofs,
And the long curtains blow into the room.

RELATING TO ROBINSON

Somewhere in Chelsea, early summer;
And, walking in the twilight toward the docks,
I thought I made out Robinson ahead of me.

From an uncurtained second-story room, a radio
Was playing *There's a Small Hotel;* a kite   5
Twisted above dark rooftops and slow drifting birds.
We were alone there, he and I,
Inhabiting the empty street.

Under a sign for Natural Bloom Cigars,
While lights clicked softly in the dusk from red to green,   10
He stopped and gazed into a window
Where a plaster Venus, modeling a truss,
Looked out at Eastbound traffic. (But Robinson,
I knew, was out of town: he summers at a place in Maine,
Sometimes on Fire Island, sometimes the Cape,   15
Leaves town in June and comes back after Labor Day.)
And yet, I almost called out, "Robinson!"

There was no chance. Just as I passed,
Turning my head to search his face,
His own head turned with mine   20
And fixed me with dilated, terrifying eyes
That stopped my blood. His voice
Came at me like an echo in the dark.

"I thought I saw the whirlpool opening.
Kicked all night at a bolted door.   25
You must have followed me from Astor Place.
An empty paper floats down at the last.
And then a day as huge as yesterday in pairs
Unrolled its horror on my face
Until it blocked—" Running in sweat   30
To reach the docks, I turned back
For a second glance. I had no certainty,
There in the dark, that it was Robinson
Or someone else.
                                    The block was bare. The Venus,   35
Bathed in blue fluorescent light,
Stared toward the river. As I hurried West,
The lights across the bay were coming on.
The boats moved silently and the low whistles blew.

SARATOGA ENDING

I

Iron, sulphur, steam: the wastes
Of all resorts like this have left their traces.
Old canes and crutches line the walls. Light
Floods the room, stripped from the pool, broken
And shimmering like scales. Hidden   5
By curtains, women dry themselves
Before the fire and review
The service at hotels,
The ways of dying, ways of sleep,
The blind ataxia patient from New York,   10
And all the others who were here a year ago.

II

Visconti, mad with pain. Each day,
Two hundred drops of laudanum. Hagen, who writhes
With every step. The Count, a shrunken penis
And a monocle, dreaming of horses in the sun,   15
Covered with flies.—Last night I woke in sweat
To see my hands, white, curled upon the sheet
Like withered leaves. I thought of days
So many years ago, hauling driftwood up from the shore,
Waking at noon, the harbor birds following   20
Boats from the mainland. And then no thoughts at all.
Morphine at five. A cold dawn breaking. Rain.

III

I lie here in the dark, trying to remember
What my life has taught me. The driveway lights blur
In the rain. A rubber-tired metal cart goes by,   25
Followed by a nurse; and something rattles
Like glasses being removed after
A party is over and the guests have gone.
Test tubes, beakers, graduates, thermometers—
Companions of these years that I no longer count.   30
I reach for a cigarette and my fingers
Touch a tongue depressor that I use
As a bookmark; and all I know
Is the touch of this wood in the darkness, remembering

The warmth of one bright summer half a life ago—
A blue sky and a blinding sun, the face
Of one long dead who, high above the shore,
Looked down on waves across the sand, on rows of yellow jars
In which the lemon trees were ripening.

WILLIAM STAFFORD
(1914–   )

TORNADO

First the soul of our house left, up the chimney,
and part of the front window went outward—pursued
whatever tore at the chest. Part of the lake
on top guyed around the point, bellied
like a tent; and fish like seeds ripened felt   5
a noiseless Command around their gills, while
the wheatfields crouched, reminded with a hand.

That treble talk always at the bottom of the creek
at the mouth, where the lake leaned away from the rock
at the mouth, rose above water. Then Command moved   10
away again and our town spread, ruined
but relieved, at the bottom of its remembered air.
We weren't left religion exactly (the church
was ecumenical bricks), but a certain tall element:
a pulse beat still in the stilled rock   15
and in the buried sound along the buried mouth of the creek.

AUNT MABEL

This town is haunted by some good deed
that reappears like a country cousin, or truth
when language falters these days trying to lie,
because Aunt Mabel, an old lady gone now, would
accost even strangers to give bright flowers   5
away, quick as a striking snake. It's deeds like this
have weakened me, shaken by intermittent trust,
stricken with friendliness.

Our Senator talked like war, and Aunt Mabel
said, "He's a brilliant man,
but we didn't elect him that much."   10

Everyone's resolve weakens toward evening
or in a flash when a face melds—a stranger's, even—
reminded for an instant between menace and fear:
There are Aunt Mabels all over the world,
    or their graves in the rain.   15

AT THE CHAIRMAN'S HOUSEWARMING

Talk like a jellyfish can ruin a party.
It did: I smiled whatever they said,
all the time wanting to assert myself
by announcing to all, "I eat whole wheat bread."

The jelly talk stole out on the cloth   5
and coated the silver tine by tine,
folding meek spoons and the true knifeblades
and rolling a tentacle into the wine.

And my talk too—it poured on the table
and coiled and died in the sugar bowl,   10
twitching a last thin participle
to flutter the candle over its soul.

Nothing escaped the jellyfish,
that terror from seas where whales can't live
(he could kill sharks by grabbing their tails   15
and neither refusing nor consenting to give).

Oh go home, you terrible fish;
let sea be sea and rock be rock.
Go back wishy-washy to your sheltered bay,
but let me live definite, shock by shock.   20

THE SUMMONS IN INDIANA

In the crept hours of our street
(repaired by snow that winter night)
from the west an angel of blown newspaper
was coming toward our house out of the dark.

Under all the far streetlights   5
and along all the near housefronts
silence was painting what it was given
that in that instant I was to know.

Starting up, mittened by sleep, I thought
of the sweeping stars and the wide night,   10
remembering as well as I could the hedges
back home that minister to comprehended fields—

And other such limits to hold the time near,
for I felt among strangers on a meteor
trying to learn their kind of numbers   15
to scream together in a new kind of algebra.

That night the angel went by in the dark,
but left a summons: Try farther west.
And it did no good to try to read it again:
there are things you cannot learn through manyness.   20

WRITTEN ON THE STUB OF THE FIRST PAYCHECK

Gasoline makes game scarce.
In Elko, Nevada, I remember a stuffed wildcat
someone had shot on Bing Crosby's ranch.
I stood in the filling station
breathing fumes and reading the snarl of a map.   5

There were peaks to the left so high
they almost got away in the heat;
Reno and Las Vegas were ahead.
I had promise of the California job,
and three kids with me.   10

It takes a lot of miles to equal one wildcat
today. We moved into a housing tract.
Every dodging animal carries my hope in Nevada.
It has been a long day, Bing.
Wherever I go is your ranch.   15

RICHARD WILBUR
(1921–   )

THE DEATH OF A TOAD

A toad the power mower caught,
Chewed and clipped of a leg, with a hobbling hop has got
  To the garden verge, and sanctuaried him
  Under the cineraria leaves, in the shade
    Of the ashen heartshaped leaves, in a dim,   5
      Low, and a final glade.

The rare original heartsblood goes,
Spends on the earthen hide, in the folds and wizenings, flows
  In the gutters of the banked and staring eyes. He lies
  As still as if he would return to stone,   10
    And soundlessly attending, dies
      Toward some deep monotone,

Toward misted and ebullient seas
And cooling shores, toward lost Amphibia's emperies.
  Day dwindles, drowning, and at length is gone   15
  In the wide and antique eyes, which still appear
    To watch, across the castrate lawn,
      The haggard daylight steer.

4. *cineraria:* a plant with ash-colored leaves. Cf. cinerarium, a place for depositing the ashes of the dead.   **14.** *emperies:* absolute dominions.

STILL, CITIZEN SPARROW

Still, citizen sparrow, this vulture which you call
Unnatural, let him but lumber again to air
Over the rotten office, let him bear
The carrion ballast up, and at the tall

Tip of the sky lie cruising. Then you'll see   5
That no more beautiful bird is in heaven's height,
No wider more placid wings, no watchfuller flight;
He shoulders nature there, the frightfully free,

The naked-headed one. Pardon him, you
Who dart in the orchard aisles, for it is he   10
Devours death, mocks mutability,
Has heart to make an end, keeps nature new.

Thinking of Noah, childheart, try to forget
How for so many bedlam hours his saw
Soured the song of birds with its wheezy gnaw,   15
And the slam of his hammer all the day beset

The people's ears. Forget that he could bear
To see the towns like coral under the keel,
And the fields so dismal deep. Try rather to feel
How high and weary it was, on the waters where   20

He rocked his only world, and everyone's.
Forgive the hero, you who would have died
Gladly with all you knew; he rode that tide
To Ararat; all men are Noah's sons.

---

24. *Ararat:* the mountaintop where Noah's ark came to rest after the Flood.

LOVE CALLS US TO THE THINGS OF THIS WORLD

The eyes open to a cry of pulleys,
And spirited from sleep, the astounded soul
Hangs for a moment bodiless and simple
As false dawn.
               Outside the open window   5
The morning air is all awash with angels.

Some are in bed-sheets, some are in blouses,
Some are in smocks: but truly there they are.
Now they are rising together in calm swells
Of halcyon feeling, filling whatever they wear   10
With the deep joy of their impersonal breathing;

Now they are flying in place, conveying
The terrible speed of their omnipresence, moving
And staying like white water; and now of a sudden
They swoon down into so rapt a quiet   15
That nobody seems to be there.
                   The soul shrinks

From all that is about to remember,
From the punctual rape of every blessèd day,
And cries,   20
    "Oh, let there be nothing on earth but laundry,
Nothing but rosy hands in the rising steam
And clear dances done in the sight of heaven."

Yes, as the sun acknowledges
With a warm look the world's hunks and colours,   25
The soul descends once more in bitter love
To accept the waking body, saying now
In a changed voice as the man yawns and rises,

"Bring them down from their ruddy gallows;
Let there be clean linen for the backs of thieves; 30
Let lovers go fresh and sweet to be undone,
And the heaviest nuns walk in a pure floating
Of dark habits,
              keeping their difficult balance."

10. *halcyon:* a bird whose nest built on the sea during the winter solstice
was said to calm the waves.

SHE

What was her beauty in our first estate
When Adam's will was whole, and the least thing
Appeared the gift and creature of his king,
How should we guess? Resemblance had to wait

For separation, and in such a place   5
She so partook of water, light, and trees
As not to look like any one of these.
He woke and gazed into her naked face.

But then she changed, and coming down amid
The flocks of Abel and the fields of Cain,   10
Clothed in their wish, her Eden graces hid,
A shape of plenty with a mop of grain,

She broke upon the world, in time took on
The look of every labor and its fruits.
Columnar in a robe of pleated lawn   15
She cupped her patient hand for attributes,

Was radiant captive of the farthest tower
And shed her honor on the fields of war,
Walked in her garden at the evening hour,
Her shadow like a dark ogival door,   20

Breasted the seas for all the westward ships
And, come to virgin country, changed again—
A moonlike being truest in eclipse,
And subject goddess of the dreams of men.

Tree, temple, valley, prow, gazelle, machine,   25
More named and nameless than the morning star,
Lovely in every shape, in all unseen,
We dare not wish to find you as you are,

Whose apparition, biding time until
Desire decay and bring the latter age,   30
Shall flourish in the ruins of our will
And deck the broken stones like saxifrage.

20. *ogival:* formed like an ogive, a flame-shaped arch common in Gothic
architecture. The same configuration often occurs in Gothic representations
of women.   **32.** *saxifrage:* literally, "broken stone"; a dwarf herb with tufted
foliage which grows in the clefts of rocks.

ALLEN GINSBERG
(1926–   )

From "HOWL"

for carl solomon

I

I saw the best minds of my generation destroyed by madness,
 starving hysterical naked,
dragging themselves through the negro streets at dawn looking
 for an angry fix,
angelheaded hipsters burning for the ancient heavenly   5
 connection to the starry dynamo in the machinery of
 night,
who poverty and tatters and hollow-eyed and high sat up
 smoking in the supernatural darkness of cold-water flats
 floating across the tops of cities contemplating jazz,
who bared their brains to Heaven under the El and saw   10
 Mohammedan angels staggering on tenement roofs
 illuminated,
who passed through universities with radiant cool eyes
 hallucinating Arkansas and Blake-light tragedy among
 the scholars of war,
who were expelled from the academies for crazy & publishing   15
 obscene odes on the windows of the skull,
who cowered in unshaven rooms in underwear, burning their
 money in wastebaskets and listening to the Terror through
 the wall,
who got busted in their pubic beards returning through
 Laredo with a belt of marijuana for New York,   20
who ate fire in paint hotels or drank turpentine in Paradise
 Alley, death, or purgatoried their torsos night after night
with dreams, with drugs, with waking nightmares, alcohol and
 cock and endless balls,
incomparable blind streets of shuddering cloud and lightning   25
 in the mind leaping toward poles of Canada & Paterson,
 illuminating all the motionless world of Time between,
Peyote solidities of halls, backyard green tree cemetery dawns,
 wine drunkenness over the rooftops, storefront boroughs
 of teahead joyride neon blinking traffic light, sun and   30

moon and tree vibrations in the roaring winter dusks of
   Brooklyn, ashcan rantings and kind king light of mind,
who chained themselves to subways for the endless ride from
   Battery to holy Bronx on benzedrine until the noise of
   wheels and children brought them down shuddering   35
   mouth-wracked and battered bleak of brain all drained
   of brilliance in the drear light of Zoo,
who sank all night in submarine light of Bickford's floated out
   and sat through the stale beer afternoon in desolate
   Fugazzi's, listening to the crack of doom on the hydrogen
   jukebox,   40
who talked continuously seventy hours from park to pad to bar
   to Bellevue to museum to the Brooklyn Bridge,
a lost battalion of platonic conversationalists jumping down the
   stoops off fire escapes off windowsills off Empire State out
   of the moon,   45
yacketayakking screaming vomiting whispering facts and
   memories and anecdotes and eyeball kicks and shocks of
   hospitals and jails and wars,
whole intellects disgorged in total recall for seven days and
   nights with brilliant eyes, meat for the Synagogue cast   50
   on the pavement,
who vanished into nowhere Zen New Jersey leaving a trail of
   ambiguous picture postcards of Atlantic City Hall,
suffering Eastern sweats and Tangerian bone-grindings and
   migraines of China under junk-withdrawal in Newark's   55
   bleak furnished room,
who wandered around and around at midnight in the railroad
   yard wondering where to go, and went, leaving no broken
   hearts,
who lit cigarettes in boxcars boxcars boxcars racketing through
   snow toward lonesome farms in grandfather night,   60
who studied Plotinus Poe St. John of the Cross telepathy and
   bop kaballa because the cosmos instinctively vibrated at
   their feet in Kansas,
who loned it through the streets of Idaho seeking visionary
   indian angels who were visionary indian angels,   65
who thought they were only mad when Baltimore gleamed in
   supernatural ecstasy,
who jumped in limousines with the Chinaman of Oklahoma on
   the impulse of winter midnight streetlight smalltown rain,
who lounged hungry and lonesome through Houston seeking   70
   jazz or sex or soup, and followed the brilliant Spaniard to

converse about America and Eternity, a hopeless task, and
     so took ship to Africa,

who disappeared into the volcanoes of Mexico leaving behind
     nothing but the shadow of dungarees and the lava and ash
     of poetry scattered in fireplace Chicago,

who reappeared on the West Coast investigating the F.B.I. in
     beards and shorts with big pacifist eyes sexy in their dark
     skin passing out incomprehensible leaflets,

who burned cigarette holes in their arms protesting the narcotic
     tobacco haze of Capitalism,

who distributed Supercommunist pamphlets in Union Square
     weeping and undressing while the sirens of Los Alamos
     wailed them down, and wailed down Wall, and the Staten
     Island Ferry also wailed,

who broke down crying in white gymnasiums naked and
     trembling before the machinery of other skeletons,

who bit detectives in the neck and shrieked with delight in
     policecars for committing no crime but their own wild
     cooking pederasty and intoxication,

who howled on their knees in the subway and were dragged
     off the roof waving genitals and manuscripts,

who let themselves be fucked in the ass by saintly
     motorcyclists, and screamed with joy,

who blew and were blown by those human seraphim, the
     sailors, caresses of Atlantic and Caribbean love,

who balled in the morning in the evenings in rosegardens
     and the grass of public parks and cemeteries scattering
     their semen freely to whomever come who may,

who hiccupped endlessly trying to giggle but wound up with
     a sob behind a partition in a Turkish Bath when the blonde
     & naked angel came to pierce them with a sword,

who lost their loveboys to the three old shrews of fate the one
     eyed shrew of the heterosexual dollar the one eyed shrew
     that winks out of the womb and the one eyed shrew that
     does nothing but sit on her ass and snip the intellectual
     golden threads of the craftsman's loom,

who copulated ecstatic and insatiate with a bottle of beer a
     sweetheart a package of cigarettes a candle and fell off
     the bed, and continued along the floor and down the hall
     and ended fainting on the wall with a vision of ultimate
     cunt and come eluding the last gyzym of consciousness,

who sweetened the snatches of a million girls trembling in the
     sunset, and were red eyed in the morning but prepared to

sweeten the snatch of the sunrise, flashing buttocks under   115
    barns and naked in the lake,
who went out whoring through Colorado in myriad stolen
    night-cars, N.C., secret hero of these poems, cocksman and
    Adonis of Denver—joy to the memory of his innumerable
    lays of girls in empty lots & diner backyards, moviehouses'   120
    rickety rows, on mountaintops in caves or with gaunt
    waitresses in familiar roadside lonely petticoat upliftings
    & especially secret gas-station solipsisms of johns, &
    hometown alleys too,
who faded out in vast sordid movies, were shifted in dreams,   125
    woke on a sudden Manhattan, and picked themselves up
    out of basements hungover with heartless Tokay and
    horrors of Third Avenue iron dreams & stumbled to
    unemployment offices,
who walked all night with their shoes full of blood on the   130
    snowbank docks waiting for a door in the East River to
    open to a room full of steamheat and opium,
who created great suicidal dramas on the apartment cliff-banks
    of the Hudson under the wartime blue floodlight of the
    moon & their heads shall be crowned with laurel in   135
    oblivion,
who ate the lamb stew of the imagination or digested the crab
    at the muddy bottom of the rivers of Bowery,
who wept at the romance of the streets with their pushcarts
    full of onions and bad music,   140
who sat in boxes breathing in the darkness under the bridge,
    and rose up to build harpsichords in their lofts,
who coughed on the sixth floor of Harlem crowned with flame
    under the tubercular sky surrounded by orange crates of
    theology,   145
who scribbled all night rocking and rolling over lofty
    incantations which in the yellow morning were stanzas
    of gibberish,
who cooked rotten animals lung heart feet tail borsht &
    tortillas dreaming of the pure vegetable kingdom,   150
who plunged themselves under meat trucks looking for an egg,
who threw their watches off the roof to cast their ballots for
    Eternity outside of Time, & alarm clocks fell on their heads
    every day for the next decade,
who cut their wrists three times successively unsuccessfully,   155
    gave up and were forced to open antique stores where
    they thought they were growing old and cried,

who were burned alive in their innocent flannel suits on
    Madison Avenue amid blasts of leaden verse & the tanked-
    up clatter of the iron regiments of fashion & the   160
    nitroglycerine shrieks of the fairies of advertising & the
    mustard gas of sinister intelligent editors, or were run
    down by the drunken taxicabs of Absolute Reality,
who jumped off the Brooklyn Bridge this actually happened
    and walked away unknown and forgotten into the   165
    ghostly daze of Chinatown soup alleyways & firetrucks,
    not even one free beer,
who sang out of their windows in despair, fell out of the
    subway window, jumped in the filthy Passaic, leaped on
    negroes, cried all over the street, danced on broken   170
    wineglasses barefoot smashed phonograph records of
    nostalgic European 1930's German jazz finished the
    whiskey and threw up groaning into the bloody toilet,
    moans in their ears and the blast of colossal steamwhistles,
who barreled down the highways of the past journeying to   175
    each other's hotrod-Golgotha jail-solitude watch or
    Birmingham jazz incarnation,
who drove crosscountry seventytwo hours to find out if I had
    a vision or you had a vision or he had a vision to find out
    Eternity,   180
who journeyed to Denver, who died in Denver, who came
    back to Denver & waited in vain, who watched over
    Denver & brooded & loned in Denver and finally went
    away to find out the Time, & now Denver is lonesome
    for her heroes,   185
who fell on their knees in hopeless cathedrals praying for each
    other's salvation and light and breasts, until the soul
    illuminated its hair for a second,
who crashed through their minds in jail waiting for impossible
    criminals with golden heads and the charm of reality in   190
    their hearts who sang sweet blues to Alcatraz,
who retired to Mexico to cultivate a habit, or Rocky Mount
    to tender Buddha or Tangiers to boys or Southern Pacific
    to the black locomotive or Harvard to Narcissus to
    Woodlawn to the daisychain or grave,   195
who demanded sanity trials accusing the radio of hypnotism &
    were left with their insanity & their hands & a hung jury,
who threw potato salad at CCNY lecturers on Dadaism and
    subsequently presented themselves on the granite steps of

the madhouse with shaven heads and harlequin speech of   200
    suicide, demanding instantaneous lobotomy,
and who were given instead the concrete void of insulin
    metrasol electricity hydrotherapy psychotherapy
    occupational therapy pingpong & amnesia,
who in humorless protest overturned only one symbolic   205
    pingpong table, resting briefly in catatonia,
returning years later truly bald except for a wig of blood, and
    tears and fingers, to the visible madman doom of the wards
    of the madtowns of the East,
Pilgrim State's Rockland's and Greystone's foetid halls,   210
    bickering with the echoes of the soul, rocking and rolling
    in the midnight solitude-bench dolmen-realms of love,
    dream of life a nightmare, bodies turned to stone as
    heavy as the moon,
with mother finally ******, and the last fantastic book flung   215
    out of the tenement window, and the last door closed at
    4 AM and the last telephone slammed at the wall in reply
    and the last furnished room emptied down to the last piece
    of mental furniture, a yellow paper rose twisted on a wire
    hanger in the closet, and even that imaginary, nothing but   220
    a hopeful little bit of hallucination—
ah, Carl, while you are not safe I am not safe, and now you're
    really in the total animal soup of time—
and who therefore ran through the icy streets obsessed with
    a sudden flash of the alchemy of the use of the ellipse the   225
    catalog the meter & the vibrating plane,
who dreamt and made incarnate gaps in Time & Space through
    images juxtaposed, and trapped the archangel of the soul
    between 2 visual images and joined the elemental verbs
    and set the noun and dash of consciousness together   230
    jumping with sensation of Pater Omnipotens Aeterna
    Deus
to recreate the syntax and measure of poor human prose and
    stand before you speechless and intelligent and shaking
    with shame, rejected yet confessing out the soul to   235
    conform to the rhythm of thought in his naked and
    endless head,

231–232. *Pater . . . Deus:* "Almighty Father, everlasting God."

the madman bum and angel beat in Time, unknown, yet
    putting down here what might be left to say in time come
    after death,   240
and rose reincarnate in the ghostly clothes of jazz in the
    goldhorn shadow of the band and blew the suffering of
    America's naked mind for love into an eli eli lamma lamma
    sabacthani saxophone cry that shivered the cities down to
    the last radio   245
with the absolute heart of the poem of life butchered out of
    their own bodies good to eat a thousand years.

243–244. *eli . . . sabacthani:* "My God, My God, why hast thou forsaken me?" Jesus' words from the cross (Matthew 27:46).

DENISE LEVERTOV
(1923–   )

SONG FOR ISHTAR

The moon is a sow
and grunts in my throat
Her great shining shines through me
so the mud of my hollow gleams
and breaks in silver bubbles   5

She is a sow
and I a pig and a poet

When she opens her white
lips to devour me I bite back
and laughter rocks the moon   10

In the black of desire
we rock and grunt, grunt and
shine

LOSING TRACK

Long after you have swung back
away from me
I think you are still with me:

you come in close to the shore
on the tide
and nudge me awake the way

a boat adrift nudges the pier:
am I a pier
half-in half-out of the water?

and in the pleasure of that communion
I lose track,
the moon I watch goes down, the

tide swings you away before
I know I'm
alone again long since,

mud sucking at gray and black
timbers of me,
a light growth of green dreams drying.

COME INTO ANIMAL PRESENCE

Come into animal presence.
No man is so guileless as
the serpent. The lonely white
rabbit on the roof is a star
twitching its ears at the rain.   5
The llama intricately
folding its hind legs to be seated
not disdains but mildly
disregards human approval.
What joy when the insouciant   10
armadillo glances at us and doesn't
quicken his trotting
across the track into the palm brush.

What is this joy? That no animal
falters, but knows what it must do?   15
That the snake has no blemish,
that the rabbit inspects his strange surroundings
in white star-silence? The llama
rests in dignity, the armadillo
has some intention to pursue in the palm-forest.   20
Those who were sacred have remained so,
holiness does not dissolve, it is a presence
of bronze, only the sight that saw it
faltered and turned from it.
An old joy returns in holy presence.   25

THE SECRET

Two girls discover
the secret of life
in a sudden line of
poetry.

I who don't know the
secret wrote
the line. They
told me

(through a third person)
they had found it
but not what it was
not even

what line it was. No doubt
by now, more than a week
later, they have forgotten
the secret,

the line, the name of
the poem. I love them
for finding what
I can't find,

and for loving me
for the line I wrote,
and for forgetting it
so that

a thousand times, till death
finds them, they may
discover it again, in other
lines

in other
happenings. And for
wanting to know it,
for

assuming there is
such a secret, yes,
for that
most of all.

A PSALM PRAISING THE HAIR OF MAN'S BODY

My great brother
> *Lord of the Song*
wears the ruff of
> *forest bear.*

Husband, thy fleece of silk is black,   5
> a black adornment;
lies so close to the turns of the flesh,
burns my palm-stroke.

My great brother
> *Lord of the Song*   10
wears the ruff of
> *forest bear.*

Strong legs of our son are dusted
> dark with hair.
Told of long roads,   15
we know his stride.

My great brother
> *Lord of the Song*
wears the ruff of
> *forest bear.*   20

Hair of man, man-hair, hair of
breast and groin, marking contour as
> silverpoint marks in cross-
> hatching, as river-
> grass on the woven current   25
> indicates ripple,
praise.

OUR BODIES

Our bodies, still young under
the engraved anxiety of our
faces, and innocently

more expressive than faces:
nipples, navel, and pubic hair
make anyway a   5

sort of face: or taking
the rounded shadows at
breast, buttock, balls,

the plump of my belly, the   10
hollow of your
groin, as a constellation,

how it leans from earth to
dawn in a gesture of
play and   15

wise compassion—
nothing like this
comes to pass
in eyes or wistful
mouths.   20
      I have

a line or groove I love
runs down
my body from breastbone
to waist. It speaks of   25
eagerness, of
distance.

      Your long back,
the sand color and
how the bones show, say   30

what sky after sunset
almost white
over a deep woods to which

rooks are homing, says.

THE MUTES

Those groans men use
passing a woman on the street
or on the steps of the subway

to tell her she is a female
and their flesh knows it,   5

are they a sort of tune,
an ugly enough song, sung
by a bird with a slit tongue

but meant for music?

Or are they the muffled roaring   10
of deafmutes trapped in a building that is
slowly filling with smoke?

Perhaps both.

RESTING FIGURE

The head Byzantine or from
Fayyum, the shoulders naked,
a little of the
dark-haired breast visible
above the sheet,   5

from deep in the dark head
his smile glowing
outward into the
room's severe twilight,

he lies, a dark-shadowed   10
mellow gold against
the flattened white pillow,
a gentle man—

strength and despair
quiet there in the bed,   15
the line of his limbs
half-shown, as under stone
or bronze folds.

HYPOCRITE WOMEN

Hypocrite women, how seldom we speak
of our own doubts, while dubiously
we mother man in his doubt!

And if at Mill Valley perched in the trees
the sweet rain drifting through western air   5
a white sweating bull of a poet told us

our cunts are ugly—why didn't we
admit we have thought so too? (And
what shame? They are not for the eye!)

No, they are dark and wrinkled and hairy,   10
caves of the Moon . . .   And when a
dark humming fills us, a

coldness towards life,
we are too much women to
own to such unwomanliness.   15

Whorishly with the psychopomp
we play and plead—and say
nothing of this later.   And our dreams,

with what frivolity we have pared them
like toenails, clipped them like ends of   20
split hair.

BEDTIME

We are a meadow where the bees hum,
mind and body are almost one

as the fire snaps in the stove
and our eyes close,

and mouth to mouth, the covers   5
pulled over our shoulders,

we drowse as horses drowse afield,
in accord; though the fall cold

surrounds our warm bed, and though
by day we are singular and often lonely.   10

A DAY BEGINS

A headless squirrel, some blood
oozing from the unevenly
chewed-off neck

lies in rainsweet grass
near the woodshed door.   5
Down the driveway

the first irises
have opened since dawn,
ethereal, their mauve

almost a transparent gray,   10
their dark veins
bruise-blue.

THE JACOB'S LADDER

The stairway is not
a thing of gleaming strands
a radiant evanescence
for angels' feet that only glance in their tread, and need not
touch the stone.   5

It is of stone.
A rosy stone that takes
a glowing tone of softness
only because behind it the sky is a doubtful, a doubting
night gray.   10

A stairway of sharp
angles, solidly built.
One sees that the angels must spring
down from one step to the next, giving a little
lift of the wings: 15

and a man climbing
must scrape his knees, and bring
the grip of his hands into play. The cut stone
consoles his groping feet. Wings brush past him.
The poem ascends.   20

Designed by Michel Craig
Set in Janson and Helvetica
Composed by American Book–Stratford Press, Inc.
Printed and bound by The Murray Printing Company
HARPER & ROW, PUBLISHERS   71 72 73 7 6 5 4 3 2 1